A Hundred Years
of
ROYAL STYLE

Queen Alexandra, as Princess of Wales,
in a hand-tinted photograph by S. Begg.

A Hundred Years of ROYAL STYLE

COLIN McDOWELL

MULLER, BLOND & WHITE

First published in Great Britain in 1985 by Muller, Blond & White
55 Great Ormond Street, London WC1N 3HZ.

British Library Cataloguing in Publication Data
McDowell, Colin
   A hundred years of royal style.
   1. Costume—Great Britain—History—19th
   century 2. Costume—Great Britain—History
   —20th century 3. Great Britain—Kings and
   rulers
   I. Title
   391′.022′088042   GT1755.G7

ISBN 0 584 11071 5

Printed and bound in Great Britain by
Purnell and Sons (Book Production) Ltd.,
Member of the BPCC Group, Paulton, Bristol

Editing, design, picture research and production by
Bull Publishing Consultants Limited and Eric Drewery,
South Croydon, England.

CONTENTS

For my sister

ACKNOWLEDGEMENTS

In writing this book I have been given a great deal of assistance by a wide variety of people but, as so many of them spoke off the record and did not wish their names to be mentioned, it would be invidious to single out any for specific thanks. I am, however, profoundly grateful to all for the help they gave.

I was allowed to consult Queen Mary's dressers' diaries by gracious permission of Her Majesty The Queen. I also wish to record my grateful thanks to Queen Elizabeth The Queen Mother for allowing me access to her dresser's diaries.

I want to take this opportunity to acknowledge the help of all the designers and milliners who talked to me and lent me material. I am particularly grateful to the houses of Hartnell and Amies for allowing me to comb through their archives and take my pick.

Finally, my thanks to Muriel Ross and her staff at the London College of Fashion; and to others without whose help and assistance this project would have been immeasurably more difficult, if not impossible, especially Timothy Cooke, Kate Duffy, Gloria Ferris, Peter Hope-Lumley, Jaine McCormack, Chris Motley, Vivienne Philips and Judy Rumbold.

Colin McDowell

The Queen: "By Grace of her position, doyenne of the cult of personality: an exposed, lonely woman forced to fulfil an astonishing round of engagements and symbolic duties that make little concession to the twentieth century, in order to sustain an institution that, rationally, should have as much relevance to the modern world as other ancient British customs such as 'Rolling The Waffle'."

Andrew Duncan

The Monarchy: "I do not think that any of us who are monarchists at heart would expect a King or Queen to be exactly like one of ourselves ... we would hope and expect of them that they would be a little aloof from us ... if we did not feel nervous we would feel a little disappointed. For they are, and should be, a caste apart by race and marriage."

Sacheverell Sitwell

The Court: "There are arguments for not having a court and there are arguments for having a splendid court; but there are no arguments for having a mean court."

Walter Bagehot

INTRODUCTION

Of picture books about the Royal Family there is no end. They have become a considerable industry, and press photographers have grown rich by servicing it. These books clearly fulfil a demand: like modern icons, they fuel the faith of the royal worshippers. This book aims to get behind the hagiography. It has been written on the assumption that many readers who are interested in modern royalty and its appearance would like their interest fed with something more substantial. Although it includes photographs and drawings, these are carefully designed to illustrate and compliment the text. In a sense it is a complete reversal of the normal approach.

The Queen and the rest of the Royal Family would be as remote as the portraits in Hampton Court were it not for their public appearances and what we see of their way of life – in short their style – which gives us glimpses of who they are and what they stand for. As the title indicates, the subject is style: that is, an attitude of mind which affects clothes and appearance but which is also an approach to life. Style involves things other than dress and one of the most characteristic aspects of royal style is its smoothness of operation. The book examines how this is achieved.

The discussion of royal style is confined to crowned heads, but it includes Mrs. Simpson, later Duchess of Windsor, who quite possibly might have become Queen and, in a special chapter, the Princess of Wales, the Queen of the future. The fact that other princesses, royal duchesses and the male members of the Royal Family are not included is not to suggest that they lack style but rather that they do not represent royal style in the same distinct and all-embracing way as do those we have concentrated upon.

The following brief biographical details are included to show the changes of title involved in 'promotion' up the royal ladder towards monarchy passing through hierarchical positions on the royal chess board. The Duchess of Windsor and the present Princess of Wales are not included. The Princess of Wales will continue with that title until she is crowned Queen Consort and, like the Duchess of Windsor, her position vis-à-vis the crown is unchanging.

WHO'S WHO

QUEEN ALEXANDRA
Born: 1 December 1844, Copenhagen
Died: 20 November 1925, London
Christened: Alexandra Caroline Maria Charlotte Louise Julia
   Second daughter of Prince Christian of Schleswig-Holstein-Sonderburg-Glücksburg and
   Princess Louise of Hesse-Cassel
Married: Edward, Prince of Wales 10 March 1863
   Princess of Wales 1863–1901
Coronation: 9 August 1902 (Queen Consort)
Death of King 1910:   as Queen Dowager, lived at Sandringham

QUEEN MARY
Born: 26 May 1867, London
Died: 24 March 1953, London
Christened: Victoria Mary Augusta Louise Olga Pauline Claudine Agnes
   Only daughter of Prince Francis, Duke of Teck and Princess Mary Adelaide of Cambridge,
   Duchess of Teck
   Normally referred to as Princess Mary of Teck
Engaged: 1. Prince Edward, Duke of Clarence, heir presumptive, December 1891, who
              died in January 1892
         2. Prince George, Duke of York, May 1893
Married: Prince George, 6 July 1893
   Duchess of York 1893–1901; Princess of Wales 1901–1910
Coronation: 22 June 1911 (Queen Consort)
Death of King 1935:   as Queen Dowager, lived at Marlborough House

QUEEN ELIZABETH
Born: 4 August 1900, London
Christened: Elizabeth Angela Marguerite Bowes-Lyon
   Ninth child of 14th Earl of Strathmore and Kinghorne, Lord Glamis and Cecilia, Countess
   of Strathmore (née Cavendish-Bentinck)
Married: Prince Albert, Duke of York, 26 April 1923
   Duchess of York 1923–1936
Coronation: 12 May 1937 (Queen Consort)
Death of King 1952:   as Queen Elizabeth, the Queen Mother, lives at Clarence House

QUEEN ELIZABETH II
Born: 21 April 1926, London
Christened: Elizabeth Alexandra Mary
   Eldest daughter of the Duke and Duchess of York; Duke of York crowned King George V
   in 1936 following the abdication of King Edward VIII
Married: Prince Philip of Greece, 20 November 1947
   Duchess of Edinburgh 1947–1952
Coronation: 2 June 1953 (Queen)

1
STYLES FOR A ROYAL WAY OF LIFE

When Queen Victoria wrote to the ten-year-old Prince Edward that "dress is a trifling matter", she immediately qualified it by adding, slightly reluctantly no doubt, that "it is of some importance particularly in persons of high rank". In fact, dress is of great importance in persons of high rank, especially those who are royal. Whether members of the public see the royal figure in person or on film, they make up their minds about the individual and, possibly, royalty in general on the basis of the royal look. Queens rarely offend by their actions or words; they are too constrained by protocol and the proprieties of a parliamentary institution. But their clothes can please or annoy, impress or amuse, delight or horrify. Their greatest liberty is in their choice of clothes and even that is, at best, a controlled liberty. They must always be discreet. As Queen Victoria counselled Princess Helene: "a little rose in front, dear child, because of the footmen."

Dressmakers and milliners are more important for royal women than speech writers because clothes are the most important element in the public projection of their personalities. The choice of life partner, job, house and holiday often tells us more about ordinary people than their clothes. With royalty, none of these criteria apply. There may be sixteen royal homes, but they are all inherited and they and their contents are unlikely to change very much; the royal family almost always holidays at home, never in hotels; the job is passed on, not chosen, and leaves little scope for other jobs; husbands are taken from the narrowest and most exclusive menu in the world.

For the majority of her subjects, a Queen is known by her dress and it is by her appearance that she is remembered. Queen Alexandra's name instantly brings to mind pearl chokers; Queen Mary is symbolised by what were aptly described as "those terrifying toques"; Queen Elizabeth the Queen Mother is flowered hats and floating chiffon; the Queen is stiffly embroidered grand evening dresses and tiaras; Princess Diana, future Queen, is hats and clutch bags; and Mrs Simpson, nearly a Queen, is Paris dresses and rather too much good jewellery.

Much of the impression of the royals as perfect people living perfect lives is created by the immaculately unruffled appearance which royal women project.

The Queen, dressed by Hardy Amies, in Canada in 1984.

11

Never flurried or ill at ease, they can exercise an almost hypnotic effect upon the public. When Alexandra, "the sea-king's daughter from over the seas" as Tennyson called her, arrived from Denmark, her looks and charm captivated everyone. As Queen Victoria said, "I never set eyes on a sweeter creature! Her voice, her walk, carriage and manner are perfect. You may go far before you find another Princess like Alix."

In the Edwardian era society revolved around the court to a much greater extent than it has since. Sitwell's view that royalty was "a caste apart" was commonly held. The King and Queen were leaders of fashion to an extent that has not been maintained. The chain of influence was simple: the King and Queen were the arbiters of taste, not only by their own dress, but by their approval of the appearance of those within their circle; from that tight court circle their influence spread to those members of the aristocracy who were not part of the court and also to the wealthy but not well-born members of London society; from them it spread to the middle classes and became "Pooterised". Queen Alexandra was able to create fashion fads to an extraordinary extent. Rheumatic fever had left her with a slight limp: certain society women thought it chic to affect a limp also. To cover a scar on her neck she wore tight 'choker' necklaces: fashionable women flocked to their jewellers to have them copied. Wherever she and the King appeared society went crazy. The highest born in the land pushed and shoved, climbed on chairs or stood on tiptoe in their carriages to catch a glimpse of the smallest details of the royal apparel. Society women rushed home and consulted their dressmakers about instantly copying a particular sleeve or sent their maids scurrying to the Oxford Street shops to search for the exact shade of ribbon trimming the royal bonnet. If such behaviour seems bizarre and unbelievable today, it must be remembered that society women at that time had few other ways to fill their time. Fashion was an obsession. Clothes were changed many times a day and several hours were spent on perfecting each toilette.

A beautiful, warm and fashionable Queen was the ideal head of such a world and Alexandra fulfilled the role almost perfectly. Her one drawback was her figure: she was really too thin for the taste of the time. But this was a minor flaw – for the rest she was complete. Her taste was strong and individual. Perhaps she had taken note of Queen Victoria's advice not to vie "in dressing with the fine London ladies but rather to be as different as possible by great simplicity", for her clothes were less baroquely flamboyant than those of many society beauties. This does not mean that her clothes were not richly ornamented and embroidered. She was, after all, a daughter of her time. In fact, as Cecil Beaton pointed out in _The Glass of Fashion_, "it was Alexandra who started the tradition that royalty could wear anything at any time and get away with it". She wore spangled, bejewelled and beaded outfits in the middle of the day. The formal Queen wearing evening clothes in the daytime surrounded by women wearing normal day clothes is now such a cliché that no one remarks on the discrepancy or comments on its implausibility. But at the time it was new, and paradoxically, considering how accessible her personality was, Alexandra

Queen Alexandra's Edwardian styles were ideal for drawing attention to her fashionably narrow waist.

An early photograph of Princess
Alexandra and her sister Dagmar,
dressed identically in the height of fashion.

helped to distance the court by wearing clothes in which no one else dared to appear. As she grew old she began to show signs of an endearing eccentricity: she is reputed to have appeared at a family dinner party wearing white and silver with a real orange pinned into her hair. She slowly declined into a deaf and rather dotty figure, known to her family as "Motherdear", whose monotonous life at Sandringham, surrounded by her dogs, was enlivened by her enduring interest in her clothes and appearance. She retained her looks late into life, but in 1924, the year of her death, she wrote poignantly to a friend urging him to "think of me as I used to be, now that I am breaking up".

In a memorable phrase, Henry 'Chips' Channon said that to meet Queen Mary was "like talking to St. Paul's Cathedral". Although he was referring to her demeanour late in life, Mary was, even as a young woman, an imposing, statuesque figure. She appeared to be tall and had an excellent carriage. When she and her family lived in financial semi-exile in Florence she was described as "a remarkably attractive girl, rather silent, but with a look of quiet determination mixed with kindness". As a young woman she was noted for her sense of humour. Keir Hardie commented that "when that woman laughs, she does laugh"; Princess Mary said that she had to be careful not to "because you see I have such a vulgar laugh". Before her marriage she spent little money on clothes because, as she herself said, her family was always in "queer street". Many of her clothes were made by a small dressmaker in Kingston-on-Thames. Madame Mangas, who came to London from her Paris base, provided the more important toilettes and her bonnets were from another French woman, Madame Meurice of Mount Street. Costs were always watched. The traditional appearance that evolved over the years into the 'Queen Mary look' which everyone knows has sometimes been interpreted as the result of early indifference to clothes, but, in fact, as a Princess she was as interested in clothes as anyone, and although she found the hours spent at the dressmakers a great bore, her taste developed early. The list of the clothes made for her in coronation year (1911) discloses the preference for soft pastel or neutral colours which remained with her all her life. The cost of her clothes in that year – a rather staggering £2,000 – does not argue an indifference to them.

Queen Mary's appearance developed and then ossified into what Beaton calls "the all-weather model" because of the King. George V was a conservative who wished everything to remain as far as possible the way it was when he was young and he was passionately keen that his wife should retain the appearance she had when they were married. She was happy to comply, although she did now and then 'test the water' by attempting to modify her appearance. On one famous occasion Lady Airlie, acting as guinea-pig, shortened her skirts slightly to show an ankle, and when the King reacted unfavourably the Queen knew it was useless for her to follow. (George also vetoed wide-brimmed hats.) As a result, Queen Mary developed a remarkably stable and stylised form of dress which, far from seeming eccentric, became the very embodiment of regality. Such sartorial reliability may even have helped the royal family to survive the uncertainties of the abdication

The classic Queen Mary 'look' consisted of a softly-draped toque, a long coat with fur trim and, almost invariably, a parasol.

crisis. As long as the old Queen was around, looking as she always had, the people felt that the monarchy was secure.

For the last forty years of her life, as skirt lengths moved up and down, hair went short and long and women's appearance altered more than it had in all previous centuries put together, Queen Mary wore almost the same style everywhere she went. For evening, she favoured heavily beaded gowns (dress would be too flippant a word for her very stately creations), while for day she wore tailored suits, long-toed buttoned slippers and large toques. She frequently carried a parasol. The muslin of her youth was replaced by velvet, satin and silk in mauve, rose pink, delphinium blue and beige. It is perhaps her tall, dressed hair and toques which are most memorable. The story goes that her milliner in Great Portland Street never bothered with fittings, but kept blocks of the Queen's head with her wigs on them on a special shelf. The hats were made, sewn onto the wigs and sent to the Palace: hair and hat were complete and ready to wear. Throughout her life Queen Mary was the exemplar of Beaton's contention that "since royalty by its very definition is above the crowd, it stands to reason that the fashions of Kings and Queens should be individual and unique, abiding by their own rigid laws and prohibiting imitation by the lower classes". Her successor, Queen Elizabeth, the Queen Mother, has, in a very different way continued the tradition.

Landseer's *Dignity and Impudence* could be taken as the title for a double portrait of the straight-backed, straight-laced and inhibited Queen Mary and the relaxed, warm and humorous Queen Elizabeth. The contrast between the two Queens was as great as that between the painter's bloodhound and Scotch terrier. The young Queen brought a new approach to the role of consort, one which, in many respects, overturned the values of her predecessor. Elizabeth's attitudes were right for their time and helped the monarchy to move forward with the people after the difficult abdication period. Shy as the young Duchess of York, she gained great popularity as Queen and has become a superstar as Queen Mother. If the notion that subjects 'love' a member of the royal family has any real meaning, the Queen Mother may be said to be genuinely loved by vast numbers, not only in Great Britain but throughout the world. She is loved by people even though they do not know her nor very much about her. What they are in love with is her demeanour and her image. Events in her life have, of course, helped to attract sympathy, admiration and devotion. Coming to the throne after the débâcle of the abdication she, with her husband and children, re-affirmed the importance of the family unit in society and thereby gained the grateful affection of the people. Throughout World War II she remained at the side of the King, making sure they were seen together visiting bombed areas and supporting the war effort. Widowed at an early age, she had the sympathy of the nation in her period of grief and in the long days of recovery which followed. But much of the adoration for her has also simply been a response to her appearance.

The Queen Mother's clothes have always tended towards the theatrical – as indeed has she, in the nicest way possible. She adored acting as a girl and her

Even in the thirties the Queen Mother had her own style: gently draped bodice, three-quarter length coat and extravagant fur. All project a soft and feminine appearance.

delight in dressing up was carried into adult life and motherhood (she even passed it on to her daughters in the famous Palace pantomimes into which the young Princesses threw themselves with such enthusiasm). Andrew Duncan described royal appearances in public as "the everlasting wedding photograph" and, in a sense, the Queen Mother has always dressed in that heightened fashion which weddings encourage. George VI understood his consort very well and he suggested to the Royal dressmaker, Norman Hartnell, that he should base his designs for the Queen's evening dresses on Winterhalter's portraits of Eugénie of France and Elizabeth of Austria in Worth crinolines. They were ideal: magnificent, romantic and flattering, but in no way titillating or revealing. They had a make-believe, dressing-up quality which created the fairy-tale illusion of the beautiful Queen in all her glory, and their rich embroidery enabled them to stand up to the priceless jewels worn as a matter of course by royal women. By absorbing the impact of very large gems in a general glitter and shine, the dresses softened the potential tactlessness of displaying such opulence in a way that Wallis Simpson's simple and more sophisticated evening dresses, for instance, could not. Cecil Beaton described the Queen Mother's evening appearance as having "all the unreality of a spangled fairy doll on top of a Christmas tree. The effect she creates ... is dazzling in its effect upon her devoted but dazed beholders." The comment is still true today.

Down the years the Queen Mother has hardly changed her style in evening wear and even in her eighties she is still wearing off-the-shoulder, full-skirted evening gowns for grand occasions. Perhaps she pushes credibility to the limit, appearing in public dressed in a way which in any other woman of her age, even the most glamorous Hollywood star, would seem unwise; but she triumphs because she is not attempting to appear glamorous as a film star might. She is simply projecting her version of regality and what in others would seem bizarre – in her seems no more than mildly and lovably eccentric. Her style in day wear was not formed so quickly, but it has had consistent elements and has varied little over the years. Not that the Queen Mother is a follower of fashion. Like Queen Mary, she has given passing fashions only the most cursory of nods. She realised at an early age that fashion fads and regal dignity do not match and that a consistent approach to dressing is essential for royalty. The measure of her success is that in photographs taken over forty years ago she projects a convincing royal image, recognisably in her own style, and only the hats tend to raise eyebrows. Only rarely do the photographs provoke the laughter commonly provided by the fashions of a bygone age.

The hats, however, do present a problem. They were chosen, as were her amazing high-heeled, thick-soled shoes, to make her appear taller. Hats which were swept up high to one side gave the illusion of height. Unfortunately, they now appear extraordinary in their contrived theatricality.

Even as a young woman, the Queen Mother was attracted to softness. Tailored precision has never been her style: dressmakerly drapes and fluttering panels are consistent aspects of her image, plus fur and feather trimmings. In choosing these elements she created a larger-than-life appearance, as if she were on a stage giving a performance. They proved very flattering as her figure became more matronly and, as she grew older, she heightened the effects. Hardly ever seen in a fur coat, Queen Elizabeth realised that fur trimming could add the right degree of softness and luxury without destroying the pliability and movement of the silhouette. Fur trimming has always been part of the regalia of Kings and subconsciously it emhasises her regality in the eyes of her subjects. Feathers are equally soft, pliable and feminine and Queen Elizabeth has been especially fond of using osprey and ostrich in hats and stoles and as trims and hem weights for her famous floating panels.

Her real triumph came with her gradual blossoming as Queen Mother, when she found the unique image which makes her appearance unlike that of any other woman on earth. As her figure has become comfortably and reassuringly plump, so she has become the archetype for mums and grandmas throughout the land, even though they are unable to dress like her. We can view her life as a two-act play. Act I ended with her widowhood, which was followed by an interval of a year during which she wore only black. Act II has built up to a richly coloured climax through which she sweeps like a fantastically caparisoned Gloriana. Her appearance for the past twenty years has transcended the narrow confines of fashion and the norms of good taste. She is her own arbiter. Everyone thinks that she is 'marvellous' and indeed she is. More than any other member of the royal family she has a strong and uniquely personal style. She knows precisely what is right for the image she has created. The cliché is true: she has star quality.

Queen Elizabeth's appearance was a direct contrast to that of the woman whose presence made her Queen, Mrs Wallis Simpson. Chic, super-sophisticated and seriously fashionable, Mrs Simpson was unsuitable for the throne as much by the way she dressed as by her background and behaviour. It is arguable that the public, who loved the new King, Edward VIII, might have been prepared to accept his choice of Queen. She was foreign, but then, most Queens were; she was fashionable, but so had Alexandra been; she was American, but America was considered glamorous; she was divorced, but it is questionable whether the population at large cared much about that. Established, aristocratic England, however, would not have her. It was not because Mrs Simpson was the King's mistress – if, indeed, she was. As Prince of Wales, his affairs with women had been accepted quite happily by society. His relationship with Mrs Dudley Ward lasted for sixteen years; that with Lady Furness actually included her joining him on safari in 1928. Society had discreetly closed ranks and confined its gossip within its own circles. The press was equally discreet, and, for a long time, was so even with Mrs Simpson. But the ladies in the Prince's life, before Mrs Simpson came along, were from the highest ranks of society and knew how to behave. They dressed the part and knew how to treat the servants. Mrs Simpson was different.

She met the Prince at a hunting weekend in Melton Mowbray in 1931, where it was apparent to everyone that, for all the impression which she made on the Prince

A sensible walking costume by Redfern for Queen Mary, ideal for visits to agricultural shows, flower exhibitions and all country occasions.

by her brittle and cynical wit, she was not one of them. Even though excuses could be made – Mrs Simpson had a terrible cold – it was obvious that she was city, not country, based. Her world was that of the little black dress, not the tweed suit. The English upper classes have always been happy to accept the super-wealthy (many are that themselves and all aspire to be), but the money must get acres behind it. One look at Mrs Simpson was enough to confirm that Paris, New York, London and Rome were her ambience, not Yorkshire, Leicestershire, Perthshire or Aberdeen. She was not quite 'right' and the thought of curtseying in front of her as Queen of England was dismaying. Wallis Simpson was unsuitable by the standards of court society and it showed in what she did and what she wore. Had she come earlier, in the more relaxed court of Edward VII and his pliant Queen, Alexandra, she might just have succeeded. But against the frosty formality of George V and Queen Mary she had no chance. No one had more rooted views on how a lady should dress than George V and his wife took pains to present a public appearance which personified royal dignity both in dress and manner. The coolness of the sophisticate was not the same thing. Wallis Simpson was much cleverer than most members of the royal circle: she was better read, more informed and more aware. But these things did not matter. She upset the royal servants by entering the kitchen to show them how to make the new-fangled American sandwiches she liked to serve when entertaining at Balmoral. She was over-familiar, almost patronising, with the King. Worst of all, she was chic: she cared about her appearance and figure far too obviously and she wore too much jewellery. She loved jewellery. "I said what had struck me most," Marie Belloc Loundes once recalled, "were her perfect clothes and that I had been surprised, considering that she dressed so simply, to see that she wore such a mass of dressmaker's jewels."

Of course they were not dressmaker's jewels, made of paste and glass; they were the real thing. The Prince of Wales is reputed to have given her £110,000 worth of jewels in less than a month. He also gave her family heirlooms left by Queen Alexandra for his future Queen. Mrs Simpson hastily had them re-set in a modern style. Lady Diana Cooper remembers her as "glittering" and Chips Channon writes of her "dripping with rubies . . . literally smothered with emeralds". Like Anita Loos' heroine, Lorelei Lee, in *Gentlemen Prefer Blondes*, Mrs Simpson surely knew what were a girl's best friend! They were a preoccupation even during World War II. Major 'Fruity' Metcalfe visited the Duke and Duchess of Windsor when the fall of Paris seemed likely and was shocked to find that their major concern was for the safety of the Duchess's jewellery and wardrobe. Wallis Simpson was thirty-eight in 1934, neither beautiful nor pretty but, as Lady Furness said, although "she did not have the chic she has since cultivated . . . she had a distinct charm and a sharp sense of humour". She raises the fascinating speculation . . . what if? Had she become Queen what sort of a royal image would she have projected?

Mrs Simpson, asked once what the Duchess of York could best do to promote British fashion abroad, is reputed to have replied, "stay at home". She had a lady's maid from the Duchess and complained that "all she can do is press frills and all I

An early portrait of Queen Mary when still Princess Mary of Teck, before her marriage to the Duke of York.

want is a plain black frock done properly". Therein lies the different approach. Fairy-tale, make-believe clothes would not have been Mrs Simpson's approach to dressing as a Queen. To confine herself to British dressmakers, as most royal ladies do, would have been repugnant to her. She believed in fashion and she knew that the best fashion designers were in Paris. To have turned her back on them would have been impossible. Not that her favourite designers were all French. Mainbocher was a fellow American, Molyneux was British, Schiaparelli was Italian. But they all lived and worked in Paris along with Patou and Chanel, whose clothes also appealed to Mrs Simpson. They understood that simplicity and sophistication of line comes from perfect cutting, meticulous sewing and skilled draping. With the exception of Schiaparelli, they avoided unnecessary surface details and fussiness. Their dresses made a well-bred and elegant backdrop to displays of impressive jewellery.

Mrs Simpson not only knew that "elegance is refusal" and that the smart woman preserved a clean and uncluttered line, she realised that sophisticated clothes used a very limited colour palette. Plain fabrics were her choice for day (Molyneux's grey being a particular favourite) and richly subdued fabrics with a controlled sheen for evenings. She would never have worn the bejewelled and spangled crinolines of Queen Elizabeth and multi-coloured, floating chiffon would equally have displeased her. She did, however, like blue and was married to the Duke of Windsor wearing, as Lady Metcalfe described it, "a long blue dress, short-fitting tight coat, blue straw hat with feathers and tulle, the loveliest diamond and sapphire bracelet which was his wedding present". The dress was very simple and relied for its impact on the perfect way it hung. It was created by Mainbocher and was a masterpiece of cut. The shade of blue was immediately dubbed 'Wallis blue" and had a great vogue throughout the world.

Even as she grew older the Duchess of Windsor remained a slim and exceedingly chic fashion figure in Paris and New York, in her Givenchy suits, Norell coats and Balenciaga evening dresses. It is hard to imagine her putting on weight and allowing herself to become matronly. Almost certainly she would not have enjoyed the huge popularity that attends Queen Elizabeth, simply because her image was too cool and too perfect. People need to identify with the object of their adulation and the average middle-aged English woman scorns sacrificing everything for an elegant appearance – she puts on weight, wears clothes which are not in the height of fashion and does not care about creating a ruthlessly logical fashion image. Pearl-smooth and weasel-thin, the Duchess of Windsor would have been far too elegant a Queen to inspire loyalty and love. How would she have dressed to visit blitzed East End lanes during the war? What would she have worn at Badminton? Her brittle slimness would have raised an insuperable barrier between her and her subjects. As she grew older her perfectly fashionable dressing submerged any warmth of personality she might have had.

The role of Princess, waiting in the wings to become Queen or Queen consort, is not an enviable one. There is a tightrope to be walked. Indifference to clothes or

In this Beaton portrait Mrs Simpson is given all the trappings of eighteenth century princely magnificence. However, they do not overwhelm her Mainbocher dress, diamond necklace and diamond and emerald bracelet: the trappings of twentieth century success.

appearance would soon have the popular press shrieking about 'sloppy royals'; on the other hand, an ostentatious display of new and extravagant styles would elicit equally strong censure. The present Queen, when she was Princess Elizabeth, showed little interest in clothes, as those close to her in her late teens and early twenties testify. As a teenager, she was uncertain how to dress. Peep-toed shoes, sling-back sandals, draped busts and floating panels, middle-aged hats, fur stoles: all showed the clear influence of the Queen Mother's taste. Marian Crawford, the royal nanny, wrote that "the Princess was always conservative about her dress, and content to wear whatever was laid before her". The same writer gives an interesting insight into the constraints placed upon a young Princess in the exercise of her personal taste. "Choosing a wardrobe is taken out of her hands by her dressmaker, shoemaker and milliner. The exact colour of the main garment is given to the tradesmen and then the accessories arrive, perfect, beautiful, costly, without the personal effort which makes shopping so large a part of the whole intriguing adventure of a woman's life. I did not say that Princess Elizabeth did not choose her own clothes. Of course she did but within prescribed limits. She had to remember, for instance, that however she might long to wear a certain colour, she could not do so if it was a shade that would tone in and get lost among a large crowd and so make it difficult for her to be easily and immediately seen by the loyal crowd who congregate wherever she is to make a public appearance. There might be times too when in the interest of trade she was asked to wear a certain material, a certain style of shoe to give it that boost that would make the whole world buy it". The picture created by 'Crawfie' of a compliant girl prepared to do as she was told in matters of dress certainly does not suggest that, as a Princess, the Queen had any great interest in her clothes.

In fact, at the age of eighteen, she clearly had a healthy indifference to clothes which was a characteristic of the daughters of her class: the landowning aristocracy whose confidence is so complete that they do not require beautiful clothes as a booster. Indifference was encouraged by the privations still prevalent in post-war England. Even a Princess had only a certain amount of government clothing coupons per year and the allowance was not generous. The restrictions on the purchase of new clothes meant that the Princess moved towards her coming of age with a smaller wardrobe than any previously known in royal circles. It has been calculated to have consisted of three coats, some hats, half-a-dozen frocks in wool, silk or crêpe and excellent shoes. Louis Wolff in *Queen of Tomorrow* contends that some of the Princess's clothes were made from her mother's old ones – especially some of the full-cut ones made for the 1939 Canadian Tour "from which enough material could easily be taken to make evening dresses in the present severe styles". In a country of post-war dowdiness the Princess could get away with being similarly dressed: in fact, anything else would have been tactless. However, she did possess something which would have been the envy of all girls of her age: a pair of nylon stockings. No one who did not live during the war and the post-war period can begin to imagine the excitement generated by the first nylons. They were so

The Queen Mother increasingly favours softly coloured chiffons for an evening appearance less grandiose than the full-blown crinoline.

desirable and yet so scarce that they acquired the status of totem objects. The Princess was given hers after a tour of the first nylon stocking factory in England. Queen Mary, who was also given a pair, held them up to the light and said: "They look as though they might be rather cold to wear".

Norman Hartnell told Godfrey Winn, who told the world in *Illustrated*, 1 March, 1952, that when he made "her Royal Highness's first party dress just at the end of the war she accepted the fitting as part of her official duties but one did not feel that she was interested in clothes as such or in creating or even following the latest fashions ... Princess Elizabeth was happiest, one felt, in country tweeds or very simple things and always would be ... when choosing her trousseau, she made few positive suggestions except to ask me to make several dresses in her favourite lime green." The taste which the Princess's clothes exemplified was that of three women: herself, her mother and Margaret 'Bobo' MacDonald, her maid. In those early days the last two were surely the most influential. The Princess was introduced to her mother's dressmaker and milliner and seemed content to be dressed in a watered-down version of her mother's idea of regality. 'Bobo' MacDonald had an exceptionally powerful voice for one in her position, largely because Princess Elizabeth had few opinions of her own as far as her appearance was concerned. It is very hard for a Princess to develop her taste if she has no particular interest in clothes. Whereas most girls are told very quickly by their friends when they have made a bad choice, a future Queen has no peers to tell her if she looks dreadful. She is beyond criticism. It is this role of honest critic that those with palace links say was taken by 'Bobo'. Especially after the Princess's marriage and slow separation from her mother's taste, 'Bobo' helped her mistress to choose colours, patterns and styles.

So the Princess, who had led a sheltered life, and who was advised on her clothes by her maid, was not a fashionable figure. Magazine and newspaper editors, who knew that increased circulation could be obtained if the future Queen could be presented as a fashion leader, had to fall back on emphasising the beauty and charm of her appearance. Given the lack of any real information, there was little else they could do, and in this regard nothing has changed in the last thirty years. Journalists still largely know only what they see: Palace moles are few and they are notoriously unreliable. Rumours might hint at bad temper or sarcastic petulance, but editors rarely publish them. They are aware that highlighting such defects of character could mean a slump in circulation. Emphasis on appearance is safe and can even give scope for some gentle chiding over a dress without causing readers much annoyance. But editors know that for their readers Princesses are as lollipops for children: unless they are coated in sugar and made very sweet, they lose their attraction. "In the twentieth century," Kingsley Martin has written, "anyone can question the dignity of Christ, but no one attributes faults to the royal family". Kingship is based on the illusion that members of an endogamous royal tribe are morally and intellectually superior, more beautiful and more gracious than commoners are. Nevertheless, their subjects want to be given glimpses that reassure them that, even with all the grandeur, the royals are just like them. It is with relieved delight that people learn that Queen Mary, apparently remote and intimidatingly regal, had her little 'human' eccentricities like the two pockets she required to be made in all her clothes: one for her hankies and one for her secret supply of biscuits. Dieters who have nibbled feel guilty no more.

The dichotomy in the public's needs – remote magnificence and identifiable reality – can be seen by comparing the present Queen, when she was a Princess, with the Princess Diana. During the thirty years that have elapsed since Elizabeth II came to the throne, royalty has given the illusion of being more accessible, more of the people and more inclined to be treated 'normally'. Nevertheless, the public has embraced Princess Diana with the same uncritical adulation they gave to Princess Elizabeth. In both cases the reaction is largely to a myth. Because of wartime security arrangements, Princess Elizabeth spent her mid- and late-teens at Windsor remarkably out of the public gaze. After the war she was, as it were, rediscovered by press and people. Press and Palace had to create a person. From being dressed identically with her younger sister, she had to be separated as the heir and given precedence so that public identification was no longer with 'the little princesses', but with Princess Elizabeth, the future Queen, and her sister, Princess Margaret. This was achieved by dress. Lady Diana Spencer had similarly to be separated from the crowd and made unique after her engagement to the heir to the throne. Prince Charles had had many girlfriends, most of whom were from the same narrow background and most of whom dressed in the same way, wearing the accepted, Sloane Ranger kit. Diana Spencer was in the identical mould. Jeans, corduroy pants, floral skirts, kilts, cashmere sweaters, Fair Isle cardigans, T shirts, Lady Northampton Wellingtons and casual shoes were elements of the uniform and they were a camouflage. Lady Diana had to be more easily identifiable. The goal was achieved by dress.

When Princess Elizabeth became Queen and matured, the girl who had been largely indifferent to clothes began to see them as a vital part of her role and so developed her own style. But for the first few years of her reign she continued to dress as her mother and her maid suggested. Consequently, she often looked less like a twenty-five-year-old than a forty-five-year-old. Looking back, it is easy to criticise her clothes as being inappropriately old, but her problem, shared today by the Princess of Wales, was a real one: she was too young. Young girls should look casual and informal, but we expect formality of princesses. Protocol demands seriousness. The problem can be solved only by growing older.

Marion Crawford recalled the "effort it had been to persuade the Princess to change into a new hat". Yet in a sense the Queen's indifference to fashion has been a blessing to her, since she must choose outfits to fit her role, not merely to gratify her personal tastes. The Queen wears a vast wardrobe of clothes and accessories. She spends more on clothes in a year than many of her subjects do in a lifetime. In the space of a week she may visit barracks, supermarkets, playschools, hospitals, factories and theatres; she may wear ceremonial robes, grand evening dresses,

Queen Elizabeth arriving at the Festival Hall in 1953 to hear a lecture on the Ascent of Everest. Dressed by Hartnell, she is wearing her own version of the currently fashionable style.

protective clothing and crash helmets, Wellingtons and floral hats. Many hours of her life are spent in changing her clothes. If she were really interested in fashion she would be driven mad by the choices and decisions. As it is, suitability of purpose is the only real consideration. Most of her day-time appearances are, for her, unspectacular and routine. However, she never forgets that what to her is just another visit to a civic centre or opening of a play group is for the other participants a red-letter day. If they are actually to meet her, it becomes an unforgettable, once-in-a-lifetime experience. Her clothes must reflect the importance that the occasion holds for them.

Subdued drama (and visibility) can be injected by the Queen's choice of colour for her clothes on these occasions. This is where her fashion strength lies. Although she has made mistakes about styles, her colour sense is always sound. She wears vibrant, deep colours or strong pastels with great success, especially when, as she frequently does, she limits herself to a one-colour outfit. It is her colour sense that, to a large degree, defines her personality for her subjects.

In the evening her engagements are much less routine and her appearance is able to be much more spectacular. Evening affairs which royalty attends are glamorous occasions. Everyone dresses up and glitter is expected. The Queen wears clothes of a dazzling richness on these occasions and almost always outshines all others quite effortlessly. Her jewellery is unrivalled, stunning both in quantity and quality. It is quite commonplace for the Queen to wear a fortune around her neck for these gala appearances, and with tiara and earrings her jewels for a night out, if not literally 'priceless', are certainly irreplaceable. Some are her personal property, but many of the most magnificent are heirlooms which have been passed down to her and which, in turn, will be bequeathed to the Princess of Wales.

It is perhaps not easily remembered these days, when the fashion limelight shines relentlessly on her daughter-in-law, that the Queen once set fashion trends. Even when she was a small child, and her nursery was painted primrose, people flocked to follow her lead: primrose yellow became *the* nursery shade. As early as her sixteenth birthday, when she first appeared on parade as Colonel of the Grenadier Guards, she set a trend. Her hat of green felt, shaped like a beret with the top jutting forward over a small peak in a military manner, was copied and sold in shops throughout the country. Overnight the 'Princess Hat' became a bestseller. For the Royal Command Performance of 1953 Hartnell devised an unusually soigné evening dress for her. It was slim-fitting and its elegant black was sparked with a white panel down the complete length of its front. Nicknamed 'The Magpie Dress', it was featured on the front pages of almost all of the national papers and, within hours, versions of it were on sale in a London store. It was copied cheaply throughout the rag trade and was even made into a paper pattern. During the fifties the Queen's clothes were regularly featured in women's magazines and used for practical fashion articles of the 'how to dress like the Queen' variety.

But the Queen cannot really be made into a fashion leader. Fashion moves on and she must stand still. She must be easily recognised and she must not look ridiculous. One decade's high-fashion look is risible to the next, and even years later people are not to be alarmed, amused or puzzled by royal garments. Comparison with two other women is instructive. Mrs Jackie Kennedy and Princess Grace of Monaco were both more beautiful and more fashionable than the Queen. Mrs Kennedy, in particular, was dedicated to fashion. But in photographs with the Queen she looks faintly comic now simply because her clothes were in the height of the current fashion. Princess Grace of Monaco was a beauty and, due to her experience as a film star, had more understanding of the need for timelessness than Mrs Kennedy did. Films are meant to have a long life. They lose credibility if the actors are unconvincing because of their clothes. Designers for modern-dress films have to create clothes which are of the moment, but which will also look contemporary three or more years later when the film is still being shown. The great Hollywood designers, like Travis Banton, Irene Sharraff and Edith Head, understood this. Edith Head's costumes for Grace Kelly in *Rear Window*, although designed in 1953, have still not dated. Discussing clothes with designers of this calibre helped Princess Grace to dress in a timeless way and still be elegantly of the moment.

The golden rule in royal dressing is that clothes must be comfortable, becoming and acceptable. The first canon of good taste is to dress in a way that is fitting for the occasion. A Queen does not dress to impress. Having no social superiors, she does not need to. Her choice of clothes is based on their suitability. She cannot be seen smoothing down her skirt or adjusting straps. Every time she gets out of a car she is met by a barrage of flashguns and a cacophony of cheers: she does not want the added complications of adjusting her hat or worrying about her hemline. When she sits down it is on a raised platform: she cannot be worrying about the length of her skirt. It is taken for granted that under no circumstances will the royal slip be showing. The dilemma for her dressmakers is how to make the Queen look regal in modern clothes. Evening dress presents little difficulty; the richly embroidered gown and much jewellery fit the received image of royalty. It works. It is more difficult to make day wear look regal, since anything other than an elegant look in the middle- and upper-class way would be blatantly vulgar. Both by personal inclination and force of circumstance, therefore, the Queen has inherited none of her mother's extrovert style. Apart from her evening gowns, she dresses in such an everyday way that she could have stepped as easily out of a Sunningdale villa as a royal palace.

Over the years the Queen has slowly developed her own style. It is basically a fifties image, strongly reminiscent of Balenciaga's softly tailored jackets and Givenchy's dresses with their gentle collars. Her heyday of looking correctly, but unexceptionally, dressed was the seventies. Since then there have been some worrying lapses. The blue-and-white dress-and-jacket outfit worn in California in 1983 was alarming, all the more so because the Queen could not comprehend how unsuitable and slightly ridiculous it was. Although the designers now admit that "it was a bit busy" and have altered it, the Queen is reputed to have said about the fuss

The Queen looks happiest in Hardy Amies' tailored coats.

it caused, "stupid people – there's nothing wrong with it". The idea of a monarch with her head forever buried in a fashion magazine is distasteful, but the North American tour showed that she cannot ignore style with impunity. The evening dresses in which she deserted her traditional look and tried to make a fashion statement were fussy and confused compared with the elegant line of Mrs Reagan's outfits. Simplicity is the keystone for the Queen and she and her designers must resist the temptation to fuss. The Queen will probably never develop as unique a style of dress as her mother and grandmother, but it is to be hoped that she can steer between the Scylla of dowdiness and the Charybdis of bad taste which loom up every now and again for anyone.

2
THE ROYAL SUPPLIERS

The story goes that Queen Victoria, who believed wholeheartedly in buying only those goods made in Great Britain or the Empire, unwittingly wore foreign clothes, the creations of the Parisian designer, John Frederick Worth. Outfits were ordered by the Queen from her London dressmakers, who proffered ranges of materials for her Majesty's selection, showed her 'their' latest designs, waited on her decision, measured her – and promptly sent the details to Worth in Paris. He then made the dresses from the designs he had originally provided for the court dressmakers. When the completed creations arrived in London the Worth label was snipped out before the garments were delivered to Windsor.

If true, it was an innocent deception, though a very profitable one for Worth's establishment, since it is said that the Queen was reluctant to wear a dress more than once. A minimum of three hundred and sixty-five dresses per year was a considerable order even in the days when a society hostess might change her outfit five times a day. (Apparently, Queen Victoria was diplomatic about her choice of styles and had dresses copied identically or with only the slightest alterations so that her subjects could not accuse her of vanity or extravagance.) But even had the deception been uncovered, Queen Victoria could not have been accused of disloyalty, for Worth was really more English than she.

He was born in Lincolnshire. His father was a lawyer who ruined himself by his gambling. Worth was sent to London at the age of twelve to be an apprentice in the haberdashery department of Swan & Edgar. From there he moved to France, with little money and even less French, but with a lot of ambition and determination. He eventually obtained work in the fashionable store, Gagelin et Opiqez, which sold dress materials and exclusive cashmere shawls. He was a great success and soon began designing clothes which made the shop even more fashionable. Having decided to found his own establishment with a partner from the firm of Gagelin, he needed a patron. His 'break' came when his wife showed some of his designs to Princess Metternich, the wife of the Austrian Ambassador to France. The Princess ordered two dresses at the very low cost (which the Princess imposed) of 300 francs each. She wore one at court and the rest of the story is like a fantasy. The Empress

Norman Hartnell, photographed in his Bruton Street premises in 1953, at work on clothes for the Queen's World Tour.

Eugénie, possibly the first modern 'fashion freak', demanded to know who had created the Princess's *robe de style*. On being informed that it was an Englishman, she commanded his presence and ordered some dresses to be made. From then Worth's future was secure and, as the eleventh edition of the *Encyclopaedia Britannica* put it, he "set the taste and ordained the fashion of Paris" for many years. His rule was more absolute and secure than that of any of the crowned heads he served. Not only was he dressmaker to the Empress Eugénie, he also dressed nine European Queens and all of the Russian Princesses. Worth was patronised by all, regardless of nationality, because he was considered the best designer in Paris, and Paris was the city where the grandest ladies went for their important clothes.

At the beginning of the century Queen Alexandra, as the lists of her warrant holders clearly show, relied on Parisian couturiers for many of her more important items. She patronised the couturier, Doeuillet, and the Maison Laferrier, both of which were Paris-based houses although Doeuillet had a London branch. But for serious clothes the English were clearly considered best: Durrant of Edinburgh for tailoring, Gent and Son of Birmingham for ladies tailoring, Albert Phillips and John Morgan and Son (of Cowes, Isle of Wight) also for tailoring; Seymour and Molyneux for embroidery. The delicate area of corsetry was in the hands of Madame Lambert in London and Madame Drion Regnier in Paris.

Over the years, other royal ladies have been known to dip a coy toe into the potentially hot water of Paris couture. Generally speaking, however, most royal clothes originate in London and are designed by appointed dressmakers. There are advantages for the Palace in this. There is the convenience of having the couturier within hailing distance. And the press is prevented from making capital out of the disloyalty implied by choosing foreign goods in preference to British-made ones. Palace circles still recall the chauvinistic hysteria in the late fifties when Princess Margaret bought from Dior. If the court were still the trend-setter in fashion, as it was in the reign of Edward and Alexandra, there might be a case to be made for a Queen who dressed in the latest styles. She would then have to buy her clothes in Paris or Milan. But over the last fifty years fashion and the Palace have become separated to such an extent that a super-fashionable Queen, wearing Parisian clothes, is undesirable. The purpose of her clothes is to emphasise continuity and stability. Fashion contains neither. Hence, the fact that royalty has chosen a designer is no guarantee of his fashion status. If creative ability and originality were the criteria, almost certainly no English designer would be chosen. Chanel, Dior, Balenciaga, Yves Saint Laurent, Lagerfeld, Armani... it would be a very long list indeed before an English designer's name appeared on a roll-call of the world's great designers. Even then, it would almost certainly not be the name of a 'By Appointment' designer.

Another advantage of buying British is the measure of control it provides. Most of what goes on between dressmaker and client is a secret between the two. A woman allows her dressmaker to know about figure problems that it is his job to mask on the assumption that he will be discreet. There are many people who are eager to

Layered chiffon on floating panels, topped off with an extravagant hat: archetypal 'Queen Mum' dressing.

learn intimate details known only to dressmaker, vendeuse and fitter. If foreign couturiers allowed their tongues to wag, the Palace could not prevent them. London designers are in a different position. Any desire they might have to blurt out secrets, such as the amount the Queen pays for her clothes, can be kept in check through the office of the Lord Chamberlain. Mention of that august name causes fear to settle like a miasma around a nervous designer and staff. If a designer is indiscreet, he will be reprimanded; if the indiscretion is grave, he could lose the royal custom.

It is not surprising that royal designers, who face problems that their fellows do not have to, become devoted to their clients. They are extremely reluctant to discuss anything to do with their royal connection. They no doubt remember the true tale of a young shoemaker who visited America after the war and was fêted by the New York press as the son of the royal shoemaker. During a party a determined female journalist asked him various questions about the royal feet. To all questions the young shoemaker politely, but firmly, answered, "I am not allowed to say". Undeterred, the journalist went around other guests saying, "if I were so tall what size shoe would I take?", or, "how much would I have to pay to have a pair of shoes made in London?" In this way she made guesses of such shrewd accuracy that she was able to write an article under the heading, 'Queen's Cobbler Tells All', which professed to have details directly supplied by the young man. When he returned to London he was upbraided by his father and summoned by the Lord Chamberlain to be dressed down. To this day, all designers with a royal warrant play their cards close to their chests.

Of the more recent warrant holders the most interesting for the purposes of this book are the dressmakers and milliners, and of these no one has given more proof of excellence than Norman Hartnell. The story of Hartnell and the establishment of his couture house is chronicled in his autobiography, _Silver and Gold_. His beginning in fashion was not easy. Born in London in 1901 into a solidly middle-class family, he went up to Cambridge with the intention of becoming an architect. However, as he had been excited by the theatre since his youngest days, it was not long before he became side-tracked into the world of amateur dramatics. By designing costumes for the 'Footlights Revue', the famous university production, he slowly realised what his true _métier_ was. He came down from Cambridge, before taking a degree, pretty well convinced that his future lay in designing dresses. His father, though none too thrilled at the idea, acquiesced.

Encouraged by his sister, Hartnell began the soul-destroying process, known to most tyro designers, of tramping around fashion houses to show his designs. Minnie Hogg, a journalist who had seen his costume designs at Cambridge, got him a job with Mrs Hughes, a dressmaker who had taken as her trade name the rather improbable French one of Madame Désirée. She loosely termed herself 'court' dressmaker. This title meant that she had made dresses for ladies who were to be presented at court. It did not denote a royal connection. Young Hartnell cared little about that: he was sufficiently excited to have obtained any job and especially

31

pleased to be working for a prestigious Mayfair establishment. The optimism was brief. He was sacked after three months. Although they dwell in perfumed halls there is nothing effete about the majority of successful designers. They are very tough and very determined. The materials with which they work may be soft and malleable; *they* are not. The reason is simple. Fashion is one of the hardest fields to break in to. The aspirant designer has to line up with many others, a proportion of whom will be just as talented as he; the designer for whom he wants to work will be very busy and rather suspicious of new talent; the protective ring of very fierce ladies who surround him will try to discourage any interruption of the maestro's precious time. Any young designer who survives, therefore, has to be more steel than velvet. Hartnell was just that. Undeterred by his short-lived association with Madame Désirée, he decided to go to the top. This meant arranging to meet London's grandest couturier: Lucile.

Lady Duff Gordon, for this was Lucile's real name, was an immensely successful and exceedingly important personage, both by her own estimation and that of others. She had a strong business head and an eye for talent. Her business included branches in New York, Chicago and Paris and she had employed Molyneux in his early days. "I trained and made Molyneux," she told Hartnell, with the utmost grandeur. "I can train and make you." She was graciously pleased to look at the young Hartnell's designs, liked them and offered him a job. Nothing happened for some weeks and then Hartnell saw one of his designs reproduced in a newspaper, as designed by Lucile 'just for you'. He wrote to ask when he was to start work in the couture house, but received no reply. When two more designs of his appeared in the press under the Lucile name, he realised that he was being plagiarised. The matter was brought to court and, advised by his solicitor, Hartnell accepted a paltry £50 in compensation. He could, of course, have demanded a considerable sum in damages, which would have helped him set up on his own, but, out of ignorance of his rights, he did not. Nevertheless, after failing to get an interview with Reville, London's other grand couturier, and Paquin, the French designer who had a branch in London, Hartnell and his sister decided that the only answer *was* for him to set up on his own. This he did in April, 1923, when he moved into Bruton Street, his father having paid the year's rent in advance. At first euphoria buoyed him up, but soon he realised that no customers were coming. Faced with receivers threatening to take over, he gladly agreed that 'to put him on the map' a dress show was required. It was a success and from that moment his business prospects showed promise.

It is hard now to imagine how totally the French dominated the fashion world of the twenties and thirties. Snobbish clients felt that their money had been safely spent only if they were making purchases from a French designer. London designers frequently changed their names to give their clothes more *cachet*. Many a cockney Alf, when he opened his own little dressmaking or tailoring establishment 'for the quality', was suddenly transformed into a Monsieur Adolph. Although not prepared to change his name, Hartnell realised that in order to prosper he needed

Major royal designers:

Hardy Amies, CVO, RDI

Simone Mirman

Aage Thaarup

Frederick Fox

a Parisian connection. He decided to show his collection in the capital of fashion, did so in 1927, and received sufficient acclaim for his name to be taken seriously back in London despite its distressingly English ring. By 1934 he was financially secure enough to move into grander Bruton Street premises – Number 26, where his house still continues today.

Hartnell's clientele was not solely aristocratic; it also included all of the grand ladies of the theatre. His favourites were Gertrude Lawrence, Norma Shearer, Isabel Jeans and Beatrice Lillie. He dressed them on and off stage and worked on many Cochran revues. So it was to a highly experienced designer that the royal family turned in the thirties. Hartnell first became involved with designing for royalty when Queen Mary's dresser, Miss Weller, telephoned to make an appointment to visit his Bruton Street salon in order to make a selection of gowns to submit to her Majesty. The Queen needed three dresses and the young couturier submitted water colours of his designs with, to use his own words, "a loyal heart". The sketches met with approval, but the prices did not. Queen Mary did not consider that 35 guineas was correct for the blue embroidered dress and she insisted upon paying 45 guineas each for all three! It very soon became apparent that this young man, who had suffered so many difficulties when first setting out, was to take over the major role of dressing royalty and to have his fortunes permanently intertwined with those of the new young Queen, Elizabeth of Glamis. In fact, his first major dress for a member of the royal family was the gown which Queen Elizabeth wore for the state banquet to mark the Belgian King's visit in 1936. It was a *"robe de style* of gleaming silver tissue over hooped *carcasse* of stiffened silver gauze with a deep *berthe* collar of silver lace encrusted with glittering diamonds". He was next asked to create the dresses for the Maids of Honour who were to attend Queen Elizabeth at George VI's Coronation in 1937.

A year later Hartnell's involvement with the royal family was confirmed when a summons from the Palace invited him to create the wardrobe for the Queen's state visit to Paris in 1938. This was his great opportunity to show that English designers were the equal of their French counterparts. Things progressed smoothly until, just as he was beginning the final fittings, disaster struck. The Queen's mother, the Countess of Strathmore, died and the court went into mourning. The state visit was postponed, but the revised dates still fell within the period of mourning. None of the beautifully coloured materials which had been so carefully chosen by the Queen and her couturier could be used. Yet the thought of dressing the Queen in black or purple for a visit in the height of summer was repellent. Hasty consultations with the Palace yielded the solution: everything was to be kept in the same style, but re-made in white. The impact on Paris was sensational and Hartnell's connection with the Queen was sealed. From that time until his death in 1979 he created all of her public outfits and to this day she remains loyal to his house.

Norman Hartnell created thousands of royal clothes. He designed major wardrobes for the present Queen, beginning when she was a young Princess, and for many years produced most of Princess Margaret's 'big' evening dresses. His

During the thirties and forties Queen Elizabeth's appearance became reassuringly predictable. For evening, heavily embroidered crinolines were enhanced with fur capes or stoles and convincing displays of jewellery; during the day the effect was soft, relying on draping, flying panels, embroidery and fur and feather trims.

service to the royal ladies was recognised by the Neiman-Marcus Award which he received in 1974. This honour, bestowed by the famous Dallas Store for excellence in the field of fashion, was eclipsed by the ultimate honour: he received a knighthood in 1977. His ability to create heavily embroidered state and evening dresses for the Queen Mother and her daughter, Queen Elizabeth II, kept him in the forefront of royal designers until his death. He was, in fact, responsible for the modern vision conjured up by the phrase 'The Queen of England': the unchanging picture of a woman in a richly ornate, glittering and bejewelled evening dress, tiara and Garter ribbon. These elements are as much an example of royal icon dressing as the clothes in any portrait of Elizabeth I. They constitute what Hartnell himself called "the regal renaissance of the romantic crinoline" for formal and state occasions – a fairy-tale, romantic look which uses chiffon, net and velvet to create majesty with glamour.

In its heyday the Bruton Street workrooms had a staff of four hundred cutters, seamstresses and embroiderers to carry out the complicated and delicate handiwork involved in couture. The work force has dwindled as the number of customers for this expensive and exclusive form of dressing has diminished and now there are only thirty full-time workers. The Queen and Queen Mother still use the House of Hartnell and Princess Margaret is an occasional customer; but the Queen has, for many years, used Hardy Amies and Ian Thomas in addition.

Hardy Amies began his association with the royal family in 1950, when he created two overcoats, two day dresses and two evening dresses for Princess Elizabeth's Canadian tour. This was the beginning of a partnership which has continued for thirty-five years and a high point in a design career which dated from 1934, when, at the age of twenty-four, Amies had begun to work in the high-fashion sportswear establishment of Lachasse. Although his mother had worked in dressmaking establishments in London, it was chance that brought him into the world of fashion. When he finished school it was decided that journalism was the career he should follow and, on the advice of the editor of the *Daily Express*, he went abroad to learn languages. He began in the south of France, teaching in a language school, but moved to Paris to work for an international delivery firm for a salary of one pound per week. From there Amies moved to Germany, where he worked in a glazed tile factory before returning to Birmingham to be trained as a salesman for Avery Scales. He hoped that his fluent German would get him sent back to that country. He remained, however, in the London, Reading and Oxford areas, becoming more and more frustrated, until his life changed quite suddenly and unexpectedly in 1933. His mother had worked for a dressmaker called Miss Gray, who had married and become Mrs Shingleton. Her husband had amalgamated her firm with his own French couture house, called Paulette, to create the firm of Gray & Paulette. Its sportswear division was called Lachasse.

In 1933 the designer for Lachasse, Digby Morton, set up his own establishment. Lachasse was therefore without a designer when a letter from Amies to a family friend in Nice described a dress worn by Mrs Shingleton with such feeling that it was sent to the lady herself. Impressed by the description, she persuaded her husband to take on the totally inexperienced Amies as a designer. Amazingly, he agreed and in 1934 Amies began work at Lachasse. There he first learned his craft, allowing his talent to unfold as he came to understand Morton's approach and eventually developing his own individual statement as a couturier. The speciality of Lachasse was tailoring and this has been Amies' strength throughout his career.

World War II interrupted and Amies joined up. Bad feeling between the designer and Mr Shingleton came to a head in 1940 and he was sacked. However, he continued designing, initially having his clothes made up by Bourne & Hollingsworth and sent to South America. He then came to an agreement with the London branch of Worth to make up and sell his suits. This arrangement lasted until the end of the war, when he decided that the time had come to establish himself under his own name. Friends and clients produced the backing and premises were found in Savile Row, in a bombed, but salvageable, Georgian house where the dramatist, Sheridan, had once worked. It was so perfectly in tune with Amies' taste that he has not moved since locating his new firm there in November, 1945. The first Hardy Amies show took place two months later. Amies was more than an expert tailor. He also had the imagination to produce sophisticated day and evening dresses and his firm flourished. In 1954 he branched out into menswear and designed a range for Hepworths. This association proved so satisfactory that Hepworths put money into the Amies business. When Hepworths became part of Debenhams, the Debenhams directors decided to buy Hardy Amies Ltd., which they did in 1973. Amies bought them out in 1980, since which time he has had ownership.

With his partner and fellow designer, Ken Fleetwood, Amies has created a major part of the Queen's wardrobe over the years and he continues to do so. He is the sole survivor from a time when London was able to support haute couture and boasted a number of top designers like Paterson, Cavanagh, Stiebel and Digby Morton. He alone has withstood the advance of the meretricious and tawdry fashion of London in the sixties and early seventies.

Hardy Amies' fashion philosophy is simply that, to be elegant, clothes must have a low waist. His clothes for the Queen, as for his other customers, are cut so that the waistband is slightly lower than the natural waist level just above the hipline. He has said that clothes "are not to be displayed, they are to be used" and that his job "is to do honour to cloth". Amies believes that, if difficulties are to be avoided, all good design must grow from an understanding of the cloth. This practical approach appeals to the Queen, who once spoke to him about clothes for "going about my business". She must be able to put on her clothes and then forget them, secure in the knowledge that they are comfortable and will behave predictably. Of course, she also wants them to be attractive and for her Amies' belief "in soft, fluid dresses, covering the knee and caressing the calf", combined with his no-nonsense approach, is ideal.

Ian Thomas completes the triumvirate of dressmakers 'By Appointment' to the Queen. He was born in Middle Barton, Oxfordshire, and attended Oxford Art

Hardy Amies chose opulent oyster white satin for this slim evening dress and large half crinoline over-skirt for the Queen.

Sketches from the house of Hartnell showing the romantic evening dresses created for the Queen's Royal tours during the fifties.

College, where he specialised in fashion in his last year. On completion of his course he wrote to the secretary of the Incorporated Society of London Fashion Designers to discover what were the prospects of work with a London designer. This society, now defunct, was set up during World War II with government backing to promote British clothing exports. It included all of the best London designers and in 1952, when Thomas left college, it was still flourishing. The secretary suggested that Thomas should show his work to John Cavanagh who, having worked with Molyneux and Balmain, was just setting up shop in London. Although he liked Thomas' work very much, Cavanagh could afford to pay an assistant only £2.10.0 a week. Keen as he was to be taken on Thomas knew he could not live on that amount. He declined the offer and asked Cavanagh where there were other designers' establishments within walking distance of his Curzon Street premises. On learning that Hartnell in Bruton Street was the nearest, he promptly took his folder there. With the confidence of youth he strode through the luxurious portals of the most important London fashion house of the day, left his sketches and walked out. The following day he was offered a job at £3.0.0 a week. Feeling that he could just manage to live on that, he accepted.

Thus began an association with the House of Hartnell which lasted seventeen years, Thomas working for his first seven years without a pay rise. He became Hartnell's personal assistant and they grew very close. Hartnell once said "Ian is my second skin", but Thomas recalls that, close as they were, Hartnell guarded his Palace privileges jealously and did not bring him directly to the notice of the Queen. When, in 1970, Thomas decided that the time had come to set up under his own name, Hartnell was very upset and took a long time to recover and forgive. Shortly before leaving Hartnell, Thomas was summoned to the Palace to meet the Queen, who presented him with a pair of gold cuffflinks bearing the royal cypher and a signed photograph. She wished him good luck and this, he assumed, ended his connection with royalty.

Though Thomas' own establishment in Motcomb Street started off in a very small way, it was successful from the beginning. The clients with whom he had worked in Bruton Street soon began to track him down. Within six months Miss MacDonald telephoned on behalf of the Queen and asked him to submit some designs. Since then he has created clothes for the Queen to wear on both official and unofficial occasions. The Thomas name is based on 'one-off' creations for private clients, although he designs a ready to wear line for a Japanese manufacturer. Thomas is not interested in London's smart or fashionable life. He escapes from duchesses to dressage at every opportunity and spends as much time as he can at his house in Warwickshire, where he breeds horses. He wistfully recalls the grand days at Hartnell when they designed formal ball gowns and spectacular dresses for specific occasions and the memory of specific dresses – like the one in black velvet and taffeta worn by the Queen when she visited the Vatican – gives him particular pleasure. But in these less formal days there is less scope than formerly for the royal designers. Thomas is proud of the fact that his clothes are much less expensive than

This photograph of Queen Alexandra, by the fashionable photographer Downey, shows her at her most glittering. Her dress and train, entirely embroidered with pearls, have the decorative boldness of the Ballets Russes allied with an operatic grandeur far removed from the clothes of her subjects. This is royalty at its most distant and, paradoxically, its most modern.

those of other couturiers: he claims that he can produce outfits for the Queen at half the price of the other royal designers.

Aage Thaarup was for many years milliner to the royal family. A Dane, he was born in Copenhagen, but has lived a peripatetic life. When he was a boy, he was kicked in the leg while playing football, and for some time he was dependent on a bath chair and crutches. Indeed, the leg troubled him all of his life and was eventually amputated. His ambition was to be a schoolmaster or a priest, but since his parents could not afford the required education, he went to a commercial school. After a year he was apprenticed to the ladies' hat department of Fonnesbeck's, Copenhagen's biggest store. At the end of three years he moved to Berlin to continue his training. The next port of call was Paris, where he worked for Maison Lewis in the rue Royale. This training had been arranged by his Copenhagen store and at the end of it he had to return to Denmark, which seemed so dull after all the excitement that he lost no time in escaping to London. There things went so badly that, encouraged by friends, Thaarup set off for India to try his luck. He set himself up in Bombay, where he enjoyed immediate success with the British and continental expatriot community, and then opened a shop in New Delhi. In 1932 he returned to Europe to set up a business in London. Despite fashionable premises in Mayfair – the shop was in Berkeley Street – few customers came to him, and his business was saved from ruin only by Cecil Beaton, who used his hats for photographs in *Vogue*. The magazine credited the milliner and he was 'made'. He moved to Grosvenor Street and soon he was making hats for every smart head in London.

Thaarup's royal connection goes right back to the thirties. With his tiny salon next to the Berkeley Hotel and a grand 'raj' clientele from his days in India, Thaarup had only to send a girl wearing his latest creation to the Berkeley Buttery, which was the smart meeting place, for everyone to be talking about it in an instant. Not surprisingly, society flocked to his door. One of his customers was Lady Doris Vyner, a Scot who had the traditional large skull of the Scots and therefore had difficulty finding hats that were comfortable and stayed put. Thaarup, as a Scandinavian, understood the large, round skull of the notherner (he insists that it can be as much as 2½ inches bigger all round than English skulls) and his hats pleased Lady Vyner very much. One of her closest friends was her fellow Scot, the Duchess of York, and it was not long before a telephone call came from Lady Vyner. Would the milliner be in if the Duchess called to view his hats? He would. Red carpet, hastily borrowed from the photographer next door, was secured with drawing pins, curtains were draped across stock and, in a primitive way, things in the tiny salon were prepared. The Duchess arrived with a lady-in-waiting, overwhelmed Thaarup with her charm and chose some of his creations. He remembers being struck, on that first encounter, with her vivacity, and also her calm, which Hartnell called "the intentionally measured and deliberate pace of Royal ladies". Thaarup's association with the royal family became very close: he not only continued to design for the Duchess when she became Queen, he also

Queen Mary, dressed for a fashionable wedding in 1927. The appliqué velvet flower which decorates her coat and collar are typical of the sumptuous garments created for her by Reville and Handley Seymour.

designed for her daughters and her mother. He always went to the Palace individually to show his hats and recalls his first visit there, with Princess Margaret Rose "shooting" him from behind a chair and Princess Elizabeth excitedly talking about an old groom at Windsor of whom she was so much in awe that her father used to joke, "Don't ask me, what does – say?"

Thaarup was a friend of Schiaparelli and her boyfriend, Kurt Weill, and was therefore no stranger to the excitements of surrealism. His hats using trimmings of tiny plastic vegetables caused the Duke of York to laugh. "You're mad!" he said. Underneath the fantasy, however, was an extremely talented milliner who took a very practical approach to hat-making. Thaarup designed with the figure in mind and at a first meeting insisted on seeing his customers walk across his salon. It was essential to observe how they moved and to note the breadth of their hips. This, he maintains, is the most important measurement to consider if the hat is to be to scale and correctly balanced for the figure. In addition, he would note down the customers' colouring and hairstyle and take smears of their favourite lipstick and mascara. Another important aspect of his service was to make the sometimes tricky art of wearing a hat easier by showing the customer how to place it on her head: a mark inside the hat lined up with the wearer's nose if the hat was worn correctly. And each hat was provided with two hatpins covered with the same material, to ensure that it stayed on! With all of this, it is not surprising that during the thirties Aage Thaarup hats were worn by everyone: even the super-sophisticated Wallis Simpson, introduced to him by Lady Furness, became a regular customer, matching his hats to her Mainbocher and Molyneux outfits from Paris.

Thaarup approached the task of producing millinery for royalty with total professionalism. Understanding the Queen Mother's height problem, he created 'lifting' shapes for her. A Breton style was returned to many times. It consisted of a soft roll ("it helps the cheekbones") like a "sticking-out sausage" which bevelled out from the forehead and was then built outwards and upwards. An exaggerated form of this style was used for the Queen Mother when she needed the illusion of extra height for sitting next to General de Gaulle in a carriage. Thaarup believes that a tilt best suits the Queen Mother's face and he points out that her flower hats are much more subtle than one might imagine. "You can't just plonk flowers on the head. You have to build out the shape from a net cap using very fine fuse wire so that you can bend leaves and flowers forwards, then the hat stands out from the face and flatters it." He considers that the Queen wears hats well "because her neck is beautiful". Thaarup always worked closely with the dress designers, who would show him sketches of the outfit and give him samples of the materials so that he could design to the correct colours and patterns – either to match or tone. He 'sculpted' hats on the block and then followed their progress through the workroom. His team of specialist girls stitched and draped, but since very few of them were good at placing trimmings at the correct angle, he normally did that bit himself. For a special tour he would create as many as eighteen to twenty hats; a normal order would be much fewer, perhaps only five or six. Only once did the

Queen Mother say, "my husband did not like that hat". Praise was much more usual. "Your hats are so nice," the Queen once remarked; "they sit perfectly and are right from the back." Although long retired, Thaarup continues to receive Christmas cards from the royal family, and he regrets that, although they are still delivered by hand, a limousine has supplanted the old horse-drawn carriage.

Aage Thaarup was London's most fashionable and successful milliner for many years and much of his fame rested on the highly creative partnership he had with the Queen Mother, for whom he created some of his very best hats. In those days, a chic hat was an integral part of a smart woman's outfit and added the same 'fizz' as lemon in a gin and tonic, so a fashionable milliner's work was constantly plagiarised. Thaarup's was no exception. To overcome this piracy, which always took place at the blockmakers, he decided to make his own French-style spartre blocks. Since they were made on the premises, they could not be copied. A spartre block is made by plaiting the grass, wetting it, and stretching or moulding it into shape. It is built up with more spartre, newspaper or whatever until the shape is right, when it is wired and, to give it solidity, a coat of plaster of Paris is added. It is then lacquered. The process is laborious, but once made the block is good for up to a dozen hats and no-one can steal the idea as it has not left the house.

Thaarup had a brilliant flair for publicity. He regularly put on shows and diversions for the press and he knew how to capitalise on his royal connection in the most diplomatic and inoffensive way. When he had created hats for a tour, say to Australia, he would fly out in advance to do a promotional tour of his own. Thus he would snatch up a great deal of work making hats for ladies invited to royal functions who wanted something correct, chic and European. Who better to design a hat in which to meet a Queen than the man who had designed the Queen's hat? Sadly, Thaarup went bankrupt in the mid-fifties and his business never recovered. He retired, but remained in London, where he still lives.

Simone Mirman is a Frenchwoman. Her mother was a dressmaker who hoped that her daughters would go into business together. To that end, she apprenticed Simone to a milliner when she was fifteen and her sister to a dressmaker. The plan failed because Simone eloped to London. Having worked for the famous Parisian milliner, Rose Valois, she had no difficulty in finding work in Schiaparelli's London branch, where she was hired as a charge hand in a workroom. In 1947, encouraged by her husband, Serge, who became a director at Dior and was responsible for setting up Dior-London, she opened her own millinery establishment. By 1952 she was making two collections a year, of about 150 hats each, to show to the press when, out of the blue, the Queen Mother's lady-in-waiting asked her to present some hats for Princess Margaret. She provided fifteen hats, all in white or black (the royal family was just coming out of mourning for George VI), and the Princess, who had always thought Thaarup too expensive, bought them all. As Princess Margaret was still living at Buckingham Palace at the time, Madame Mirman arrived at the front door and signed the visitors book in the grandest style before being ushered into the royal presence by a page. Only later did the petite Frenchwoman learn that

Soft silk crepe with fullness at the sleeves, formal gloves and parasol make up the Queen Mary look for garden parties and summer season events such as Wimbledon.

her entrance was the tradesman's!

In 1960 the Queen Mother began to buy from Madame Mirman. She instantly put the designer at ease by speaking very good French and whenever they meet for fittings that is the language they use. The Queen Mother becomes very involved, is extremely interested in her hats, loves all materials – especially chiffon and velvet – and is fascinated by the trimmings. She eagerly awaits the delivery of new hats and becomes very excited as each box, containing several hats, is opened to reveal the newest Mirman creations. Her involvement makes fittings a rewarding experience and Madame Mirman has always felt that, far from dealing with someone awe-inspiring, she is fitting a close acquaintance. When Madame Mirman was injured in a car crash in Brighton and put into hospital there, one of the first messages of sympathy, accompanied by flowers, was from the Queen Mother.

The atmosphere in a fitting for the Queen, who, through Hartnell, became a Mirman client in 1965, is calmer and much more formal but, again, the personal involvement was demonstrated when Madame Mirman's husband died. She received a telegram of condolence from the Queen even before the obituary was published in *The Times*. When Norman Hartnell was alive, Madame Mirman was normally engaged by the Queen to design hats to go with his outfits. She was provided with a sketch of his design and swatches of the material to be used. With Hartnell she had a very professional and relaxed partnership. He would advise her, but always give way to her opinions. Together they would subtly guide their royal client, without ever forgetting that the final decision rested with the person who was to wear the clothes. Nevertheless, royal dressmakers are not always happy with the Queen's fashion independence. "At the final fitting," one complained, "she always looks like a fashion plate and then in public she spoils it by plonking her hat too far back on her head. It ruins the line." Madame Mirman's method of designing, which has remained unchanged over the years, reflects her French practicality. She never prepares sketches; instead, using a block made to the Queen's measurements, she goes to the fitting at the Palace with two or three hats made up in the correct colours for the outfits. In this way she gives that other practical lady, the Queen, something solid to react to. In fact, she now knows the Queen's taste so well that she almost always gets the hat right first time. For long tours the Queen might require twelve or more Mirman hats, but they all are made to have a long life. Some of them are worn regularly for more than five years and occasionally they are returned to be re-trimmed to go with new outfits.

Madame Mirman has frequently said to the Queen that she would love her to come to her shop but the reply is always, "Well, some day...". Princess Margaret, who is still a customer, prefers to come to the shop and try on as many different creations as she can. Like any other client, she moves around the shop picking up and trying on many hats before making her final choice. She is very flexible, as she has no particular favourite in hats, but she dislikes trilby or bowler shapes and wears nothing which has a masculine connotation. In fact, shapes reminiscent of other things do not appeal to her. She still buys fur hats – fox, Persian lamb or mink

– but this is a practice which is dying out with other members of the royal family. Certainly no pelts of wild animals or rare species would be found on the Queen's head these days!

An Australian, Frederick Fox, is the third milliner to the Queen. Born and brought up in New South Wales, Fox was the eighth in a family of nine children whose father farmed and sold tractors, bicycles and sewing machines, in addition to running the local shop. His upbringing was tough and very strict, but this did not inhibit his ambition to be a fashion artist. As a boy he became fascinated by hats and by his thirteenth birthday he had a business going, re-trimming neighbours' wives' hats, which he delivered by bicycle every Saturday. When he left school he knew what he wanted to do; determined to become a milliner, he took himself off to Sydney, where he hoped to work for the city's top milliner, Henriette Lamotte. She would not take him on, but she found him a job with a friend, J.L. Normoyle, and personally taught him many of her own skills. Like many other novice designers, Fox was abysmally paid. He earned £2.10.0 a week. After nine years of learning his craft, first with Normoyle and later with Phyl Clarkson, he was ready to leave Sydney. He arrived in London in 1958, found work with the milliner, Otto Lucas, and remained with him until 1964, when he opened his own business.

Fox designed hats for Amies' collections for five years before Amies asked him to design hats for the Queen. His first major assignment was the Queen's visit to Brazil in 1970, for which he made half-a-dozen hats. Since then he has always supplied hats for Amies' clothes for the Queen and he is also milliner to Princess Alexandra, Princess Michael, the Duchess of Kent, occasionally the Queen Mother and, increasingly, the Princess of Wales.

Although Fox points out that the Queen is no fashion freak, he knows very well that she is not indifferent to her appearance and that she takes a special interest in millinery. As he says, most photographs are of head and shoulders, even on television, so that a becoming hat is very important for the royal image. Fox starts the design process by seeing sketches and swatches of material of an Amies design, but he does nothing until after the first fitting, in case the dress design is abandoned. At the second fitting he will produce a shape or even a complete hat. He frequently takes more than one, so that the crown can be taken from one brim to another, to create the hat which finally wins approval. Although he listens to Amies, and respects his views, it is a rare day that he stifles his own better judgement. And though he knows that his client is ultimately always right, he likes to limit the number of ideas presented to the Queen, preferring to have done most of the work beforehand so that her time is taken up by only minor adjustments.

Some hats are worn only a few times; others last for five or six years. The Queen has been wearing his black Cenotaph hat, for instance, for more than ten years. She has favourites and is inclined to enthuse: "I love the pink pillbox, it looks marvellous". On the other hand, if an Amies outfit is especially successful and is worn many times, Fox may well make a new hat to give it a new lease of life. There is no royal hat pool from which the Queen mixes and matches: a hat goes with one

The Queen looks her most elegant wearing tailored coats in strong colours, such as this one by Amies.

King George VI and Queen Elizabeth leaving the church after a smart wedding at St Margaret's, Westminster in July 1950. The Queen's clothes are typical of her fashion at this time: an impressive hat, collarless coat with cape sleeves and platform soles.

outfit, or at most two, and is not swapped. The Queen takes a practical approach to outfits. For example, if she is having a light wool coat and wool dress made for winter, she will often have a silk dress made to wear with the coat in the summer. Two hats are then designed, one for summer and one for winter. In all Fox makes perhaps twenty hats each year, excluding those specially designed for tours.

A number of practical considerations peculiarly affect the design of royal hats. The Queen will normally not wear fur hats, both to forestall charges of extravagance and, more important, to avoid angering animal protection societies. Fox likes her in big hats, like the white, medium-brimmed one she wore in Germany in 1978. The Queen, however, favours small, off-the-brow hats, because large ones make it awkward for her to get out of cars. She is particularly unhappy with foreign cars, which are much lower than a Rolls-Royce and do not give her enough headroom when she is getting out. (American cars with their low-slung, highly-sprung lines are especially tricky.) Fox always takes great care over the depth of the crown of a hat, not only because in his experience this is what dates most quickly, but also because photography distorts crowns, making them look higher than they really are. Royal hats are not to be dislodged; whatever their shape or size, they are, as Fox puts it, "firmly anchored with every device known to man". All these considerations help to explain why Fox often dresses the Queen in berets.

The Queen does not normally tell her designers when or where she is going to wear her outfits; in fact, like most women, her decision is made on the day. Even on royal tours, clothes are rarely designated in advance for particular occasions. The royal family gets no discount. It is billed just like anyone else and the Keeper of the Privy Purse, unlike some private customers, Fox wryly comments, pays on the dot. The Queen likes to keep a check on costs. It does not take a very observant eye to realise that not all clothes and hats for a tour are specially designed. Outfits from previous tours are often re-used, particularly if the country visited is little interested in Western fashion. A sharp-eyed journalist, noticing that most of the clothes on a tour of India and Pakistan were second-hand, remarked that "Brenda doesn't believe in wasting money on a flashy new wardrobe just to impress a load of Sikhs and their provincial wives". In fact, it would be wrong to imagine that, immensely rich though most members of the royal family are, they are spendthrifts. From the Queen down they are price-conscious and they always want to know prices in advance. It is, after all, an ancient fear of the aristocrat that tradespeople will get fat at his expense. The length of time taken over a hat, and hence its price, varies according to the Queen's movements. A milliner may have to travel to Balmoral or Sandringham for fittings. From June to October is not an uncommon length of time for the making of a hat. This is time well spent, for, in the iconography of dress the hat is surely the most important item. It not only denotes authority it is, in royal terms, a substitute for the ultimate symbol of power: the crown.

Queen Mary at a garden party at St James's Palace in 1939. This is the way she will always be remembered and is a testimony to her strongly individual views about her appearance.

3
THE PRACTICALITIES

Throughout the century, appointed dressmakers have waited on the royal ladies at Buckingham Palace, Windsor or any of the other royal homes. The royal connection has frequently brought them fame. Hartnell's name became known throughout the land, even to those whose interest in fashion was almost non-existent. Before him, the centre of the stage was shared by Reville and Mrs Handley-Seymour, who were court dressmaker to Queen Mary for many years, Reville being listed as a royal warrant holder as early as 1930 and Mrs Handley-Seymour still appearing on Queen Mary's list as late as 1947.

The royal ladies must always look less for a creator who will produce fashion fireworks and more for one who is reliable, and discreet, both in his designs and in his conversation. Even the very grandest of designers need to remember their place when they do business with the Palace or Clarence House. They are treated with kindness, consideration and courtesy, frequently with fondness, but there is a social gulf between them and their royal clients. To the vendeuse, as, in the French manner, the saleswoman is called, a subservient manner comes naturally. She functions in the traditional role of the royal servant who is relied upon to be discreet and tactful and to whom affection and warmth are shown. She remains with her royal mistress for many years. One vendeuse has been with the Queen for fifteen years and has become very close to her. As she says, "I spend more continuous time with Her Majesty than almost anyone, including her family". Fittings can last as long as two-and-a-half to three hours, during which time she stands close to the Queen, looking in the mirror and noticing every glance and every change of expression. As Hartnell did, she finds the Queen's personality warm and radiant: "after a fitting you feel as if you've had a tonic – you feel as if you've been on holiday for a fortnight". She has worked with the Queen at Buckingham Palace and at Windsor, Balmoral and Sandringham. Like the Queen herself, she likes the homely Norfolk house best.

The Queen's interest in and involvement with everyone 'outside' is seen in her extraordinary kindness to her vendeuses, with whom she has a trusting and, within the confines of royal protocol, natural relationship. There are two sides to the Queen: the woman who has been known to perch on a chair munching a Mars bar and chatting in a totally relaxed way and the woman who, when displeased by a breach of etiquette or a piece of over-familiarity, can freeze her victim with 'the look', famous in court circles and never forgotten by the unfortunate recipient.

Undoubtedly the person outside the royal family who knows the Queen best is her nurse, dresser, confidant and adviser, 'Bobo' MacDonald, a Scottish woman of humble birth. Like her mistress, 'Bobo' has been cut off from the 'world outside' in a myriad of ways. She does not have to shop for food, cook her family a meal or wait for a bus. She has had more influence on the royal image than anyone apart from Hartnell. 'The Little Lady', as she has been known to call the Queen, has listened to her advice on clothes and many other things since she was a child. She has great power. As one designer put it, when Miss MacDonald is present "if she takes to you life is pleasant, if she doesn't, it is not". Fittings may be relaxed affairs, but they have their own protocol. One is not allowed to turn one's back on the royal presence. Pins, feathers or whatever are groped for after taking a few steps backward to the table, and this movement may be difficult if corgis, the greatest hazard after 'Bobo', are lying in the way! When leaving the room the designers back away from the Queen and bow at the door. Yet for all the protocol, Freddie Fox's experience of fittings is typical. Initially over-awed by the atmosphere, he now finds them very easy and enjoyable. When Miss MacDonald telephoned him after his first fitting, and he apologised for doing all the wrong things, she waived his misgivings aside: "The Queen likes natural people, Mr Fox". It is perhaps unfortunate that the Queen makes up her mind about people at a first meeting, when they are at their most nervous and unnatural, for having done so, she rarely changes her opinion. On the other hand, if she and the redoubtable Bobo take a liking to someone, no kindness is too much. Towards the end of his life Hartnell felt unsteady during a fitting, but knew that protocol forbade him sitting on the sovereign's presence. When he told his vendeuse that he felt unwell she told the Queen who immediately said, "He must have a chair and some water". As the vendeuse made for a chair the Queen stepped ahead saying, "No, no, you get the water. I'll carry the chair, it's far too heavy for you".

The process of creating royal dresses begins with the submission of sketches as much as six months in advance of when they are needed. Having been given a brief for a royal tour or itinerary, designer and vendeuse arrive at the Palace with a selection of fabrics and drawings, and spend a considerable amount of time with the Queen discussing her needs. The Queen, who takes her wardrobe very seriously and is knowledgeable about fabrics and the climates in which they will be worn, will spend two or three days with the sketches before making her decision. Cost as well as suitability is taken into account. People close to her feel that the Queen has little idea of the real cost-of-living outside; she sometimes appears to believe that seamstresses are still working for £5 a week. The Queen Mother is more carefree. Faced with a choice of ten designs, she is quite inclined, as a member of the household once said, "to have the bloody lot". The Queen is likely to look quizzical and ask "expensive?" Once a decision is made the Queen writes

In the fifties Hartnell used black and white satin for two dramatic outfits for the Queen. She wore the evening dress at a Charity Performance in1953 and the coat for her visit to Paris in 1957.

'yes' or 'no' on each sketch and the dressmakers get to work, having been given a very clear, though rarely detailed, brief. The Queen Mother used to give Hartnell an extremely detailed itinerary, so that he could create specific outfits for particular purposes. This no longer happens. Only for the grandest occasions are clothes designed specifically.

Few women who have couture clothes made for them have to endure fittings as arduous as the Queen's. Whereas they might, at most, try two dresses in a fitting, the Queen, whose time is at a premium, pushes through as many outfits as possible in the time available. Normally, for a two-hour fitting, say, a rail containing anything up to a dozen dresses will be taken to the Palace. Times of fittings vary, but the pattern remains unchanging. A considerable amount of work towards the finished garment has already taken place before the first fitting. The materials chosen by the Queen have gone to the head cutter, who uses a paper pattern of the design, cut to the Queen's measurements, to produce a garment which he fits on to a dressmaker's dummy also made to the Queen's measurements. Parts of the garment are normally basted together with loose stitches, so that if it needs to be dismembered during a fitting it comes apart easily. Collars and sleeves especially are often required to be taken off and re-pinned. Skirt and back seams are usually permanently sewn, as it is unlikely that the garment will need to be re-made to that extent, but hems are left to be decided upon during the fitting. If the garment is an embroidered evening or state gown, a sample panel will have been prepared to pin on to the garment so that the complete effect can be judged.

The clothes to be tried during a fitting are packed with tissue paper to prevent creasing. They are placed on hangers in protective covers, which are opaque so that prying eyes cannot see the garments when they are being loaded and unloaded. If there are many different outfits, they are delivered to the Palace in advance. If only a few, they are taken by the couture workforce – the couturier, the vendeuse and one or two seamstresses. No matter how many fittings they have attended the couturier and his colleagues never become blasé. Everyone admits to a feeling of nervousness, excitement and elation as they swing through the gates to Buckingham Palace and enter through the Privy Purse doorway. (The clothes enter through the tradesmen's entrance. It is not permitted to carry them through the Palace.) Fittings take place in the Queen's dressing room, on the second floor. Surrounded by mirrors, the couturier's assistants array the clothes on hangers and when all is prepared a page rings to inform the Queen's maid that things are ready. The Queen arrives to greet the couturier and his team and the couturier withdraws to the waiting room while the Queen puts on the first garment.

The secret of couture does not lie merely in beautiful and costly fabrics, hand-sewn. What raises it above ordinary tailoring is the perfection of the cut and the precision of the fit. These very things tend to make all royal clothes look slightly old-fashioned. They are formal and stiff whereas the way most women now dress is casual and relaxed. There are certain vital areas in a couture garment: the collar and the way it lies, the sleeves and the way they are set into the garment (which affects

The essence of the Queen's mature style for day wear is that she dresses in clothes which the majority of her female subjects in her age group could wear anywhere throughout the land. Tasteful, understated and unostentatious, they are conceived to be uncontroversial and seemly.

the way they hang and the shoulders sit) and the hemline, which is measured by a ruler to ensure that every point on it is the same distance from the floor. Adjustments are usually small, but much time is spent with scissors, pins and tailor's chalk in getting them absolutely precise. During this time the Queen must stand perfectly still (normally in her stockinged feet) and everyone must concentrate. There are long periods of silence while everyone's attention is on the work in hand; but in between there is a certain amount of chatting. The workforce do not speak until spoken to. The Queen is always interested in hearing about 'normal' happenings of the sort that never happen to her. Much of the talk is about the garment and the Queen gives her opinion and listens to what the experts say. She never fusses, is extremely logical and is exceptionally good at conveying her needs. She is always open to suggestions. "Might I suggest that the top button be fractionally higher, Ma'am?" "Do you think so … yes, you're quite right." As each garment is approved the couturier exits, walking backwards, and remains in the waiting room until the vendeuse calls him back. When all the dresses have been fitted the Queen departs and tea and cakes are served to the couturier and his team. If the fitting is before lunch dry sherry will be offered.

A second fitting will check that all alterations are correct and that the garment fits and hangs perfectly. After any minor adjustments or last-minute alterations it goes back to the couture house to be finished. For very important or complicated outfits such as a state gown there might be three fittings, but normally the third visit to the Palace is to deliver the completed garment. The collars will be perfectly rolled, the seams will not be puckered, the hem will be even, the button-holes will be precisely aligned and the sleeves will join the shoulders without a trace of a wrinkle. To help the fit, the garment is lined with silk. Usually it is sewn largely by hand.

The Queen understands the importance of maintaining a consistent appearance, but no more than any other woman does she wish to be boringly predictable. She is lucky, for she has such a marvellous complexion and colouring that she can wear almost any colour, including, despite her age, very bright and strong ones. She is not fond of navy and normally wears black only for mourning. This may be a pity. "She looks her best – absolutely marvellous – in black velvet," says one of her designers. "With her colouring the effect is stunning." The Queen seems to have phases with colours, sometimes yellows ("a difficult colour which few women can wear – but she can" says a vendeuse), sometimes greens and frequently the 'royal' colour, blue. Pastels must never be wishy-washy: "They won't see me". Of course, the days when a Queen could have unique colours and exclusive patterns are long gone, and when someone remarked how nice she looked in a blue printed wool outfit on a tour of America, she said, with ironic amusement, "and another woman, too". Contrary to popular belief, there is little to-ing and fro-ing among the royal ladies to ascertain what colours they are wearing for a particular occasion. If, as happens, the Queen and her mother have both decided to wear blue to church they are both of sufficiently strong character not to change.

Queen Mary's low-revered, single-buttoned coats with fur collars became as instantly recognisable a trademark as her toques and buttoned shoes.

Colours, materials and types of design are chosen according to the work they are required to do. Foreign Orders and military uniform affect the choice of colour, temperature governs choice of materials ("it is always so hot" the Queen has been known to sigh) and suitability of purpose is uppermost when style is considered. Designers are set two basic problems in making clothes for the Queen. The first, shared also by her mother and her sister, is to create the illusion that she is taller than she is. The second is to minimise the fact that she is what is known in the trade as a 'clinger'. Due to her static electricity, her favourite materials, silk, crêpe de chine and chiffon, have a tendency to cling. The solution is an interlining of organza.

The Queen does not have as many dress-and-coat outfits as her mother and she chooses many more single dresses. These are known as 'investiture dresses' and are worn indoors, for investitures, lunches or audiences. Favourite clothes are worn over and over; occasionally they have their length altered, although they are rarely remodelled. As with colours, the Queen's choice of clothes often goes in cycles: if one three-year-old outfit re-appears, others from the same period almost invariably follow.

Since Hartnell died the Queen Mother has, in a sense, created her own clothes, keeping to the lines developed over the years. Very early in their association, Hartnell solved the problem posed by her slight stature and the need for clothes which gave dignity without submerging the warmth of her personality. An illusion of height was created by three-quarter length loose coats, a straight silhouette, and panels floating uninterrupted from the shoulders. Fur and feathers for large collars, or weights to the panels, combined softness with regality. Her look is largely unchanging and although she is open to suggestions, she invariably returns to the very feminine look which is her trademark, especially flattering cross-over tops and draped skirts. It is important that the material of a draped skirt can be wrapped around and across when she is sitting down and it often has bows or ties at the waist. Always the Queen Mother chooses soft fabrics. Her favourite is pure silk and she finds it difficult to comprehend that good silks are now extremely hard to find and exceedingly expensive. She brings out dresses which are over ten years old and says to her vendeuse, "this is such a marvellous silk, why don't they make it any more? There must be a fortune waiting for anyone who produces material like this today." Many of her dresses are made of soft wool, frequently trimmed with silk. That the Queen Mother almost always wears pearls must be taken into consideration when designing the bodice: the pearls must be allowed to fall unhindered and the neckline must be low to accommodate them. "I have my style," she says firmly, though she tries to understand modern clothes and is tolerant of the way her friends' sons and daughters, as well as her own family, dress. She and Hartnell struck up an immediate rapport and many a cosy afternoon was spent at fittings, where gestures often took the place of words, "A little...?" he would say, patting his waist and she would know that he wanted a skirt gathered or draped; or she would say "perhaps some...?" with a motion towards her shoulder and that would be enough for the couturier to add trimmings to the dress.

Client, designer and vendeuse must be very conscious of certain things. If the Queen Mother is in Germany presenting leeks to the Welsh Guards, for example, or pinning on decorations, the vendeuse tries to make sure that a buttoned coat is worn, to prevent one side of it from rising up when the Queen Mother stretches up or forward. Again, foreign orders and decorations must be borne in mind when choosing colours. In Canada, for instance, when Mounties in their scarlet tunics are present, reds, pinks and oranges are normally proscribed. Jade, blue and cream are used instead. Sometimes the rule is broken. On her 1984 visit to Canada the Queen wore a red coat and white-and-red hat, echoing the colours of the Mounties' uniforms and paying a carefully judged compliment to the Canadian flag. The Queen Mother likes pastel shades, but not timid ones. Her pinks, soft yellows, apricots and blues, like the mauves, purples and turquoises she so loves, are strong. She was once described by a guest at a garden party as looking like "a bunch of freshly picked sweet peas". As she gets older she likes white less and less – she has a pale complexion – and prefers shades of pink for evening. Other colours with which she is not happy are brown, beige, black and navy blue. Of the last she says, "I don't want to look like the Mums in the high street in Eton". She also dislikes fur, except as a trim, and is hardly ever seen in a fur coat, although she does wear a grey, "sort of broadtail" coat.

The Queen Mother knows that she is expected to look glamorous and goes out of her way to please. She tells her vendeuse that she dresses for the people. "They expect it of me; they have taken a lot of trouble for me." Nevertheless, she dresses with tact: she would not dress for a visit to factory towns with high unemployment in the same way as she would for Ascot. She has always, in addition, to bear the cameras in mind. Photographers frequently have to climb over the heads of crowds to photograph her from above, and since she measures about the same from head to waist as from waist to ankle, foreshortening can make her appear dowdy if a skirt is too long. The skirt must nevertheless be longer than the bodice. The scar on her leg which she got when her brother pushed her out of an apple tree is the 'maximum length line'. For various reasons, then, the Queen Mother largely ignores fashion length. If she has a straight skirt, the waist is slightly lifted, and she favours full chiffon skirts to give the illusion of bulk and length below the waist.

Her vendeuse knows the Queen Mother's taste very well and frequently chooses fabrics for her in Bond Street. If there is something in an exclusive fabric shop which she feels would be right, she obtains a sample. The Queen Mother is not afraid to experiment. "Let's take a chance," she will say. "Let's see – nothing ventured, nothing gained". In this way she discovered that cherry red and plum red were flattering colours for her. The rapport which she has established with the house of Hartnell is so close that, in all their association, only two dresses have been returned. The Queen Mother turns to soft, fluid looks over and over again. 'Floaters' from the shoulders, which help to make her seem taller, are now part of a standard look. As with the Queen, the exclusive use of a fabric is a thing of the past,

The appearance which endeared Queen Elizabeth to middle-aged women worldwide during the forties. Soft, accommodating and comfortable, it proved that plump women could still look smart.

The Windsor 'house style' on display at the V. E. Day celebrations in 1946. The Queen and Princess Elizabeth are in extravagant hats by Thaarup which use ostrich feathers and veils to amazing effect.

although Hartnell will not repeat for other customers anything she has chosen.

The vendeuse begins to choose a wardrobe for the Queen Mother by going through a new collection, picking out anything she feels her client might like, and adding what she calls one or two 'fashion-of-the-year looks'. The Queen Mother, who knows her own mind, usually greets them with "Oh no, not me!" Together they make a choice from the sketches, laying 'possibles' to one side and definite 'noes' to the other. Inevitably there are four or five which are basically the same and juggling begins. If there are too many blues other colours must be substituted; if there are too many chiffons, something more solid is needed. The final choice will probably be two or three country outfits ("Her Majesty would *never* wear checks in town"), several 'reception' outfits, Ascot clothes and some evening wear. This number is 'topped up' over the year and in July, before leaving London for her holiday, the Queen Mother chooses her autumn clothes. She is especially fond of 'trio' dressing, which consists of a thin dress, a thin coat and a thick coat. Although, unlike Princess Margaret, the Queen Mother does not feel the cold, she does, as a Palace official once said, "use helicopters like taxis" and she is therefore exposed to rapid changes in temperature. When she travels by helicopter, flimsy coats give way to heavy ones which will not be swept up in the draught from the propellers.

What the Queen Mother calls "my smart outfits" are created for the receptions which, for reasons of economy, are more and more taking the place of grand evening banquets as a means of royal entertaining. Her evening dresses are very grand, with hand embroidery for state occasions, simpler for private functions. The vendeuse, who supervises and advises on everything, uses certain 'tricks' to achieve the final look. Chiffon dresses, for example, are given a silk yoke to prevent them from 'sliding all over' at the shoulder. The tube which would normally be worn under a chiffon evening dress is omitted: it is impractical to have anything tight on the thighs as the Queen Mother must be able to sit and stand with perfect ease and no tugging.

Fittings take place at Clarence House, where vendeuse and fitter arrive with the clothes in big boxes – known by the designer's staff as coffins – at about 11 a.m. Along with a maid and, sometimes, a dresser, the women work as a team. Occasionally they have Radio Two on, when they discuss Jimmy Young's recipe of the day; frequently they are hampered by dogs. The session is punctuated by enthusiastic remarks from the Queen Mother. "Oh yes, why don't we do that?" she will say when the vendeuse makes a suggestion. The Queen Mother will stand, walk around and sit to test that everything works. Very much a 'man's lady' (in the nicest possible sense) and very feminine, she responds to a compliment – especially a male one. Her favourite dresses are, not surprisingly, ones which have earned her the most compliments. Rather endearingly, like her daughter, she has 'phases' with her clothes – a current one being the fad for off-the-face hats provided by the milliner, Joy Quested-Noel.

All royal designers, from Hartnell on down, have had to learn one basic lesson: no matter how beautiful, original or memorable a design, it is a good *royal* design only if the person wearing it is able to fulfil her role with absolute smoothness, precision and efficiency. This is what the endless time and trouble taken over royal clothes is about. The dictates of fashion, the whims of the designer and the taste of the royal client are all secondary to the overriding requirement: a design which is suitable for its function.

4
HISTORIC ROYAL MOMENTS

Over the centuries royalty has cast aside many of the trappings of magnificence which were at one time standard weapons in the regal arsenal. Dress is used less and less as a means of distancing King from commoner and, for reasons of political and financial expediency, the occasions when a modern monarch dons ceremonial robes are now very few.

Splendour at court is seen most dramatically at coronations, weddings, jubilees and funerals. All have the effect of raising royalty to a level above their subjects. The coronation is the most mystical ceremony. It is also the most extravagant. With the utmost gravitas and glitter the new monarch is anointed by the Church and acclaimed by the people. In the days when Kings actually ruled and when, as often happened, they came to their great office by 'right of conquest', the coronation of a new monarch signalled that the peace and order of the state were guaranteed. Then, as now, it contributed greatly to the "cult of the monarch as hero", as Sir Roy Strong has put it. Cloth of gold, fine stuffs, velvets and jewels are all used to heighten the magnificence of the occasion. Sumptuousness both distances royalty from their subjects and excites deference to the Crown. More than at any other time royal wealth and power are on display. Splendid dress, priceless jewels and prodigal expense are all part of the elaborate showing-off of princely power. As Sir Harold Nicholson commented: "through pageantry . . . the sovereign . . . acquires an aura of grandeur".

Down the centuries coronations have followed the age-old pattern with remarkable faithfulness. Since the coronation of Harold in 1066 all monarchs who have remained King long enough have been crowned in Westminster Abbey. (The exceptions were Edward V, who was murdered in the Tower, and Edward VIII, who abdicated in 1936.) The ceremony is performed, after the form laid down in the *Liber Regalis* of 1382, by the Archbishop of Canterbury. (The exceptions were the coronation of Mary Tudor by the Bishop of Winchester and the coronation of Elizabeth I by Bishop Oglethorpe of Carlisle.)

The central act of the rite is the anointing, which is followed by the investiture with the royal robes before the new sovereign is handed the regalia. The order of

Queen Mary had this portrait, wearing her coronation gown, painted by Henry Macbeth-Raeburn for presentation to the House of Lords.

the handing is the ring, the armills (bracelets), spurs, sword, sceptre and rod and, finally, the placing on the head of St Edward's Crown. The order has changed in one respect: the sceptre, the symbol of kingly power, was handed to the monarch last in medieval times.

St Edward's Crown, of solid gold set with precious stones, was for many years thought to have been made by Sir Robert Vyner for Charles II, but it is now generally accepted that it was made for George I in 1715. It was too heavy for the young Victoria, who had a lighter model made for her in 1838, but George V revived its use in 1911. For the coronation of George VI in 1937 the present state crown was made. The consort's crown was formerly set with hired jewels, it being considered wasteful to use royal jewels for a crown which was to be worn only once. William IV's wife, Queen Adelaide, found this quite unacceptable. She had her crown set with her own jewels and the last consort to walk up the aisle of the Abbey with a crown studded with hired jewels was Queen Alexandra in 1902.

Alexandra could always be relied upon to take an independent stand – and on nothing with greater certainty than her dress. As she crisply, and probably justly, said when arrangements for her coronation were being made: "I know better than all the milliners and antiquaries. I shall wear exactly what I like and so shall my ladies – basta!" The traditional colour for a Queen of England's velvet coronation robe is violet shot with crimson; for the Princesses it is blue. Alexandra, however, instructed M. Dorée, an old Huguenot weaver, to create a velvet cloth in her own shade of purple (Princess Louise christened it 'petunia'); the Princesses wore violet. Alexandra also broke with tradition by insisting that, although not entitled to them, she would have *all* the royal emblems, just like her husband, on her embroidery. They were designed at her express command by the architect, Frederick Vigers, and executed by the Ladies' Work Society, watched over anxiously by Princess Louise. Underneath the embroidered robe the fifty-seven-year-old Queen wore a dress of gold tissue. It was woven in India, a country she had always longed to see, at a fraction of what it would have cost in England. The over-dress, made in Paris by Thorin-Blossier, was of white net embroidered with gold spangles and gold and silver floral sprays. Lady Curzon, wife of the Viceroy, designed the embroideries. The out-standing collar, of gold bobbin lace, was wired and covered with gilt, diamanté and pearl embroidery. The Queen, who, despite her years, still had a 23-inch waist, looked magnificent. Lady Jane Lindsay described her as being "like a vision coming through the dark archway of the screen. I never saw anything more beautiful. Her left hand was supported by the Bishop of Oxford in a wonderful gold and white cape, the Bishop on her right in dusky red damask… Words fail to say how marvellous she looked moving down with her crown glittering with diamonds, a sceptre in each hand". Her white kid gloves, embroidered in gold and lined with purple velvet, were made to her design by the King's glovers, Messrs Harborow of New Bond Street. The future Queen Mary was present at Edward VII's coronation as the Princess of Wales and wore a heavily embroidered cream satin dress and train made for her by Frederic of Eaton Square. Over this she wore a purple velvet robe which, in itself, was destined to have a long history. She wore it at the Delhi Durbar in 1912, after her own coronation, and the Queen Mother wore it at the present Queen's coronation in 1953.

Traditionally the consort is anointed, like the monarch, by the Archbishop of Canterbury, but as Archbishop Temple was old and frail, the Archbishop of York anointed and crowned the Queen. Alexandra, to whom the religious significance of the ritual was of the utmost importance, demanded that the oil be placed, not on her head (where it would touch only her toupé), but on her forehead. One of her attendants, the Duchess of Marlborough, recounted the scene behind the canopy when it came to the sacred moment. She "watched the shaking hand of the Archbishop as, from the spoon which held the sacred oil, he anointed her forehead. I held my breath as a trickle escaped and ran down her nose. With a truly royal composure she kept her hands clasped in prayer; only a look of anguish betrayed concern as her eyes met mine and seemed to ask 'Is the damage great?'." Alexandra, who had a ready sense of the ridiculous, probably enjoyed this moment in retrospect, as she did telling people how she got soaked on her way to the Abbey because she did not think it right to put up an umbrella on such a day.

The coronation of George V, which took place in 1911, was attended by what his wife, Queen Mary, called a "quite overwhelming" number of members of the European royal families. "*All* George's first cousins of all nationalities have asked to come," she wrote to the Grand Duchess Augusta. "It will be a motley gathering." George V came to the throne only because his elder brother, Prince Edward, had died in 1892, and in the weeks preceding his coronation Alexandra made a nuisance of herself by continually saying, "*Eddy* should be king, not Georgie!". Georgie, however, it was, and he wrote of his Queen Consort, "Darling May looked so lovely ... it was indeed a comfort to me to have her by my side". She 'looked so lovely' wearing a purple velvet robe with an eighteen-foot train and a shoulder cape and edging of ermine, but lined with rabbit for economy. It was embroidered with gold emblems designed by Miss Jennifer Robinson, who had supervised the embroiderers who worked on Queen Alexandra's robe for her coronation. The Ladies' Work Society, under the eye of Princess Louise, again carried out the embroidery work. Wilkinson and Son of Maddox Street made the robe. Underneath it the Queen wore a dress made by the royal dressmakers, Reville and Rossiter. It was of cream satin heavily embroidered in gold thread, with a border of 'waves' symbolising the oceans of the Empire, a lace neckline and gold lace trimming on the sleeves. The Queen's medium-heel shoes, made of white kid with gold embroidery, were the work of the Bond Street firm of Hook Knowles and Co.

Coming after the abdication crisis, the coronation of George VI in 1937 was a popular affair greeted with relief as well as the excitement that such an event engenders. The royal family had been so shaken by the abdication that even that stickler for protocol, Queen Mary, broke with tradition and became the first Queen Dowager to attend the coronation of her husband's successor. Her Majesty appears to have enjoyed it. Sitting in a glass coach with Queen Maud of Norway, she smiled

Alexandra's strongly individual approach to her appearance was eclectic: she assimilated all the Edwardian fashion trends in her dress.

and nodded generously to the enthusiastic crowds on the way to the Abbey. Once inside, as she has written, "I sat between Maud and Lilibet, and Margaret came next, they looked too sweet in their lace dresses and robes, especially when they put on their coronets".

Queen Elizabeth, who might have turned to one of the chic, new Mayfair designers for her coronation gown, instead remained loyal to Mrs Handley-Seymour. The dress was made of white satin, cut on the cross and embroidered with spangles, gold thread and diamanté in the form of the emblems of Scotland, Ireland, Wales and England. There were, in addition, maple leaves for Canada, ferns for New Zealand and mimosa for Australia. These symbols also appeared on the Queen's purple velvet robe which was made by Ede and Ravenscroft. To give her added height the Queen wore high-heeled white satin shoes, embroidered with oak leaves and thistles in gold thread. They came from the Shaftesbury Avenue shoemaker, Jack Jacobus.

If the Queen's coronation dress was not the most stylish, that worn by Princess Marina certainly was. It came from her dressmaker, Captain Edward Molyneux, the flamboyant and elegant Irishman who had been wounded three times in World War I and awarded the Military Cross. Trained by Lucile, he had taken Paris by storm with his understated clothes for true connoisseurs of fashion. Princess Marina's clinging dress, made in his Grosvenor Street workrooms, was of fawn lamé with an embroidered feather motif of beads and rhinestones. The neckline was low and the sleeves short.

For the coronation of Queen Elizabeth II in 1953, Norman Hartnell was called upon to design the Queen's gown and the dresses of all the royal ladies in attendance. He also designed a modern version of the peeresses' robes. The Queen's gown is surely the most famous and the most magnificent created this century. Hartnell was eager that his dress should match the uniqueness of Elizabeth's coronation: she was the first Queen since Victoria and the first monarch to be proclaimed Head of the Commonwealth. The royal dress had to have nobility, but also mobility; presence, but minimum weight; and refinement, but enough strength to avoid being swamped by the rich ecclesiastical vestments surrounding it. For the first time the ceremony was to be televised and the dress had therefore to 'work' under the battery of lights. It had to look good on the television screen. In coping with this last problem Hartnell was helped by his experience in designing many wardrobes for the theatre.

Hartnell solved all the problems and created a dress which has been rightly described as his masterpiece. His brief from the Palace was sufficiently loose to allow his imagination free rein. All the Queen asked for was a dress in white satin cut on more or less the same lines as her wedding dress had been. (See page 62) Hartnell produced eight different ideas for her and together they went over his sketches. A design in white satin with silver embroidery was the favourite, but the Queen felt that the colours were too close to her wedding dress. Hartnell then came up with a ninth idea, which was to retain the full skirt and embroidery of the

A Lady of the Bedchamber's badge issued by the Royal Household to the Dowager Countess of Morton to commemorate Coronation Day, 9 August, 1902. A small card inscribed in the Queen's hand reads "for dear Lady Morton from her affte. friend Alexandra".

Queen Elizabeth chose Sir Gerald Kelly to paint her State portrait wearing her Coronation gown in 1937.

eighth design, but to carry out the flower motifs in colour instead of silver. The flowers were to symbolise the United Kingdom and, at the Queen's suggestion, they were augmented with the emblems of all her Dominions. The Welsh symbol presented a difficulty. Hartnell assumed that a daffodil would be acceptable, until the Garter King of Arms informed him that only a leek would do. To give it elegance it was embroidered in pale green with diamond dewdrops. There were eleven emblems in all, embroidered in pale silks and highlighted with crystal, pearls and opals. The end result was a richly shimmering, heavily embroidered dress in pastel colours: pale pink roses, mauve thistles, delicate green shamrocks (including a lucky four-leafed one) for the United Kingdom; green and gold maple leaves for Canada; green ferns for New Zealand; yellow mimosa for Australia; pink protea for South Africa; an opal and mother-of-pearl lotus flower for Ceylon; and lotus flowers, jute and wheat-ears in pearls, gold and green for India and Pakistan. The mass of embroidery made the dress quite heavy, but even so, to ensure that it fell properly with no distortion of the embroidered motifs, the skirt was lined with taffeta reinforced with horsehair. Very late in the preparations it was realised that the Queen would need an underdress for the Anointing Ceremony and a simple white pleated shift was designed. Time was so short that everyone at the salon, including the mannequins, was involved in sewing.

Although all eyes were on the Queen's magnificent gown, other members of the royal family were impressive in their Hartnell dresses. The Duchess of Kent remained true to her style in a slim white satin dress with a skirt of embroidered gold panels. Her daughter, Princess Alexandra, chose white tulle and lace embroidered with gold flowers. Princess Margaret wore a heavy white satin dress with a full skirt and low square neckline, the whole richly embroidered with pearls, rhinestones and silver thread. The most magnificent dress was worn by the Queen Mother, who chose a crinoline of satin, embroidered with gold and diamanté and trimmed with a broad band of gold tissue at the hem. All the royal ladies were liberally bejewelled in a conspicuous display of wealth capable of bringing tears to the eyes of the most hardened Hatton Garden jeweller. The Imperial State Crown alone contains 2,783 diamonds, 277 pearls (some reputedly from Queen Elizabeth I's earrings), eighteen sapphires (including one from the ring of Edward the Confessor), eleven emeralds and five rubies (including the Black Prince's ruby). The major diamond was the second Star of Africa, cut from the Cullinan Diamond and weighing 309 carats. In addition, the Queen wore Queen Victoria's diamond necklace (as her mother had at her coronation) which consisted of twenty-eight large stones and a large drop diamond.

The coronation of 1953 was a superbly timed, precisely organised state affair. Rehearsals began in the White Drawing Room at Buckingham Palace on 1 May. This room was chosen because it was near enough in size to the coronation area in the Abbey for distances to be measured. The Queen was able to judge the speed of her walk and the length and number of steps required to get from station to station during the service. As rehearsals progressed they were moved to the state ballroom,

Queen Elizabeth II with the Duke of Edinburgh photographed in the throne room of Buckingham Palace after her Coronation in 1953.

marked out in precisely the measurements of the Abbey so that the Queen could practise every movement from the moment she would enter the West Door. At the same time, rehearsals were taking place outside the Palace. The coronation coach was twice timed along the route to the Abbey and there were three trial runs of the service inside the Abbey, with the Duchess of Norfolk playing the part of the Queen. The Queen herself took part in only two rehearsals: the first was on 22 May and the second – the final dress rehearsal – on 29 May. A measure of the success of the forethought and planning is the fact that, three months before the day, the Duke of Norfolk, who was in charge of all the arrangements, scheduled the Queen's crowning at "approximately 12.34". In fact it took place at 12.33 and thirty seconds. No wonder after all this preparation that an over-excited cleric declared the coronation to be "a miracle which might save civilization"!

The breeding of princes is an important part of kingship. The stability of the monarchy, and the perpetuation of a royal line, are made more secure when there is a smooth transition from father to son. Hence the age-old cry, 'The King is dead, long live the King'. Continuity depends, of course, on marriage, since only sons or daughters of 'lawful issue' can succeed to the throne. Royal marriages are therefore as much public as private events. And a prospective royal bride or groom must be judged capable of bearing a heavy public burden. "None but those trained from youth to such an ordeal," Queen Victoria's grand-daughter, Princess Alice, once remarked, "can sustain it with amiability and composure." Prince Charles said much the same thing in 1969: "You've got to choose somebody very carefully. The one advantage about marrying a princess, for instance, or somebody from a royal family is that they know what happens." And he chose his wife from the ranks of the English nobility only after unsuccessful sorties into the royal houses of Europe.

When the search was on for a bride for Prince Edward, his mother, Queen Victoria, had reports sent to her about most of the European royal princesses, and very useful they must have proved to be in her job as Royal Quality Controller. Elizabeth of Wied was described by Stockmar as "to use a homely English expression, rather dowdy". Princess Alexandrine of Prussia fared little better: "poor Addy, *not* clever or pretty". Of Princess Maria of Altenburg the report ran "shockingly dressed and always with her disagreeable mother". The Weimars were considered "very nice girls but delicate and not pretty". The Princess of Sweden was "a dear little girl but much too young" and Princess Maria of Hohenzollern-Sigmaringen, who "is *quite lovely* and strikes everyone", was, alas, Catholic and therefore debarred.

The newly designed Peeress's robe created by Hartnell for the 1953 Coronation (left) and the traditional robe (right).

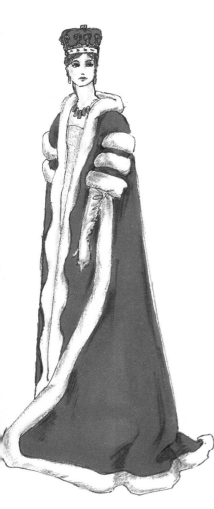

It was all very well to be fussy, but as Princess Victoria, Crown Princess of Prussia, whose task it was to scour Europe for a suitable bride for Bertie, pointed out to her mother, "Princesses do not spring up like mushrooms out of the earth and grow upon trees".

Queen Victoria was eager to get her son off her hands. Having convinced herself that her beloved Albert had died from worry over a scandal involving Bertie, she found it impossible to see her son "without a shudder". Therein lies, perhaps, the explanation for her acceptance of the King of Denmark's daughter, Alexandra, as a bride for Prince Edward. The busy Princess Victoria did her homework on the Danish Princess and was able to write to her mother that she had "seen several people who have seen her of late and who give such an account of her beauty, her charm, her amiability, her frank natural manner and many excellent qualities," adding "I thought I ought to tell you this in Bertie's interest, even though as a Prussian I cannot wish Bertie should ever marry her". Queen Victoria, who sided with Prussia in the running dispute with Denmark over the province of Schleswig-Holstein, agreed. Her reply was succinct: "The beauty of Denmark is much against our wishes. What a pity she is what she is." By temperament and emotion the Queen was pro-Prussian – "the German element is the one I wish to be cherished ... now more than ever" – but she did not need *The Saturday Review* to remind her that the Prince was "a man who can only marry seven women". The field being so narrow, she was forced to accept Alexandra. Sir Charles Phipps, Keeper of the Privy Purse, summed matters up: "It is of the *first importance* that the Prince of Wales' wife should have beauty, agreeable manners and the power of attracting people." Alexandra had all of these and the Queen came round completely. "If Bertie turns obstinate, I will ... wash my hands of him. Alfie (Prince Alfred) would be ready to take her at once and really, if Bertie refuses ... I would recommend Alfie's engaging to marry her in three years." Bertie did accept her; he met her and was bowled over, although, as Sir Charles Phipps cautioned, "it would be absurd to suppose that a real feeling of *love* could as yet exist for a person whom his Royal Highness has only seen in all for a few hours".

So the marriage was on. And a stormy affair it was. There were disagreements over everything. The bride's father was pointedly *not* invited; the date of 10 March, 1863, fell in Lent and caused a furore with the Church; since it was a private ceremony in St George's Chapel, Windsor, there was no public holiday and a severely restricted guest list; most annoyingly for the royal ladies, Queen Victoria refused to waive mourning for Prince Albert so that the wedding outfits had to be in grey, lilac or mauve.

Princess Alexandra, although not bright and barely educated, was of a highly independent mind. This was borne out when, shortly after arriving at Windsor for the first time, she was asked about cartwheels, and she promptly turned one in front of the startled eyes of the English royals. For her wedding she was equally positive. She instructed Mrs James, the dressmaker, in exactly the sort of a dress she required, down to the last detail, after a last-minute patriotic decision had robbed her of King Leopold's gift of Brussels lace for a gown. She disliked the then fashionable cage crinoline and refused to wear it. Instead she had the dress in "très bon goût, light, young and royal". It was of silver-tissue trimmed with Honiton lace in a pattern of roses, shamrocks and thistles and had a bouffant tulle skirt garlanded with orange-blossom. The train was of silver moiré antique (watered grosgrain), trimmed, like the dress, with Honiton lace and bouquets of orange blossom and myrtle. Lord Granville thought the dress "too sunk in greenery", but it established Alexandra as a fashion leader. Indeed, it foreshadowed the fashionable shape to come by at least ten years.

The Queen wore black and watched from a balcony. When the 'Swedish Nightingale', Jenny Lind, began to sing a chorale composed by Prince Albert, his widow burst into tears. After the wedding (which reminded Thackeray of a fairy tale about swans), family and guests repaired to Windsor Castle, where three luncheons were served. A general lunch took place in St George's Hall; thirty-eight royal dignitaries were seated in the dining room; and the Queen and Princess Beatrice added to the joyfulness of the occasion by eating alone in the Queen's private room! Chaos attended the couple's departure by train for the honeymoon at Osborne on the Isle of Wight. The pupils of Eton broke down palisades on the platform to get at the royal train and the guests returning to London fought for even third-class carriages – one, Count Lavradio, had his diamond star torn off him and stolen by ruffians. The new Princess of Wales looked serene in her stylish white going-away outfit with an orange-blossom trimmed bonnet – and her happiness was doubtless unalloyed by the news that, in the crowd which swarmed up Ludgate Hill that night to see St Paul's Cathedral illuminated, six people were crushed to death and a hundred taken to hospital.

The wedding of Princess May of Teck, to George, Duke of York, although preceded by dramatic events, was more decorous. In the words of Queen Victoria, "a tragedy too dreadful for words" had been suffered by the Princess. She had originally been engaged to George's older brother and heir to the throne, Edward, Duke of Clarence, but shortly before the wedding was due, he died of pneumonia. The engagement of Edward and May was no love-match, so that there was nothing very shocking in Queen Victoria's deciding that a Princess who had been suitable for one heir to the throne must be suitable for another. Her will prevailed and the wedding of George and May was set for 6 July, 1893. Strange to tell, there is little doubt that the new royal couple were deeply fond of each other. "There is nothing I would not tell you," Princess May wrote to the Prince before the wedding, "except that I *love* you more than anybody in the world and this I cannot tell you myself so I write it to relieve my feelings." He replied, "I think it really unnecessary for me to tell you how deep for you my love my darling is".

Princess May already had a trousseau, but it had been prepared in December, 1881, and quite apart from its unfortunate associations, it was no longer in the height of fashion. It was replaced by a new trousseau that was elaborate, costly and all-English, having been provided by Linton and Curtis, Scott Adie and Redfern. The

Her Royal Highness, the Princess Alexandra Caroline of Denmark, in her wedding dress.

Princess Mary of Teck, later Queen Mary, photographed on her wedding day.

wedding dress, with its train of silver and white brocade, woven in Spitalfields, was embroidered with a design of silver roses, thistles and shamrocks. The veil, a short one, had been worn by Princess Mary Adelaide, the bride's mother, at her wedding. Lady Geraldine Somerset wrote critically of the wedding: "Two things displeased me about May's entrée, first that she was not veiled *at all*!! Her veil hung in a little tiny narrow strip but a couple of inches wide *quite* at the *back* of her head only like an elongated lappet! Secondly, that instead of coming in the *exquisite, ideal* way the Pss. of Wales did at her wedding with her eyes cast down – too prettily – May looked right and left and slightly bowed to her acquaintance! A great mistake." In fact, the dress was simple and elegant and the offending veil was fastened with a diamond Rose of York.

The Princess's trousseau included "the portion" described in *Lady's Pictorial* – forty outdoor suits, fifteen ball dresses, five tea gowns and all the accessories to go with them. The bride's aunt, the Grand Duchess Augusta, sent her, in addition, some beautiful flounces of black lace. "Princess May," *Lady's Pictorial* remarked, "cannot be called a dressy woman and has no extravagant taste in dress, preferring always to look neat, lady-like and elegant, to keeping in the forefront of fashion." Considering how removed from fashion the Princess became in later life, this was an almost prophetic comment, as was the magazine's additional remark that "Princess May wears her boots and shoes with quite low heels and with pointed toes and has a very difficult taste in such matters". All the outdoor outfits had matching bonnets trimmed with feathers, velvets, bead embroidery or artificial flowers. The going-away outfit was a cream gown trimmed with gold. The wedding presents, predominantly jewels and plate, were put on public display at the Imperial Institute for the benefit of the Victoria Fund. They were valued at £300,000.

The wedding of the only daughter of George V and Queen Mary, Princess Mary, to Viscount Lascelles in 1922 was unusual for two reasons. The wedding dress, designed by Reville, was entirely of silver and so revived a mediaeval custom which had fallen into disuse since Princess Charlotte's wedding more than one hundred years previously. It was a simple design, having an underdress of silver lamé overlaid by a slip of marquisette embroidered with pearls and crystal beads to give a trellis-like effect of roses. A pearl and silver girdle went round the waist. The train of ivory duchess satin was edged with silver lotus flowers embroidered in India and bordered with the lace veil worn by the bride's mother and grandmother at their weddings. The other break with tradition was the release of information about the bride's dress, trousseau, presents and future home. The trousseau was largely the work of the court dressmaker, Mrs Handley-Seymour.

A year later Mrs Handley-Seymour was again involved in a royal wedding, that of Lady Elizabeth Bowes-Lyon and the Duke of York. This time she had the honour of creating the wedding gown. It was of ivory chiffon moiré with a mediaeval line. The bodice was banded with strips of silver lamé embroidered with seed pearls, a silver strip falling to the hemline. It had two trains, one fastened at the hips and a second,

Princess Mary's going away dress in rich cream Irish poplin, hand embroidered in pure gold thread. The skirt is embroidered in finely cut gold beads and the bodice seams are outlined with gold.

of tulle, floated from the shoulders. The veil was attached to a bandeau covered with myrtle leaves, ending in roses and orange-blossom at each ear. It was lent by Queen Mary and was the one which she had used at her wedding. Lady Elizabeth walked up the aisle of Westminster Abbey, thus breaking the tradition established in Hanoverian times that royal weddings were semi-private affairs to be solemnized in the chapels of royal residences. She was married without her bouquet of flowers: with typical impulsiveness she had placed the white heather and roses on the tomb of the Unknown Soldier. The service was not broadcast, because the Abbey chapter was afraid that "disrespectful people might hear it whilst sitting in public houses with their hats on".

Quickly dubbed 'the little Duchess' or 'the smiling Duchess', Elizabeth, Duchess of York, was an instant success with the people and the media. The wedding breakfast, so an eager country was told, was an eight-course affair, lasting for an hour-and-a-half and culminating in the 'cutting' of a nine-foot high cake which had been pre-sliced to avoid any hitches. The bride's trousseau was largely created by Mrs Handley-Seymour, with additional items by Jays and hats by Zyrot et Cie. The choice of crêpe-de-chine, kid and ermine reflect the fashion interests of the day: the colours were largely grey and beige and the only strong deviation from the current mode was the Duchess's choice of hats. She eschewed the popular broad-brimmed hats for off-the-face small ones so that she could be visible to the public. The wedding gifts were modest – no mink or sable, although the King gave her an ermine coat. The most surprising present was from the pattenmakers, who presented the Duchess with, not the old wooden overshoes from which they take their name, but twenty-four varieties of Wellingtons and galoshes. As she has been a keen fisherman and countrywoman all her life, no doubt they proved useful. The royal couple left from Waterloo station for a two-part honeymoon: the first part was spent at Polesden Lacey, and the second at the Duchess's Scottish family castle, Glamis, where she went down with whooping cough.

Possibly the most glamorous royal wedding of the century took place in 1934, when the Greek Princess, Marina, married the Duke of Kent. She was a beauty and he, by royal standards, a sophisticate. Inevitably, they were compared with the Prince of Wales and Wallis Simpson. The Kents fared better in the comparison: they were less brittle and their softness fit the mood of the thirties. They were both interested in clothes. Indeed the Duke, who had a discerning eye, frequently advised his wife about what to wear. She was not "over-dressed or boringly tweedy, but ... exceptionally elegant". It is not surprising, therefore, that she turned to the urbane Englishman abroad, Captain Edward Molyneux of Paris, for her wedding dress and trousseau. He created for her a gown of dressmakerly severity which was simple and refined. No old lace or excessive embroidery were allowed to mar the silhouette. Princess Marina's dress was the first royal wedding dress in which line and style were more important than decoration. A sheath of lamé, with a raised flower design in silver, it had a softly draped neckline, wide sleeves and was cut on a princess line. The train was also of lamé. "We are proud to find," *Vogue*

Queen Alexandra in her magnificent Coronation dress and jewels. Unconventional, as always, she waved aside the tradition that the Queen Consort's train be borne by six Earls' daughters and chose six pages instead.

Elizabeth of Glamis was married to the Duke of York in a medieval style gown in ivory chiffon moiré, created by Madame Handley-Seymour, and a veil lent by Queen Mary.

The Duchess of York's going away dress in dove grey crepe romaine, embroidered all over, was by Handley-Seymour.

commented, "that the Princess's taste chimes with ours." The wedding presents, which were delivered to the Kents' townhouse, No 3, Belgrave Square (rented from Lady Juliet Duff and chosen with the austere approval of Queen Mary) included, for the Duke, a pigskin toilet case, specially designed by Cartier and, for the Duchess, a Paquin mink coat and a vanity case set with sapphires and brilliants. Fashionable furnishings included a double-sided bookcase designed by Lady Colefax, Syrie Maugham's porcelain-handled knives and a Spanish leather screen "decorated in the Chinese manner".

The most impressive royal wedding of the century was undoubtedly that of Her Royal Highness Princess Elizabeth to Lt. Philip Mountbatten R.N. in 1947. Like her mother, the Princess was married in Westminster Abbey. Her husband had paid the standard fee of £10.2.6 to become a naturalised British subject, as a serving naval officer, and on the morning of the ceremony he was created His Royal Highness with the titles, Duke of Edinburgh, Earl of Merioneth and Lord Greenwich. Coming after a long and debilitating war and taking place in a country still suffering deprivations on all fronts, the royal marriage provided an escape from the dreary present and seemed to herald a more hopeful future. It was seen by government as good for morale at home and prestige abroad, a curtain-raiser for the Festival of Britain, the exhibition of a tired but victorious nation determined to show the world that it could succeed in peacetime as well as in a war. There was no coy nonsense about the dangers of broadcasting to people sitting in pubs. The wedding was carried by wireless around the world and raised a fever of excitement. For an example of how seriously it was taken we need only look at the action of the skipper of the New Zealand ship *Pamir*, Captain H.S. Collier, who hove to in the middle of the South Atlantic so that all his crew could listen properly to the broadcast from London.

Although the wedding took place in a period of austerity, nothing of the grandeur of the occasion was sacrificed. These were the days of rationing and the Princess's wedding dress, along with those of her bridesmaids, had qualified for extra clothing coupons. (Countless gifts of coupons from the public had been returned as it was illegal to give them away.) Norman Hartnell had to manage within the Princess's allocation of an extra one hundred coupons. Twenty dresses sent from New York were discreetly given away to girls of the Princess's age who were being married on or near the day of the royal wedding. In this way the Palace ensured that no advertising capital could be made across the Atlantic from the regal occasion.

In his autobiography, *Silver and Gold*, Norman Hartnell tells of the fuss made over the nationality of the silkworms which produced the silk for his wedding dress. So soon after World War II feelings were still very sensitive and there was public unease at the thought that the future monarch might walk down the aisle clothed in material made from Japanese or Italian silkworms. After a slight frisson of panic in his Bruton Street salon, Hartnell was able to allay misgivings with the information that his silkworms were all of Chinese nationality.

The wedding dress chosen from the twelve which Hartnell submitted was a masterpiece of the couturier's art. Hartnell's inspiration for it was Botticelli's paintings. 'Primavera' seemed a particularly good omen for what was being hailed, somewhat extravagantly, as a new dawn for Great Britain. The dress was described in an official press release:

> A Princess Gown of Ivory Duchesse satin, cut on classic lines, with fitted bodice, long tight sleeves and full falling skirt. The broad heart-shaped neckline of the bodice is delicately embroidered with seed pearls and crystal in a floral design. From the pointed waistline, formed by a girdle of pearl and embroidered star flowers, the swirling skirt is hand-embroidered in a design inspired by the paintings of Botticelli representing garlands of White York Roses carried out in raised pearls entwined with ears of corn minutely embroidered in crystals and oat-shaped pearls. Alternating between the garlands of roses and wheat and forming a final border around the entire hem of the skirt, are bands of orange blossom and star flowers appliqué with transparent tulle bordered with seed pearls and crystal.
>
> A full Court train, 15 feet long, of transparent ivory silk tulle attached to the shoulders, is edged with graduated satin flowers, finally forming the deep border at the end of the fan-shaped train. A reversed type of embroidery, as used on the Wedding Gown, is here employed on the train by the use of appliqué satin star flowers, roses and wheat, further encrusted with pearl and crystal embroideries. A voluminous Bridal Veil of crisp white tulle is held by a tiara of pearls and diamonds.

The bouquet of white orchids, supplied by the Worshipful Company of Gardeners, included a sprig of myrtle taken from the bush grown from a piece of myrtle in Queen Victoria's bouquet.

Hartnell was also responsible for the bridesmaids' dresses and again he sought inspiration in art in the Winterhalters and Hayters from the royal collection, the same paintings from which he derived ideas for the evening gowns of the bride's mother. Each of the eight bridesmaids wore an identical dress. It was romantic and soft, with a fitted bodice, a fichu of tulle swathing the shoulders and a bouffant skirt of tulle. The bridesmaids' dresses perfectly complemented the wedding dress and Princess Elizabeth stood out regally against their backcloth. To give her added stature she wore really high heels for the first time. Her open-toed sandals, lined in ivory duchess satin, had platform soles and heels two inches high. They were covered in the same material as the dress and had silver buckles studded with pearls. In order that all of this finery should look perfect before the procession down the aisle, no less than three dressers were provided by Hartnell. A small number, perhaps, when one considers that 350 girls had worked exclusively on the dress for the previous seven weeks, and more than 10,000 costume pearls and crystals had been hand-sewn on to the material. Twenty girls from the workroom were invited to the Abbey, along with Miss Mabel Syansen, who had helped in making the silk for the wedding dress.

Other guests were more exalted. Most of the remaining crowned heads and princelings of Europe were present and there were surprisingly many of them. The groom's mother, Princess Andrew of Greece, who elected for this one day not to wear her nun's habit, walked up the aisle with the bride's mother, who was in gold and apricot lamé and the Garter ribbon. They were followed by Queen Mary, stately in a dress and hip-length cape in aquamarine chenille velvet, high collar of pearls, diamond necklace and Garter ribbon. She was accompanied by the bride's great uncle, the King of Norway. The groom's sisters, having been sufficiently ill-advised to marry Germans, were punished by not being invited.

Despite the grandeur of the guest list, the wedding bore some marks of austerity. Post-war shortages of labour and, more important, materials meant that not as many special stands could be constructed as had been hoped. The number of guests was limited: only 2,250 seats were available, as opposed to the 10,000 for the coronation six years later. There were no stands along the route and people paid as much as ten guineas for window seats. 5,700 police were on duty to control the crowds and the route back to the Palace after the ceremony was shortened in response to threats of terrorism over the Palestine question.

There was little austerity about the wedding gifts. Admittedly, the Board of Trade insisted that the Glover's Company should acknowledge the difficult times by halving its traditional gift from sixty pairs of gloves to thirty. But many coupon-free presents came from abroad. They included four furs: the Hudson's Bay Company sent a full-length beaver lamb; Canada's gift was a full-length mink; a mink evening wrap came from Newfoundland; and the British rabbit-skin industry sent a grey hip-length chinchilla cape of thirty matched skins. The South African Ostrich Farmers Association provided an evening cape of lime-green ostrich feathers. Other presents were more humble. Gandhi sent a knitted shawl which so annoyed Queen Mary (who thought it was a loincloth) that Princess Margaret had to whip it away when Mary took a second look at the wedding gifts. The middle-class Marys, Alexandras and Elizabeths living in Twickenham clubbed together to buy a silver fruit basket. Royal brides always do well with jewellery and Princess Elizabeth was no exception. Her parents gave her, among other gifts, two pearl necklaces; her grandmother, among nine separate pieces of jewellery, a superb diamond tiara; the Nizam of Hyderabad a diamond tiara and matching necklace; the people of Burma a necklace of ninety-six rubies; and the Lord Mayor and the City of London a 'sunburst' diamond necklace. Looking at her jewels a few years ago, the Queen picked up an amethyst necklace still in its original presentation case and was heard to muse that she had not seen it since the wedding!

On the wedding day pearls and a diamond tiara were worn by the bride, along with the bracelet of graduated cubes of platinum which she always wore. It incorporated a tiny watch and was a gift from President Lebrun of France in 1938, presented when her parents made their state visit there. The Princess's engagement ring was also of platinum. It came from Philip Antrobus of Regent Place and was made by George Taubl. Set by Harry Marchant with eleven diamonds given by

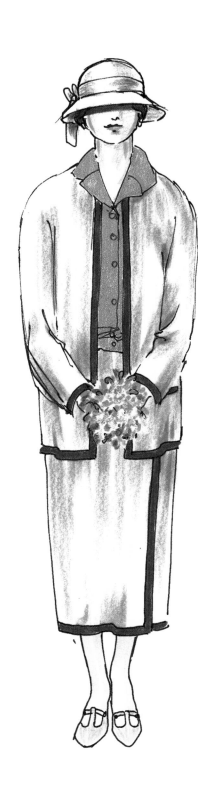

Princess Andrew of Greece, it had a central stone of three carats and five small stones on either side. The wedding ring was made by Mr W.J.L. Bertollé, the craftsman who had made the bride's mother's ring. He used gold from the same nugget of Welsh gold from which the 1923 ring had been made. The rest of the nugget was used for the wedding rings of Princess Margaret, Princess Anne and the present Princess of Wales.

The wedding breakfast, eaten off a gold state dinner service, and washed down with champagne, consisted of non-rationed food: partridge casserole, fillet of sole and bombe glacée. The Princess had twelve wedding cakes, eleven of which were cut and distributed to hospitals and institutions with which she was concerned. The official cake, weighing about 500 pounds, stood four feet high and was decorated with badges of the Royal Navy and Grenadier Guards and shields and plaques showing the couple's pastimes, including cricket for the Duke and horse-riding for the Princess. More than 7,000 telegrams were received. Boxes of carnations and mimosa arrived from the south of France. Food parcels came from America and were distributed to needy widows. The wedding dress was exhibited at St James' Palace after the event, in aid of charities, and 261,832 people paid to see it. It then toured Belfast, Cardiff and Edinburgh (where it raised £5,000 for the Lifeboat Fund) before being seen in several other major British cities. Copies toured the Dominions and the United States.

After the artistry and magnificence of what was surely the wedding dress of the century, it must have been a relief for the Princess to put on her modest, coupon-controlled going-away dress of 'love-in-the-mist' blue crêpe, also by Hartnell. Its cross-over bodice was draped to the left hip and it had a straight skirt with twin side panels, the hemline of which was fourteen inches from the ground. The ensemble was completed with a matching velour coat. It had soft revers, rounded shoulders and a gently flared skirt. Inset bands across the bodice were held with three front buttons to the waist. The whole was topped off with a high beret-type bonnet of felt trimmed with large pompoms of ostrich feathers and quills, designed by the royal milliner, Aage Thaarup.

Hartnell's design for the wedding dress of Princess Margaret to Antony Armstrong-Jones in 1960 reflected the change of royal lifestyle which the wedding itself proclaimed. On the eve of the 'swinging sixties', a secure and prosperous people did not need a romantic, fairy-tale Princess. A sophisticated simplicity was required to match the national mood. This the maestro provided. His lengthy experience as a royal dressmaker enabled him to produce whatever sort of design was demanded. Whatever the style, the results were always regal. The dress he made for Princess Margaret was exceedingly simple. It had a modestly high V-neck, a tightly-fitted bodice and long, close-fitting sleeves. The skirt was enormous. Made of white silk organza and belled out by a stiffened tulle underskirt, it required thirty yards of fabric, cut in twelve panels which formed a long train. The veil was by St. Cyr of Paris. It consisted of yards of white silk tulle, bound with organza and was held in place by a magnificent diamond tiara.

To complement the bride, Hartnell made more elaborate dresses for the bridesmaids. They were based on the design of the Princess's first ball dress which had been a great favourite of George VI. Puffed sleeves, frills, broderie anglaise panels and touches of lace made a pleasing contrast with the simplicity of the bridal gown. Hartnell's hand seemed less sure in his choice for the Queen. Her turquoise silk-and-lace, full-length outfit, with its bolero jacket and full skirt, looked strangely dowdy compared with the regal sweep of gold lamé, topped with an osprey-trimmed hat, which he provided for the Queen Mother. Not surprisingly, the most elegantly dressed royal guest was Princess Marina, who wore a sheath dress of organdie with a banded skirt of controlled fullness and a small organdie-swathed toque.

Princess Margaret chose Stiebel to provide her going-away outfit, a sunshine-yellow, silk shantung coat. It was slightly full, and its small stand-away collar and three-quarter sleeves showed the influence of the greatest designer of the time, the Spaniard, Balenciaga.

The move towards simplicity in royal wedding gowns was taken a stage further by Princess Anne, who married Captain Mark Phillips in 1973. Theirs was to be a 'no fuss and bother wedding'. Although public, it was to have the same 'feel' as royal weddings used to have when they were conducted privately in one of the royal chapels. It was not a state wedding. Heads of State were not on the guest list and, for the first time, reigning monarchs – with the exception of Prince Rainier and Princess Grace of Monaco – were not invited. In their place, the Princess invited their sons and daughters. Instead of waves of bridesmaids, the Princess opted for one. The four-tier wedding cake was made, not by McVitie and Price or Lyons as had become traditional, but by the Army Catering Corps. With all of this toning-down of the occasion, it seemed entirely fitting that Princess Anne should go to a ready-to-wear designer for her gown.

For some years the Princess had been obtaining many of her clothes from the 'up-market' ready-to-wear firm, Susan Small. It was founded by Mr and Mrs Carr Jones in the thirties and Maureen Baker had been its chief designer since the forties. Through her it had achieved a name for smart, well-made clothes which were fashionable, but not outrageously so, and always in the very best taste. Princess Anne made history by sidestepping the royal couturiers, Hartnell and Amies, and Maureen Baker came up with a dress entirely suited to the bride, the wedding and the time. It was a superb piece of dressmakerly understatement (unlike the extravagant and theatrical dress created for Lady Diana Spencer eight years later), designed with high neck and fitted bodice to subtly echo the military uniform of the groom. Miss Baker's Tudor-inspired dress was tight-waisted, with a full skirt and very large trumpet sleeves. Decoration was minimal. The collar was edged with pearls, the bodice was pintucked, and the neckline and shoulders were embroidered with pearls. The sleeves were also pintucked to the elbow, where they flared out over finely pleated chiffon undersleeves. The whole was made of white silk and the silk gauze train had a floral design of silver and pearls.

Princess Elizabeth and Lieutenant Philip Mountbatten leaving Westminster Abbey after their wedding in 1947.

But the dress was in no way as simple as it appeared. Quite apart from the embroidery and pintucking, the material itself was unique, having been woven to Maureen Baker's specifications by Stephen Walters and Sons, who called it Soie Annello. Its fineness can be judged by the fact that there were more than 1,000 threads to every inch. From this material Miss Baker cut her dress with a total mastery of her trade: the bodice and skirt were cut in one, entirely without waist seaming. Chain-store copyists who set out to reproduce the dress soon discovered that it was beyond them. (This did not, however, prevent poor imitations from mushrooming in the shops within hours of the dress's first appearance in public.)

Both the Queen and the Queen Mother were dressed by Hartnell. As this was not a state wedding they wore ordinary day clothes. The Queen's dress and jacket were in cornflower-blue Staron silk with a matching hat by Simone Mirman. The Queen Mother wore a champagne and gold silk coat with sable cuff trimming and a sable hat by Mirman. Incidentally, the versatile milliner did the wedding commentary in French for Radio Luxembourg to broadcast to the continent.

The most recent royal wedding was that of the Prince of Wales to Lady Diana Spencer in 1981. It was as extravagant in feeling (and in the feelings of hysteria the press was able to engender) as his sister's had been modest. It was also extravagant in fact. At a final estimate of around £150,000 (excluding the loss of industrial revenue caused by proclaiming the wedding day a public holiday), it was the most costly wedding in the country's history. However, it is probably true that the country got its money's worth: the gloom of living with unprecendentedly high unemployment figures was lightened by the fairy-tale, fantasy quality of the whole affair. No matter that nearly 5,000 policemen were employed to control the crowds, that marksmen were on the roofs along the route and that armed detectives rode on the coaches disguised as flunkeys! The bride looked lovely. Lady Diana Spencer was probably the most enchanting-looking bride to marry into the royal family since Alexandra.

Her dress was of silk taffeta, old lace, pearls and mother-of-pearl sequins – reputedly ten thousand of the latter! Unashamedly romantic, it was the sort of dress in which any schoolgirl might imagine herself walking up the aisle on the arm of her handsome Prince. It was created by two very young people. David and Elizabeth Emanuel had established a reputation for full-skirted, flouncy evening dresses. Lady Diana was photographed in one of their creations for *Vogue*, liked it, and . . . the rest of the story everyone knows.

The Emanuels were young and perhaps a little too eager to become rich and famous. Many of the ladies of the fashion press (a powerful and partial body) felt that they behaved in rather a cavalier fashion and took unseemly advantage of the publicity which their commission to design Diana's dress gave them. Consequently, when the dress was unveiled, it received a fair degree of criticism. Much of what was said was valid. The sleeves *were* too bouffant; the bodice *did* make the bride look top heavy; and the material *did* crease. All of these defects reflected the youth and inexperience of the designers and the bride. In fairness, it was felt that a huge

Princess Elizabeth's going away dress was in love-in-a-mist blue crepe. It had all the hallmarks of her mother's taste: a crossover bodice draped to the hip and inset panels, plus a Thaarup felt beret trimmed with an ostrich feather pom-pom and curved quills.

dress with exaggerated details was necessary to fight the vast space of St Paul's but, as a member of the Hartnell staff commented, rather haughtily, "She should have come to us; we know about these things". But although knowledgeable fashion journalists shuddered, for the vast majority of non-experts it seemed the perfect dress. For a description of the dress nothing can better the handout produced at the time:

> The Wedding Dress is made of ivory pure silk taffeta and old lace, hand-embroidered with tiny mother-of-pearl sequins and pearls. The bodice is fitted and boned with a wide frill round the gently curved neckline, and intricately embroidered lace panels on the front and back. The sleeves are full and gathered into a taffeta frill at the elbow, with an elaborately embroidered lace flounce underneath. Another lace flounce surrounds the neckline, with a taffeta bow to match those on the sleeves. The skirt of the dress is full, worn over a crinoline petticoat consisting of many layers of ivory tulle, and is trimmed around the waist and hem with embroidered lace. The sweeping train, 25 feet long and detachable, is trimmed and edged with the same sparkling lace.

To keep in line with the old rhyme, 'Something Old, Something New, Something Borrowed, Something Blue' the handout pointed out that the lace was antique, the taffeta was new, the tiara was borrowed from the Spencer family collection and the dress had a small blue bow sewn into the waistband. It also had sewn in a tiny 18-carat gold horseshoe studded with diamonds, the creation of Douglas Buchanan. The bride's shoes were designed by Clive Shilton and were of ivory silk trimmed with lace, mother-of-pearl sequins and pearls. The soles were covered in suede to prevent any undignified slipping! The bride's bouquet, which was a gift from the Worshipful Company of Gardeners, included Mountbatten roses in memory of Lord Mountbatten and myrtle and veronica grown from trees planted from Queen Victoria's bouquet.

Rumour at the time hinted that the Emanuels gave the wedding dress to Lady Diana as a gift. Informed sources within the trade, however, say that no company could afford to give away work so costly and so labour-intensive. It is, of course, quite likely that little or no profit was made on the dress, but what it did to publicise the name of the Emanuels was worth far more. It has been estimated that about 700 million people, a sixth of the world's population, watched the service on television, and the words 'dress by David and Elizabeth Emanuel' were spoken in every language across the world.

A jubilee is for rejoicing. It is a time when the monarch seems to come closer to his subjects. Formality and informality mix: state drives and thanksgiving ceremonies in St. Paul's Cathedral on one side, and, nowadays, walk-abouts on the other. It is a time when the country celebrates the enduring strength of the Crown, for many, the symbol of harmony and accord in a world threatened by chaos and disorder. Royalty has survived and subjects are relieved. A jubilee is also an outward and visible sign that the Establishment is in good repair. Some people may look upon it as an artificial occasion, mounted with a lavishness entirely out of keeping with the mere fact that the sovereign has reigned for a certain number of years, but it is celebrated with the full panoply of state and Church ritual and the extensive sale of popular souvenirs suggests that it is an appealing one.

The jubilee year of 1977 began with little enthusiasm, although manufacturers and retailers were quick to exploit its commercial possibilities. The china and glass firm, Skinners of Sutton, for example, produced a banner with the words

Oh to be in England
Now that Spring is here.
Oh to be in Skinners
In Jubilee Year.

Cajoled by television and the press, the people learned to feel excitement and by May the country was aflame with jubilee euphoria. Jubilee Day itself, 7 June, was one of strange contrasts. The procession to, and the service in, St. Paul's was followed by a luncheon at the Guildhall. To lend pomp and dignity to the occasion, it was decided to use the magnificent Gold Coach, the ornate appointments of which were matched by the dignified uniform of an Admiral of the Fleet worn by Prince Philip and the full dress uniform of Colonel-in-Chief of the Welsh Guards worn by Prince Charles. Yet the uncertainty about the role actually being played by the royals was betrayed by the Queen's choice of clothes. No long dress, no Garter sash and no tiara; instead, the Queen sat in the Gold Coach dressed as if for a wedding. There was nothing particularly wrong with her clothes, a dress and coat of strong pink silk, made by Hardy Amies for the North American tour of the previous year and worn to open the Olympic Games in Montreal. (The Queen had intended to wear a very pale green silk chiffon dress, and Freddie Fox had provided an almond green hat to match it, but, as the weather was not kind on the day, she decided on something warmer.) The pink bells hat had not pleased the couturier, who considered it too fussy, but Amies was not present at the final fitting and, in his absence, the Queen gave her approval. Amies considers this outfit to be the most important one he has made for the Queen. Important or not, the choice of it for the jubilee seems to sum up all the uncertainty about royal dressing in the increasingly informal last quarter of the twentieth century. Ancient coaches and modern couture make strange bedfellows.

Real though family grief is at the death of a King, his subjects cannot be expected to feel intimate sorrow. For them the funeral of a sovereign is, in the words of James

Cameron, "a deliberate, complex ritual, governed by precise and intricate protocol". Only with the greatest pomp and circumstance are Kings laid to rest. Pageantry, martial splendour and royal grandeur are all part of a King's funeral. The women of the royal family wear the traditional black with pearls and are normally heavily veiled. Their public ordeal is protracted. The period between death and burial is rarely less than a week and is sometimes longer. During that time family services, the lying-in-state, public ceremonies and all the sombre ritual of a state funeral must be faced with dignified self-control. When King Edward VII died, in 1910, the funeral was delayed for two weeks because the grieving Queen could not bear to part with her husband's body. Alexandra had grown accustomed to long periods between death and burial in her youth. Twice she attended funerals in Russia. In 1881, the murdered Alexander II lay in his open coffin in St. Petersburg for so many days that his bomb-damaged face was decomposing by the time of the funeral. Nevertheless, Alexandra, along with other relatives, had to obey Russian custom and kiss the dead Czar's lips. Alexander III, who was buried in Moscow in 1894, lay for seven days with his face exposed and, even then, was buried only after mass had been said thirty-nine times.

Queen Mary, perhaps remembering the harrowing fortnight after Edward VII's death, begged that George V be buried within a week. He was, but only after a ceremony at Sandringham conducted by the local vicar, the Reverend Mr. Fuller, and a thirty-six-hour period when the body lay in the church guarded by royal gamekeepers and estate workers, followed by a lying-in-state at Westminster Hall. The royal body is traditionally guarded by members of the services but, at midnight on 27 January, the Vigil of the Princes took place. The King's four sons guarded the bier for twenty minutes. After lying in state for four days, during which time more than a million mourners filed by, the body was taken to Windsor. The coffin, draped in the Union Flag and mounted on a catafalque, was pulled through the streets of London. The Imperial Crown rested on the lid, and the jolting on the cobbles dislodged the Maltese Cross which surmounts the crown and flung it into the gutter. Edward VIII, having noted in his diary, with a curious precision, that the crown was set with "a square sapphire, eight medium-sized diamonds and one hundred and ninety-two smaller diamonds", added superstitiously, "I wondered whether it was a bad omen". The King's body was followed by his four sons, four European crowned heads and the President of France. Queen Mary wore the peaked coif and thick veils of German-style mourning. Her granddaughter, Princess Elizabeth, who was aged ten, wore a black coat and a black tammy.

The death of George VI was mourned by three Queens: Mary, Elizabeth and Elizabeth II. It was the last royal funeral attended by Queen Mary, who had seen four English monarchs die: Victoria, Edward VII, George V and George VI. The royal ladies were all heavily veiled when the body of George VI arrived in the capital to lie in state at Westminster Hall. Queen Mary wore the Mary Stuart mourning cap that she had worn at Queen Alexandra's funeral in 1925. "These opaque veiled figures," as James Cameron described them, had changed their professional

Prince Charles and the Princess of Wales leaving St Paul's Cathedral after their wedding in 1981.

uniform of light pastels for dark mourning weeds. The King's subjects filed past the bier to pay their final respects and by the afternoon of the third day 80,000 people were waiting in what was probably the longest queue the world had ever seen. George died in the first week of February and court mourning was proclaimed until 31 May; his widow, however, observed personal mourning and remained in black for a year.

"There is a difference between court mourning and private mourning," Queen Victoria once told the Princess Royal. "Court mournings are short and worn here for all Crowned Heads and Sovereigns etc. who are not relations – but private mournings we wear as long as we like." Victoria, as we all know, *believed* in mourning. When the Princess Royal's mother-in-law died in 1859, even a five-month-old baby should, in Queen Victoria's opinion, have been in mourning for its grandmother. "I think it quite wrong that the nursery are not in mourning, at any rate I should make them wear grey or white or drab – and baby wear white or lilac, but not colours. That I think shocking." In 1860 she dressed her three-year-old child in mourning for her half-aunt's husband and was entranced: "Darling Beatrice looks lovely in her black silk and crepe dress". Deviation from black was, of course, permitted for royalty, as Hartnell discovered when he was able to make Queen Elizabeth the Queen Mother's white wardrobe for her State Visit to France in 1938 and still obey protocol for her while she was mourning her mother's death.

The unalterable facts of royal life are, quite simply, that whether their feelings are joyful or grieving, whether they are celebrating a magnificent occasion or marking an historic moment or tragedy, royal persons must, to a degree, allow their emotions to be on show. The personal events of their lives are played out on a public stage. Although their private thoughts are probably much like those of their subjects, royalty must parade a heightened and theatrical version of them for public consumption. In this they are aided by the trappings of royal style: age-old protocol, formalised actions and appropriate costume. The garments which they wear on these occasions help to codify the projected image, and engender an appropriate reaction from the audience, the mass of television viewers and newspaper readers throughout the world who are fascinated by royalty because they see them as 'different'.

$$5$$
THE ROYAL YEAR

Members of the royal family rarely have a day entirely to themselves. Their lives are spent travelling to and from official and semi-official occasions. Some are very grand, like the state opening of Parliament, but most of them are unspectacularly routine. Ever since the real power of monarchy faded into nothingness more than a century ago, the sovereign has had more and more of his yearly round taken up in visits to schools and factories, appearances at Commonwealth functions, attendances at charitable society events and the like. The range of occasions is wide. Yet largely missing from it is an element which at one time loomed large in the royal year: the 'Season'. The 'Season' itself is now almost dead. And what remains of it no longer revolves around the court, as it did when the monarch was the centre of high society's movements.

The object of the Season was to present daughters of the aristocracy at court and, it was hoped, to find suitable husbands for the unmarried ones before the summer was out. In Victorian times, debutantes, who were first so called in 1837, were presented at Drawing Rooms held at Buckingham Palace in the early afternoon. They were presented by a lady who had already been received at court. In those days many of the debutantes were married. They came up from the shires and normally put up at the Grosvenor Hotel, which was conveniently situated for the Palace. The business of dressing was taken very seriously and plenty of time was allowed for it. By twelve noon the hairdressers had arrived and from then until two o'clock all was energy, excitement and nervous trepidation. The completed toilette consisted of a gown of pastel shades or white (a married debutante wore her wedding gown), a bouquet of flowers and almost always a lace fan. Once inside the Palace guests assembled in an ante-chamber leading to the Throne room. The pale colours of their dresses stood out against the richer shades worn by their mothers' and presenters' gowns. The men glowed darkly in full court dress, a deep blue tunic, heavily embroidered in gold, a cocked plumed hat, silk stockings, patent shoes and a gold sword. When the Queen and royal family were assembled the presentation began. The central moment was the curtsey, which had been taught at special classes by the fashionable dancing master, Monsieur D'Eqville. He was

Royal visits are always in season and they usually lead to mutually pleasing confrontations such as this one when the Queen visited Liverpool Cathedral in October 1978.

always fully booked weeks in advance of a presentation, and he taught the girls to move gracefully by fixing a dummy train to them while putting them through their paces. The real train worn on the day was, immediately after the presentation was over, flung over the debutante's shoulder by a specially detailed court official, so that she could move on without awkward hitches. The debutantes had their photographs taken by the fashionable photographers, W & D Downey, and then, since no refreshments were served, went off to the tea-parties which completed the day.

Garden parties became a popular form of entertainment at Buckingham Palace in the nineties and between 800 and 1,000 guests were entertained at a time. Queen Victoria was drawn about the grounds in a little pony carriage which she stopped from time to time to talk to guests. The Guards' band played and the Royal Watermen in their quaint costumes stood by ready to take guests for a row on the lake. Garden parties at Windsor followed the same pattern, although there the number of guests, who travelled down by special trains and walked up to the castle, was halved. Tea was served in the grounds, after the royal family had appeared, between 4.30 and 5 p.m.

The first evening court was held at Buckingham Palace in 1902, in an attempt by Edward VII to accommodate the increasing number of those persons who considered themselves 'society' and wished their daughters to be presented. In Victorian times members of society who left their cards at the Lord Chamberlain's office had automatically been admitted to Drawing Rooms. By 1900 the increased numbers of applicants necessitated a more formal approach and rules of dress were tightened by the King. Edward VII, ebullient and 'easy' in many respects, was, in the words of a contemporary, "a martinet about attire and the perfection of detail in connection with clothes". To avoid social solecisms, ladies turned to Herbert Trendell's book *Dress Worn at His Majesty's Court*, which was published in 1908. It detailed the precise uniforms for such arcane officials as His Majesty's Swan Keeper and, in addition, had an appendix on 'Dress Regulations for Ladies Attending Their Majesties' Courts'.

Ladies attending Their Majesties' Courts will appear in Full Dress, with TRAINS AND PLUMES. For Half Mourning Black and White, White, Mauve, or Grey should be worn.

FEATHERS should be worn so that they can be clearly seen on approaching the Presence, with White veils or lappets. Coloured feathers are inadmissible, but deep mourning Black feathers may be worn. WHITE GLOVES only are to be worn, except in case of mourning, when Black or Grey gloves are admissible.

HIGH COURT DRESS. The King has been pleased to permit that a High Court Dress, according to the following description, may be worn in future at Their Majesties' Courts, and on other State occasions, by Ladies, to whom, from illness, infirmity, or advancing age, the present low Court Dress is inappropriate, viz. Bodices, in front, cut square or heart shape, which may be *filled in*

Edwardian Court Dress was sumptuous and the Courts presented an ideal opportunity to show off one's wealth and position within the Lord Chamberlain's rules. His office contained elaborately coloured sketches of the right and wrong ways of dressing at Court. One of the strictest rules concerned the three feathers, which were not to be tucked down behind the ears.

with white only, either transparent or lined; at the back, high, or cut down three-quarter height. Sleeves to elbow, either thick or transparent. Trains, gloves and feathers as usual.

It is necessary for Ladies who wish to appear in "HIGH COURT DRESS", to obtain permission through the Lord Chamberlain, unless they have already received it.

The regulations show quite clearly the process to be gone through before presentation could take place.

(1)   Ladies who have been presented and who wish to be summoned to one of these Courts are requested to make written application to the Lord Chamberlain, St. James's Palace, S.W. *on or as soon as possible after the 1st January in each year*, but not before that date.

(2)   It is not according to rule, unless under exceptional circumstances, for ladies to attend Court more than once in every three years.

(3)   When making applications, ladies are requested to state approximately the time of year that will be most convenient for them to attend a Court.

(4)   A lady attending a Court may present one lady, for whom she must be responsible, in addition to her daughter *or* daughter-in-law. The names of the ladies to be presented should be forwarded by the lady who wishes to make the presentation when she sends in her own name.

(5)   No applications can be received from ladies who wish to be presented. Their names must be forwarded by the ladies who wish to make the presentations.

(6)   Ladies may be accompanied to Court by their husbands if the latter have been presented, but gentlemen do not pass before the King and Queen. *Ladies are requested to forward the names of their husbands at the same time as their own*, in order that they may be submitted together.

(7)   Summonses are issued about three weeks before the date of each Court, and should it not be convenient for a lady to attend the particular Court to which she is summoned, it will be open to her to make her excuses to the Lord Chamberlain in writing, when her name can, if desired, and if possible, be transferred to another list.

(8)   The Dress Regulations are:- Ladies: Full Court Dress with feather and trains. Gentlemen: Full Court Dress.

This publication had the backing of the Lord Chamberlain's office and was sufficiently precise to leave little room for personal idiosyncracy on the part of those allowed into 'the Presence'. For gentlemen the regulations included a mine of information, not the least the section on 'Care of Preservation of Uniform'.

All gold and silver laced garments or articles should be folded or wrapped in tissue paper and placed in air-tight tin cases. Care should be taken that no article is put away damp. All articles liable to be eaten by moth should be unfolded at intervals and well beaten and brushed in the open air.

Alexandra wore remarkably simple gowns when at Cowes or visiting her family in Denmark.

Russia leather parings, powdered camphor, Naphthaline, carbolized paper, or turpentine sprinkled on brown paper should be placed among the articles of uniform which are to be packed away for any time. Gold Lace that has become slightly tarnished can be cleaned with a mixture of cream of tartar and dry bread rubbed up very fine applied in a dry state and brushed lightly with a clean soft brush.

The Courts were the greatest social event of the year and they were kept very exclusive. All names sent in by mothers were scrupulously checked. The chosen ones were commanded to attend. The stiff card was not an invitation; it was not to be acknowledged; it was to be obeyed. Presentation conferred social standing both at home and at European courts. A woman presented at court gained the automatic privilege "when visiting a foreign country, of being received at any Court ceremony, function or entertainment".

The first court of the season was always the Diplomatic Court and it set the tone of formality for those that followed. Presentations were held in the State Ballroom, which was 120 feet long and 60 feet wide. At the west end of the room, on a dais, stood the thrones used in Westminster Abbey for the coronation of Edward VII. Gilt Regency chairs were provided for the royal Princesses. To reach the ballroom there were two routes. The easier and less crowded one was reserved for those privileged persons who had the 'Entré' to the Palace via the Ambassadors' Entrance. They followed the route up the Grand Staircase to the first landing, where they took the second flight to the right and proceeded through the Green Drawing Room, across the Picture Gallery, then through the Music Room, the White Drawing Room, the State Dining Room and the West gallery to seats specially reserved for them in the ballroom. The others, called the 'General Circle', proceeded through the East Gallery into the ballroom, where they were seated in rotation. When the seats in the ballroom were filled, a room to the left of the East Gallery, known as the Supper Room, accommodated the remainder. A military band was stationed in the Gallery during the period of waiting and played to the nervous crowd. The King, the Queen and the royal circle then assembled in the White Drawing Room, and when the King gave the order, the great officers of the household, attended by the other ladies and gentlemen, conducted them to the Blue Drawing Room, whence they proceeded via the West Gallery to the ballroom.

A contemporary account of a court held in 1937 describes the routine, which had not changed in any significant way since the first court in 1902.

At the Courts, when their Majesties have taken their places on the Dais and the Royal family and Court officials have grouped themselves around in order of precedent, then the ceremonial is opened. At the King's pleasure, the Marshal of the Diplomatic Corps leads by the hand the wife of the Secretary of State for Foreign Affairs who, after obeisance, stands by His Majesty; after which the wife of the doyen of the Diplomatic Corps is led in by the Marshal, then the Ambassadresses, wives of Ministers and Chargés d'Affaires, together with the

During the twenties and thirties Court dress reflected the mode of the times and Court dressmakers were kept busy throughout the season creating dresses for those commanded to attend.

ladies of the Embassies and legations, and the Debutantes for whom they are responsible pass the Presence.

The Ambassadors, Ministers and Chargés d'Affaires then enter and pass the Presence. The King and Queen, having thus received the Diplomatic Corps and their ladies standing, take their seats upon the Throne and remain seated throughout the remainder of the Ceremonial.

Those with the Entré are then followed by the General Circle, including the Debutantes, each name being announced to Their Majesties by the Lord Chamberlain, who stands next the King, and everyone making their obeisance on passing Their Majesties. On the conclusion of the Court the Royal Procession is again formed and files out in like order in which it reached the Ballroom.

Did anyone actually enjoy these occasions? For the debutantes they were an ordeal which began with their being held up for two or three hours in the Mall in a queue of automobiles which inched its way towards the Palace gates. Along the way they were subjected to the comments and taunts of the crowds, many of them aggressive reflections on the luxurious lives of the 'nobs'. Eventually, during the thirties, the traffic became so congested that the rules were changed: cars were allowed into the Palace yard for the girls to alight, thus speeding up the whole process. Once they had pushed their way slowly up the broad marble stairs and recovered their composure, the debutantes had to remember the rules of the curtsey. The instructions were specific.

> The curtsey should be made gracefully and with an absence of stiffness; the left foot is drawn backwards, the knees are bent and the body gradually lowered until the left knee is within a few inches of the floor; the back is kept straight and the head kept up.

To avoid the train, it was important to get up on the correct foot. Three steps sideways, a second curtsey and the ordeal was almost over. However, before walking out the left arm had to be extended so that an usher could drape the train over it. All of this under the steady gaze of the monarch and with the additional hazards of carrying a fan or flowers or both!

No wonder that after the court and a quick visit to the photographer, the shattered girls would let their hair down and release their pent-up nerves at a dance. The announcement recorded by 'Eve' in the _Tatler_ in 1919 that "their Majesties will (weather permitting) give a series of afternoon parties in the gardens of Buckingham Palace during the months of May and June, invitations to which will be equivalent to and recorded as attendance or presentation at Court as the case may be" was followed by the comment that "an afternoon party in the gardens of Buckingham Palace just simply can't be, at worst, a function so devastatingly dull, so enervatingly ennuyant, so fearfully feminine, so tiring, so boring as a Court ... one won't feel as at the Courts that you weren't the only party bored stiff – the Royals were simply dead with it".

Yet however formal they may seem to us, British courts were lax compared with the Russian court. For example, it was prescribed by Imperial etiquette that the train of a Grand Duchess must be kept absolutely straight at all times, even when negotiating a corner. The wedding train worn by the Grand Duchess Anastasia for the Imperial Procession at Tzarskoe Selo in 1902 was twenty feet long and trimmed with trails of artificial roses. The difficulties encountered by the pages whose job it was to support these unwieldy items and keep them straight were considerable. Nor did their own constricting uniforms make the job any easier. Royal pages wore gold-and-black heavily embroidered coats, black top boots, gold-and-black helmets with a golden eagle in front and a waving white plume attached to a spike, and white knee breeches. By a strict Imperial rule the breeches had to be absolutely skin-tight with a surface unmarred by crease or wrinkle. This could be achieved only if the page thoroughly soaked his breeches in water and wore the damp garment next to his skin "without the protection of an intermediate covering". Despite great caution the tight wet breeches frequently split during the slow and complicated progress of a royal procession.

Codes of behaviour and dress were less stringent in Great Britain, but the Lord Chamberlain allowed no laxity. He did, however, move slowly with the times. Sir George Titman's *Dress and Insignia Worn at Court*, published in 1937, shows that by then the rules had been amended to exclude high-court dress.

> Ladies attending Their Majesties' Courts must wear Low Evening Dresses with Court Trains suspended from the shoulders, white veils with ostrich feathers will be worn on the head. The Train, which should not exceed 2 yards in length, must not extend more than 18″ from the heel of the wearer when standing.
>
> Three small white feathers mounted as a Prince of Wales Plume, the centre feather a little higher than the two side ones, to be worn slightly on the left side of the head, with the tulle veil of similar colour attached to the base of the feathers. The veil should not be longer than 45″. Coloured feathers are inadmissible, but in cases of deep mourning Black feathers may be worn.
>
> Gloves *must* be worn.
>
> There are no restrictions with regard to the colour of the dresses or gloves for either debutantes or those who have already been presented.
>
> Bouquets and fans are optional.
>
> Sketches of typical Court Dresses are on view at the Lord Chamberlain's Office, St. James's Palace.

The thirties saw the final flowering of the courts as the centre of the London season. Discontinued when war broke out in 1939, presentations were re-instituted in 1947. By then there was a backlog of 20,000 applicants and to ease the pressure, garden parties were held for presentations. (Bad weather in 1948 led to their being held in the State apartments.) In 1951 George VI decided to return to individual presentations, although only the debutantes, not their presenters, now curtseyed.

A Downey portrait of Alexandra taken in 1898, when still Princess of Wales. Her clothes and figure reflect the full-blown character of the fin-de-siècle period.

During the fifties the whole presentation business became an increasingly middle-class industry. Girls were taught to curtsey by Miss Beth Vacani, who had taught the Princesses to dance, and many attended a course at Cygnets House run by Mrs Rennie O'Mahoney. Here they were taught the traditional demeanour of a lady, ending the course by showing off their new skills at the Cygnet Ball at Claridges. Since fewer and fewer of the would-be debutantes had aristocratic links, finding presenters became acutely difficult. Professional presenters (who had always existed) came into great demand. A presenter, such as Lady St. John of Bletso or Lady Clancarty, often asked more than £1,000 for her services – and the charge could be nearer £2,000 if the girl were Jewish. By 1957 presentation parties had become so debased that the Lord Chamberlain's Office announced they were to cease. Instead, the Queen would hold additional garden parties.

> For some time – in fact since 1954 – The Queen has had in mind the general pattern of official entertaining at Buckingham Palace, including the problem of Presentation Parties and certain anomalies to which they give rise. Her Majesty has felt reluctant to bring these to an end because of the pleasure they appear to give to a number of young people and the increasing applications for them. These applications have now risen until it has become necessary either to add to the number of these Parties or to seek some other solution.
>
> The Queen has decided that owing to her many engagements it would not be possible to increase the number of Presentation Parties. Her Majesty therefore proposes to hold (after next year), instead of Presentation Parties, additional Garden Parties, which will have the effect of increasing the number of persons invited to Buckingham Palace, both from the United Kingdom and all other parts of the Commonwealth.
>
> In making these decisions The Queen has taken account of the increasing number of visitors from Commonwealth countries overseas who come to the United Kingdom, the large number of people who are presented to The Queen during Royal Tours and in the course of many other engagements, but who are not enrolled as having been officially presented, and the fact that the formal presentation of gentlemen, by means of Levées, has not been resumed since the war.

Despite this the traditional season opener, Queen Charlotte's Ball held in May at Grosvenor House, continued until 1977. There white-clad debutantes, apparently feeling no embarrassment, carried on curtseying to a vast, iced cake.

Crêpe romaine, broché, velvet, mousseline de soie, peau d'ange, bois de rose, velvet soleil, ripple crêpe and wind-swept satin: the very names of materials worn at courts in the thirties are redolent of a world far removed from the nylon lace of the fag-end of the season in the fifties. Records of courts held in the thirties show what very 'dressy' affairs they were.

In 1932 four courts were held at Buckingham Palace. The first, on 11 May, was preceded by the King, in full dress uniform, receiving the Emir Feizal of the Hejaz and Nejd. Queen Mary, by his side, wore a robe of silver lamé embroidered with silver and gold threads. Her silver lamé train, embroidered in a similar design, was draped with priceless old Irish lace. She wore diamonds and the Order of the Garter. The Duchess of York's robe, by Mrs Handley-Seymour, was in ivory white fleur de soie embroidered with diamanté and having a matching train. When the royal party entered the Throne Room at "precisely half past nine o'clock" as always, the dresses of the ladies arrayed before them represented every designer and good-quality fashion shop in London as well as several famous names from Paris. The Duchess of Portland and Mrs David Bruce, the daughter of the American ambassador, were dressed by Molyneux; Viscountess Brentford and Lady Hyndley had gone to Reville; Lady Crossley's white satin came from Hayward; Hartnell, Victor Stiebel, the young South African couturier, and the French house of Callot Soeurs were also represented.

By 1934 the effects of economic depression were becoming visible. Although the majority of gowns at that year's courts continued to be by fashionable and expensive London dressmakers like Elspeth Fox Pitt, Paulette, Miss Grey or the Misses Wilson or by top designers like Reville, Busvine and Handley-Seymour, more and more ladies were appearing in front of their Majesties either in copies by Harrods and Jays or original designs from Debenham and Freebody and Marshall and Snelgrove. Although even these suppliers were far from cheap, their increasing use was perhaps a reflection of the shortage of money in a year when unemployment figures reached a total of 2,126,260 in August and things were so grim that the Depressed Areas Bill, with a budget of two million pounds, was described by George Lansbury as "an attempt to bale out the ocean with a spoon".

As befitted coronation year, everyone dressed up for the five courts held in 1937 by King George VI and Queen Elizabeth. Perhaps the aristocracy felt euphoric because the new Prime Minister, Neville Chamberlain, had abolished the fifteen-shilling tax on chauffeurs, gardeners and other male servants, although there were still 1,356,598 of the King's subjects out of work. The first court of the new reign took place at Buckingham Palace on June 5. The King wore the full dress uniform of a Field Marshal. The Queen had Mrs Handley-Seymour create her an "elegant gown of deep golden brocade in a small scroll design. The corsage and the entire front of the skirt were exquisitely embroidered with scintillating diamanté. The handsome train of cloth of gold was richly embroidered with jewels in beautiful colours." With it the Queen wore the blue Garter ribbon, a tiara of diamonds and rubies and a matching necklace. The Grand Staircase and State rooms were decorated with spring flowers and flowering plants and the guests who swirled around after the presentation drank champagne or the famous royal hock cup which had been popular since Edward VII's time. Their Majesties' guests were also able to sample a Windsor Pie, "one of the specialities of the Royal table, a little appetising dainty served on a napkin". It consisted of two circular biscuits joined with a filling of cheese paste and topped with béchamel sauce and chopped ham and was a great favourite of Queen Mary. The clothes were magnificent. Mrs Baldwin wore a gown

Rich velvets, brocades and over-embroidery were typical of Alexandra's clothes at the turn of the century.

of white cloque with gold lamé flowers around the neck. Not to be outdone, Mrs Anthony Eden appeared in an ice-blue Grecian gown with classical draperies on the corsage and a narrow straight skirt. The honours for the guests' clothes were about equally shared between Mrs Handley-Seymour and Reville. The former dressed the Duchess of Northumberland in "a very elegant silver lamé gown", the Marchioness of Tweedale in a "parchment peau d'ange crêpe gown with a silver embroidery in the design of small trees" and Mrs Philip Argenti in a simple green georgette gown. Reville was responsible for Mrs Leslie Wormwald's deep cream and gold brocaded lamé gown, which she wore with a court train of very old Carrickmacross Lace, and for her daughter's gown of ivory satin.

The last two courts of coronation year took place at Holyrood House, the first to be held in Scotland since 1911. At the first of them the King wore the scarlet-and-gold uniform of a Colonel-in-Chief of the Scots Guards and the Queen the dress and train she had worn for the first and third courts. "Those favoured with the Royal summons to attend, and the large number of debutantes who made their curtseys to Their Majesties, passed out of the Throne Room, through the State Room into the Picture Gallery, where a buffet supper was awaiting them" – and thence home! On 8 July the second court was held. For it the Queen was dressed by Mrs Handley-Seymour in an ivory lace gown embroidered with sequins and paillettes with a train to match. On her head was the circlet of diamonds which had formed the lower part of her coronation crown; in the centre was the Koh-i-nor diamond. The most eye-catching of the guests' outfits was that worn by Ishbel, Dowager Marchioness of Aberdeen and Temair, a black satin dress "richly embroidered in a silver flowered design with a shoulder cape trimmed with Limerick lace and a head dress of black feathers". To complete the ensemble, she carried a black ostrich-feather fan.

Gold brocade, silver lamé, gold and silver tissue, sequins, diamanté and rich Indian embroideries … the courts showed Queens at their most majestic and, in many respects, least fashionable. Dressed as modern icons, their appearance transcended current modes. The gowns of the guests at the courts give us a very good impression of the aristocracy dressed in the height of fashion; to gain an idea of how Queens dressed to be in fashion, we must observe them at less stilted occasions. It is useful to direct our attention to the Edwardian age, which, as James Laver has pointed out, "was probably the last period in history when the fortunate thought they could give pleasure to others by displaying their good fortune before them".

Edward VII and Queen Alexandra were at the centre of social life. Her beauty and his style guaranteed their popularity after the sombre later years of Queen Victoria and they held the stage as joint heads of the most worldly and chic English court since that of Charles II. They were surrounded by people who, as a foreign resident wrote at the time, had nothing to do "but loaf through life and lounge daintily along a path strewn with roses and bank notes". Time was their great luxury. Aristocratic ladies changed their clothes as many as six times a day simply to give largely aimless lives some focal points. It was a style of life which helped to keep servants – ladies'

Alexandra in an afternoon dress which flatters her trim waist. Her famous chokers were worn to hide a scar.

maids, laundry girls, etc. – gainfully occupied. Men had many more ways of filling the empty hours but, even so, politesse and peacockery played a large part in their lives. "This was an epoch," Lord Esher said, "when men changed their evening coats before a ball if they had been in contact with tobacco smoke; when girls carried bouquets of lilies to a dance." It was also an age when society women wore tightly fitting clothes in heavy fabrics which gave little opportunity for their bodies to breathe. Deodorants did not exist; sweat had to be soaked up more or less successfully by removable dress shields worn under the arms. In an age when few dresses were washable these preservers were needed to avoid staining, especially in ball dresses which needed extra protection against the consequences of dancing in hot rooms. Few Edwardian men disliked the smell of female sweat; for many of them it was one of the attractions of the opposite sex.

Dancing was one of the great joys of Edwardian society and the King and Queen gave regular court and state balls. Even before they came to the throne their summer balls at Marlborough House, which lasted all night, were glittering affairs. A great striped tent swept out from the ballroom to create another room decorated with hydrangeas, ferns and palm trees in pots. It was carpeted in red and furnished with gilt chairs and small tables covered in the finest lace cloths. Rows of male servants stood along the canvas sides and the tables groaned with food, gold plate and crystal champagne glasses. Edward and Alexandra liked 'cuisine classique', based on lavish quantities of lobster, salmon, quail and asparagus. Often they gave fancy-dress balls; the 1874 Season ended with one at which the Princess appeared as Maria Stuart. In Queen Victoria's Diamond Jubilee year, 1897, they attended the most lavish ball of them all: the Duchess of Devonshire's fancy-dress ball. Princess Alexandra appeared as Marguerite de Valois wearing "gleaming white snowy satin and a high lace collar, with a silver-lined train of cloth of gold ... but H.R.H. refused to wear the quaint coif of the period, and consequently had a rather modern air".

These occasions, crowded as they were, held certain hazards. The Great Ball at Windsor, held in the Waterloo Chamber for Ascot week in 1903, was the first to be held at the castle for sixty-three years. Nearly 1,000 guests were packed in for this very special occasion. Princess May's letter to her Aunt Augusta tells the sad tale: "Unfortunately at the beginning of the ball while Dolly [Princess May's brother, later Duke of Teck] was dancing with Victoria his spurs caught in Mrs George Keppel's awfully long gown and he and Victoria fell heavily on their backs ... it is such a pity that ladies will wear long flowing garments made of chiffon at balls for, of course, they catch round the men's legs."

The first state ball given after the accession, held on 18 July, 1903, was distinguished by the grandeur of everything, not least the toilettes of the ladies. The tone fitted in with the old rule that a state ball could not be attended by anyone lower in rank than a peer's grandchild. It was opened in the traditional way – the Royal Quadrille performed by the King and Queen while the guests gazed on. (It was not correct behaviour to dance while royalty did.) The glamour of the occasion can be judged by the dress of the guests. The Countess of Wicklow's tulle gown had long sprays of pink roses and was covered in rose petals; the Marchioness of Lansdowne was in cream satin and "very wonderful diamonds"; the Countess of Leven and Melville's dove-coloured crêpe de chine gown was embroidered in opals; the Countess of Powis wore a blue satin dress encrusted with diamonds and the Countess of Dalkeith's blue mousseline de soie gown was hand-painted with forget-me-nots. Queen Alexandra stood out magnificently in her gown of silver tissue and a richly embroidered train. Her diamond jewellery was worth a king's ransom.

State balls continued to be the grandest of occasions throughout the twenties and thirties, although the last to open with a Royal Quadrille was the one held in 1924 in honour of the Kings and Queens of Italy and Romania. The famous Jubilee Ball of 1935 was not a state, but a court, ball. Nevertheless it upheld the level of grandeur and formality. After the arrival of the guests a procession was formed. The Lord Chamberlain, the Master of the Horse and the household officials preceded the King and Queen, and the carefully timed cavalcade arrived in the ballroom at exactly ten o'clock. At eleven the supper procession formed, the members of the royal household again preceding the King and Queen, who were followed into the supper room by the members of the Diplomatic Corps and cabinet ministers. Other guests were fed in the Green Drawing Room. Everywhere the tables were heavy with gold plate, rich food and sumptuous flower arrangements. A scented fountain decorated with pure gold horses and ebony figures, a present to Queen Victoria from an Indian Prince, perfumed the air. After supper the King and Queen sat on gold chairs on a dais draped and hung with crimson velvet to watch the guests dancing.

State banquets and dinners were further opportunities for the display of opulence. In 1902 the banquet planned for the coronation of Edward VII had fourteen courses. The chef's orders to his suppliers included 300 legs of mutton, eighty chickens and a staggering 2,500 quails – to be served in claret and brandy jelly. The fish course was to be sole in five garnishes and the dessert was liqueur jellies and caisses de fraises mirainare, jellied strawberries and vanilla cream in spun-sugar baskets which took the pastry chefs three days to make. Disaster struck when the King's appendicitis forced an eleventh-hour postponement. What to do with all the food? Perishable items were given away, sent in hampers to the Sisters of the Poor, who distributed the rich and exotic food to the poor of Whitechapel and the East End. The quail were put in cold storage and the expensive liqueur jellies were melted down and stored in magnum champagne bottles. The menu for the second coronation banquet, although reduced to twelve courses, showed all the confidence of the abandoned one. It included sole poached in Chablis and garnished with oysters and prawns, snipe stuffed with foie gras and forcemeat, and a soufflé parmesan. As a souvenir each guest was given a small spun-sugar crown. Such extravagance continued throughout the twenties and thirties, although, sadly, without the Royal Herb Strewer, whose job it was to throw flowers before the royal path at coronation banquets. Dressed in white satin with a scarlet robe, a wreath of

The sort of clothes which will always be associated with Queen Mary look quaint now but were well chosen by the woman described by a magazine as "no mere fine lady". The ephemeral fashions of the twenties and thirties were not to her taste at all – she required something more solid.

flowers on her head and garlands passing over her shoulders and under her arms, she was last employed at the coronation of George IV.

Conspicuous waste did not end with the Edwardians. The state dinner for the jubilee of King George V and Queen Mary was held in the ballroom of Buckingham Palace and it was a grand affair. A horse-shoe table with their Majesties in the centre and the guests ranged to either side was decorated with a triple row of golden flowers down its length while, in the centre, gold candlesticks arose from elaborate flower arrangements of gold and white irises and roses. The food included favourites of Queen Mary such as côtelettes de saumon à la Montpellier, asperges d'Argenteuil, sauce mousseline and soufflé parmesan.

Present-day royal entertainment has an almost frugal appearance by comparison, but in fact the luxury remains. What has gone in these more egalitarian times is the blatant ostentation. Since 1945, huge state banquets and costly state Balls have gradually diminished. For hours-long meals of many courses the writing was on the wall even before George V and Queen Mary came to the throne. The Queen was a connoisseur of food, sufficiently knowledgeable to correct French chefs. Although she liked elaborate and interesting dishes, she abhorred costly ones. She introduced a daily menu book at Buckingham Palace and wrote comments against different items on it. She disliked carrots, tomatoes and cucumbers, would not eat onions, even in a sauce, and hardly ever touched potatoes, except for the traditional Good Friday and Ash Wednesday recipes of salt cod in an egg sauce served with mealy potatoes. King George V liked simple food far removed from the exotic dishes served at his father's table: roast beef, Irish stew, apple charlotte and soup. Always soup; he even had consommé served to him each morning for 'elevenses'. The evolution of a simpler royal life-style may be illustrated by contrasting the wedding breakfast of the Duke and Duchess of York in 1923 with Princess Elizabeth's in 1947. Even allowing for post-war restrictions, it is significant that the 1923 breakfast had eight courses, whereas the 1947 one had half the number of courses and was finished in half the time. The menus also tell a tale. The Duke and Duchess of York's guests ate elaborately prepared salmon and other fish; their daughter's guests made do with pheasant casserole. The confidence of the menu cards in 1923 – a rose, thistle and shamrock entwined with gold ribbons around the cipher of King George and Queen Mary, plus the crimson and gold crests of the bride and groom – was not sustained in 1947. Princess Elizabeth's modest menu cards contained the simple letters G.R.E. beneath a crown at the top and the initials E.P. at the bottom.

Throughout the century royalty has gradually withdrawn from a central role in the traditional pursuits of the aristocracy. As Paul Thompson points out in *The Edwardians*, England in the decade before World War I was dominated by "an upper-class society, national rather than local" which followed its seasonal migrations. In Edwardian times the year was broken up into a number of seasons: the London season, which traditionally spanned the summer period from May until August 12, when the Scottish season began, immediately after Cowes week; the overlapping German bath season (August and September) when the King would visit Wiesbaden, Ems, Marienbad or Homburg; the country-house season (mid-September to mid-December); and the south of France season (mid-December to mid-May), when life was concentrated on Monte Carlo. In addition, many members of the aristocracy wintered in Cairo or Biarritz.

On these migrations the aristocracy was accompanied by an entourage of personal servants. The backstairs areas of the great houses bulged with visiting ladies' maids, valets, chauffeurs and footmen. For shooting parties the guests even brought their own dogs, which had to be fed and cared for by their owner's own staff. Few, however, went so far as the Kaiser, who, at a Sandringham shooting party, insisted that his dogs be fed from his own plate by an equerry specially chosen for this strange honour. Shooting parties were primarily for the gentlemen's enjoyment. Ladies were superfluous until the evening, when their stylish toilettes enlivened the dinner table. The high-point of the daylight events, not surprisingly in a society where preoccupation with food and drink eclipsed even the delight taken in flirting, was the shooting lunch. This, though a picnic meal, was sumptuous. At Sandringham, where shooting parties were considered "quite informal", footmen were sent out to set up a special marquee. They swept the whole area with large bristle brooms, laid a carpet of straw, and then set up the trestle tables and covered them with fine linen cloths. Silver, crystal and china were all laid out ready for the hampers of food to arrive. Sometimes they contained ambitious hot meals, ending with plum pudding, although just as stylish were the cold picnics created around the King's favourite shellfish dishes. Vintage champagne or Château Lafite (the only claret the King would drink) were served. After lunch the guns went on and the ladies returned to the house.

Lady guests at Sandringham, whether for shooting parties or house parties, spent a great deal of the day changing their clothes. They would come down to breakfast in their best day dresses, which were normally of velvet amply covered with embroidery or *passimenterie*. At shooting parties Queen Alexandra rarely appeared before lunch, by which time her guests had changed into tweeds or serge dresses for the picnic luncheon. During this part of the day the Queen often wore a simple dress with velvet trim and a small hat trimmed with a dead bird, or tweeds with a felt hat. If the weather was fine, she would herself drive to the luncheon tent in a small cart pulled by two ponies. The afternoon's event was tea, served at five o'clock. Here, elaborate and costly gowns were worn. The Queen's richly coloured tea gowns, expensively cut and trimmed, set the tone. Each day, the Queen and her guests would appear in a new tea gown. After tea, Signor Tosti would entertain or the ladies would embroider. Evenings were ceremonial. Uniforms were not worn, but full dress and decorations were. The ladies, again, had to wear a different dinner gown each evening. No wonder that those weekends involved such mountains of leather luggage. Even for a three-day visit the ladies arrived with huge, domed leather trunks, affectionately known as Noah's Arks, full of gowns, hat boxes of immense size filled with elaborate creations weighed down with decorative fruit, flowers or feathers, and heavy dressing cases with silver and crystal fittings. In addition, parasols, gloves and as many as twenty-five pairs of shoes would be required to see each lady through the visit.

At Sandringham there were normally two house parties per week: one from Monday morning to Thursday night and one from Friday morning to Sunday evening, when, all guests gone, the King and Queen would dine simply on roast beef and Yorkshire pudding. As at shooting parties, they breakfasted *en famille*; at lunch each presided over a table. The afternoon excursion was normally led by both. At all times the King kept a sharp eye on the dress and demeanour of his lady guests. He once chided the Duchess of Marlborough for not wearing a tiara, the symbol of her husband's rank and power. The Queen was also diligent. Nothing wanton or slipshod was approved. Everyone dressed carefully according to his or her rank. This often meant spending huge amounts of money. Princess Daisy of Pless recalls one occasion at Windsor when "Queen Alexandra admired my cloth of gold dress very much, and was horrified when, in answer to her question, I had to confess that the train alone was worth over £400. She said she could not possibly afford such a sum."

Goodwood, Aintree for the Grand National, Epsom for the Derby and, above all, Royal Ascot, founded by Queen Anne on her own property for races limited to hunters ridden to the Royal Buckhounds, were the glories of the summer season. King Edward and Queen Alexandra enjoyed them all and laid on elaborate picnics. The Ascot lunch of 19 June, 1908, for example, consisted of fourteen courses, including crab mousse, salmon, lamb, ham, asparagus and pigeon pie (an Ascot speciality) and ending with gooseberry fool. These meals were prepared at Windsor and brought over from the royal kitchens. The present Queen continues to provide the Ascot lunches, but the magnificent private suppers which accompanied Edward and Alexandra to the opera at Covent Garden vanished in the smoke of World War I. The suppers, brought over in the afternoon by six footmen, along with several large hampers containing cloths, silver, china and gold plate, were grand affairs. They consisted of between nine and twelve courses, all cold, including consommé, lobster mayonnaise, trout, duck, lamb cutlets, chicken ham and tongue jelly, plovers' eggs, fresh fruit and patisserie and plenty of very good champagne. For after-theatre suppers the King considered grilled oysters the perfect dish, whereas the Queen preferred a few crayfish poached in Chablis. Her favourite sweet course was Rod grod, a Danish concoction made from currants, raspberries and half a bottle of claret, served with cream and tiny sugar biscuits.

Just as the ritual of dress was highly stylised, so was the calendar of food. Derby-night dinner always included turtle soup and whitebait. The menu at Cowes had to contain shrimps and lobsters. Haggis was served once a week at Balmoral and deer pudding appeared on the menu as many as four times a week. The amount of time and money spent on food was phenomenal. Even family dinners in the Chinese room in Buckingham Palace normally consisted of twelve courses. When the royal family toured they took with them their own kitchen staff. Their Mediterranean tour of 1903 was a private one and, with the exception of sardines and blue cauliflower, the King demanded English dishes, although he graciously gave them Italian names in honour of his guests. Luxurious over-eating even stretched to Alexandra's beloved dogs, which included four Borzois given by the Czar and four Pekinese from the Emperor of Japan. Two footmen were permanently employed to brush, comb and powder them and at nine o'clock every night a tray of soup, cold chicken, quail or a cutlet was sent up to them.

Neither George V nor Queen Mary was by temperament suited to maintain Edwardian levels of ostentation. It says much for Queen Mary's attitudes that shooting parties, the endless changing of outfits and flashy days at race meetings followed by elaborate dinners appealed to her much less than the tennis championships at Wimbledon. Wimbledon was her favourite part of the London season and betwen 1919 and 1951 she missed only four championships. She understood the game and had the order of play sent to her at Buckingham Palace every night by special messenger. Her enthusiasm and her reluctance to leave after a day's play often embarrassed her hosts, as she would linger on chatting long after the centre court had been cleared. Lawn tennis, in those days an elegant game controlled by the upper classes, was in tune with Queen Mary's fastidious taste. In contrast, however, at the 1912 Command Performance she averted her gaze from the entire act of the female impersonator, Vesta Tilley, who appeared in trousers.

High style, like the Season generally, was the victim of social change as the century developed. The blatant display of wealth and privilege which were considered acceptable before World War I were tactless in the years of the depression. Although 'bright young things' behaved with an insensitivity hard to accept in the years of the Jarrow March, the royal family showed more sense. After the abdication crisis, in particular, duty became the key to the royal year, and today the Queen's annual calendar contains no features that can compare with the Edwardian pursuit of pleasure. Royal race meetings, comparatively modest shoots and the Queen's personal sport of deerstalking are virtually all that is left. The Queen's spare time is spent in breeding dogs and horses. Occasional balls still take place, state banquets continue and Command Performances are attended. (There has been an annual Royal Variety Performance since 1921 and although the rule that chorus girls could only appear if wearing stockings has gone, the ban on animal acts still remains.) Only Royal Ascot remains as a reminder of the Edwardian style of monarchy.

The Royal Ascot Week marks the high-point of what remains of the London season. The Queen holds a house party at Windsor which is a mixture of formality and informality. She and her guests take an early morning gallop down the deserted race course every morning; then at 2 p.m. they are dressed in their finery ready for the formal ride down the course. The ride is taken in open landaus, drawn by the Windsor Greys and escorted by outriders in scarlet and gold and bewigged postillions in purple, red and gold. The royal party then join the 7,000 guests in the royal enclosure, all of whom follow the Marquess of Abergavenny's strict dress

Ascot has always been an excuse for wearing the most fashionable clothes (and the most chic of hats) as these frocks from the twenties (left), thirties (centre) and forties (right) show.

The Season has diminished to almost nothing compared with its Edwardian heyday but the royal involvement with horses remains, even when they give one a shock!

code. Men must wear morning or service dress; women, immortally described by the sportswriter, Frank Keating, as having "cheeks of porcelain and voices of tin", must wear day dresses and hats "which must cover the crown of the head." Long dresses have not been worn as Ascot since the thirties. The royal box is a two-storey affair with panelled walls and bamboo furniture. Here, under the gaze of a horse's head by Lalique, the royal party eat the lunch brought over from Windsor. The highlight of the week is the super-fashionable Gold Cup day. The dinner at Windsor on that night is a full-dress affair and one of the special touches is that the flowers on the tables should be in the colours of the winner of the Gold Cup. Such a personal involvement is not found in the other remaining social event of the summer, the royal garden parties. Normally there are four per year. Three are held at Buckingham Palace and one at Holyrood House. About 8,000 guests are invited to each one with tickets strictly non-transferable. The Queen takes no part in drawing up the guest list. It is compiled by the Lord Chamberlain and is largely made up of ambassadors, politicians and worthy members of the community who have devoted their lives to the public good.

These gatherings are far removed from the society garden parties of the past. The Lord Chamberlain's rules for dress are loose: morning dress or lounge suits are acceptable. Women are expected to wear hats. The royal party emerge from the Bow Room and stand whilst the National Anthem is played. Guests take the opportunity to crane necks and subtly manoeuvre for position. With such considerable numbers converging on the Palace the lasting impression for most garden-party guests is of crowds and queues. Very few are chosen to speak to the royal party and some never even catch a glimpse of them in the crush. The tea, served by waitresses, is catered for by J. Lyons & Co. who produce, on average, 62,000 pieces of crockery, 13,000 sandwiches, 10,000 bridge rolls, 5,000 strawberry tarts, 7,000 pieces of cake and 400 gallons of tea. Strawberries and cream, once the highlight of the tea, are now considered too expensive and are not served. After tea, the Queen's party slowly returns to the Palace and, by five o'clock everything is over. The queue to leave begins as the military band, which has serenaded the guests throughout the afternoon with selections from light opera and musicals, plays on.

The Queen travels the world but is only
rarely allowed to behave like a tourist.
However, she took out her camera at the
Sultan's stables in Muscat and Oman to
snap the fine bloodstock on display.

6
ROYAL TRAVELS

Kings and Queens not only exist, they must be seen to exist. Exposure to their subjects has always been an important aspect of the job and, since the famous Indian trips undertaken by King George V and Queen Mary at the beginning of the century, the extent of foreign travel has greatly increased as transport has improved. The major change which has taken place in this century is the substitution of flight for slow sea voyages. The minimum amount of time is now spent on getting to the country to be visited and, although it means that trips are much more cost-efficient, the strain on the protagonists is much greater, since sea voyages, frequently boring, at least gave the royal party the opportunity to relax. Royal progression across the world are miracles of organisation. Most are glamorous state visits; many are gruelling and potentially dangerous; and some, like Princess Anne's 1984 Save the Children Fund Tour to some of the poorest parts of Africa, are exceedingly uncomfortable. All are important.

The dangers in not being seen regularly were realised during Victoria's reign. After the death of her beloved consort, Albert, in 1861, the Queen took up grief almost as a second profession, living a sequestered life away from the rude public gaze and surrounded by those members of the household who could be relied upon to indulge her in her protracted mourning. Her family urged her to appear in public, but their requests were almost always ignored. Republicans gained heart while the monarchy, rarely seen, slumped in popularity. Recovery began with the celebration of Victoria's golden jubilee in 1887. Jubilees, deaths and dramatic sicknesses help to keep the royals in the people's good books, and the new century, which began with all three, saw the monarchy once again on the crest of a wave of popularity. Seen again, it was loved. A lesson was learned and for the last eighty years every effort has been made by the royal family to ensure that the world sees them regularly at home and abroad.

Queen Victoria never visited the Empire, but since her day monarchs have travelled abroad as a matter of course. Travelling to the far-flung corners of the Empire, or Commonwealth, requires members of the royal family to adapt to widely varying manners and customs. Often, the more remote and smaller the country, the stronger and more unfamiliar its indigenous culture. As head of the Commonwealth the British sovereign has frequently to perform acts, especially of eating and drinking, which are mildly disagreeable or seem, at any rate, to be rather foolish.

Edward, Prince of Wales, and Princess Alexandra began their travels, which took them to many parts of Europe and the Mediterranean, with a visit to Cairo in 1869. This trip highlighted both the pleasures and the hardships of royal trips abroad. Princess Alexandra and her lady-in-waiting, Mrs Grey, arrived in Cairo after a pleasant trip in the _Ariadne_, a converted man-of-war fitted up as a yacht. The Khedive Ismail received them with considerable splendour, putting the Esbekieh Palace at their disposal. They had huge bedrooms with immense and beautifully decorated silver beds worth £3,000 each. Mrs Grey's room was so large that she could hardly hear people speaking at the other end. The curtains and covers in all the rooms of their suite were of the richest silk. The whole palace had a strange grandeur for the Princess and her companion, who were very conscious of the difference between their way of life and that of the Egyptian princesses in the harem. As a singular honour they were invited to take dinner in the harem of 'La Grande Princesse', the mother of the Khedive. They were greeted by the princess herself, attended by the Khedive's second and third wives. Princess Alexandra and Mrs Grey were each served a cherry on a gold plate, carried on a gold tray accompanied by a jewelled goblet of water. A slave then handed them a silver basin to wash their hands before dinner, while a second slave proffered a gold-fringed and embroidered napkin. Sitting cross-legged around the table (quite a feat in Victorian clothes), they helped themselves from tureens of chicken broth with rice placed in the middle of the table. For this purpose each was given a spoon of tortoise-shell with a large coral-branch handle. Other courses were eaten with the hands by tearing off pieces of meat and placing them directly in the mouth. The ladies from England were appalled. Mrs Grey wrote in her diary: "I never in my life was more disgusted or more inclined to be sick ... The taste of these extraordinary dishes as well as the sight of all these fingers dipped into the dishes ... from which I felt myself in duty bound to eat, was really too nasty. I did refuse once or twice, but the third Princess took that for shyness, and each time took a bit of the dish herself and put it into my hand – once a large onion dipped in gravy." No wine or water was served, but at the end of the meal the guests were handed a tortoise-shell cup containing vinegar, cut cucumber and herbs as a refreshing drink. As if this were not enough, the 'entertainment' of girls dancing lasted for over two hours.

A later visit was more successful. Princess Alexandra was delighted when the Khedive's four wives taught her how to paint her eyebrows and veil herself before dressing her in a burnous and leading her to the Prince of Wales, who was highly amused by the transformation. Princess Alexandra discovered what other female members of the royal family have found when abroad. They are often in countries where women must live enclosed, if not repressed, lives. As Queens and Princesses from Great Britain they are able to straddle the divide between male and female behaviour and enjoy privileges not granted to native princesses. More than a century ago, the Sultan of Selamlik, eager to propitiate his Western guests, broke the centuries-old tradition of his people when entertaining the Prince and Princess in Constantinople. Not only did he sit down to dinner with a woman, he even allowed his ministers to sit in his presence.

From the decks of the *Ariadne* the Princess was able to enjoy the exotic passing scene of the East. Whenever the ship stopped, thousands of children appeared on the shore, waving, shouting or gazing in awe. Alexandra enjoyed throwing bread and oranges to them and watching the scramble, but she was told that empty bottles were more prized so threw them instead. They were carted off to be hung up as decorations in the native huts. At night when the *Ariadne* stopped the shore was illuminated by torches stuck in the ground. At Wady Halfa their Highnesses were struck by an "ugly little boy, not very black, but rather bronze colour, and with a large silver ring stuck in one ear" who had come to watch the torches. As he apparently belonged to no one, he was taken aboard and he accompanied the Prince and Princess back to England as a pipe-cleaner, along with another trophy, a garlanded black sheep called 'Her Royal Highness's Sheep'.

Such exotic souvenirs were not collected by Queen Mary, although the long ocean voyages to India took her through some of the same areas. She and King George V were frequently away for as much as four months at a time. When they visited India in 1905, their leisurely outward journey took them by way of Genoa and the Straits of Messina and their return included a week's break in Cairo and a sight-seeing trip to Athens.

For the 1911 Durbar – the name given to royal levees for Indian princes – they set sail from Portsmouth on 11 November, 1911, on the *Medina*, after entertaining a party of fifty-three guests to lunch on board. The ship belonged to the Peninsular and Oriental Company and to run it the Royal Navy supplied thirty-two officers and 360 petty officers and men. The Royal Marine contingent consisted of four officers and 206 NCOs and men. In addition, the King and Queen had their personal suite of twenty-two persons, which included the Queen's ladies, the Mistress of the Robes, the Duchess of Devonshire, The Lady of the Bedchamber, Lady Shaftesbury, and the Maid of Honour, Miss Venetia Baring. They faced a voyage of twenty-two days. Looking back now, long sea voyages with the ship slipping silently past perfect sunsets seem the height of romance. The reality was different. The royal cabins, although luxuriously appointed, were on the third deck forward, which meant that in heavy seas the first few days were very trying. The majority of time spent at sea was a fight against tedium and so programmes of obstacle races, three-legged races and greasy-pole fights were devised to keep morale high. The Queen spent much of her time on deck reading books about India; the King occupied himself in listening to the band. They were under the watchful eyes of Mr Percy Jacomb-Hood, the official artist for the trip, who on the side, was hoping to sketch examples of the *'vie intime'* on board for readers of the *Graphic*. The Queen found it "monotonous to a degree on board"; when not reading, she passed her time in signing photographs of herself and sending her four sailor attendants, who were always within hailing distance, on little errands. She was able to dress informally during the day, frequently wearing a high-necked blouse and simple skirt. For dinner she wore a formal gown, tiara and jewels. The monotony was broken when the *Medina* passed through the Suez Canal and the royal party could admire the magnificent sentries whom the Khedive had placed for their protection at every kilometre post. They were also watched over by fierce-looking patrols of Egyptian camel corps or 'Badaween'. At Aden they went ashore to the Victoria Pavilion for a reception. The King wore the white uniform of an admiral of the fleet and the Queen was in pale blue silk. A large tent of broad stripes in pale yellow and rose madder protected the royal visitors from the heat as they made their stately progress along the red carpet to the heavily gilded, crimson-velvet thrones.

The colour, heat and magnificence were nothing compared with what the royal party found when they reached India. As they landed in Bombay a 101-gun salute greeted them and they were escorted on a seven-carriage procession into the city by dragoons and horse artillery in the lead, the Governor's Lancers as their immediate escort and the 26th Lancers in the rear. Despite the sweltering heat everyone was in full-dress uniform. Queen Mary wore a yellow-flowered chiffon gown, the Garter Star and ribbon, and a flat straw hat piled high with artificial roses. The streets of the city matched the colour of the procession with floral arches and masts and silken festoons. In the evening a state dinner was held on board. Despite a temperature of 83° in the King's cabin, full-dress uniform was worn and the Queen's heavy white satin broche dress was weighed down with gold embroidery. The heat continued throughout the visit and travel inland was made even more uncomfortable by the other hazard of the sub-continent. "India is the land of dust", a member of the party, the Honourable John Fortescue, wrote, "and it is impossible to travel there by rail in the dry season without realising the fact to the full."

On their arrival at Delhi on 9 December, the Queen was given some protection from the sun which beat down on her open carriage by a huge golden fan and a crimson and gold umbrella held over her by Indians. That night, a state dinner was held for 106 guests. The arrangements displeased the squeamish Fortescue: "The banqueting tent offended against the elements of sanitary science in the matter of ventilation . . . being very long, very narrow and low it presented neither a dignified nor an inviting appearance. The reception tent beside it, to which their Majesties and their guests withdrew after dinner, was less open to such reproach, except in respect of ventilation, being both lofty and spacious; while the roof, in broad stripes of pale blue and white, was, though somewhat paltry, at least pleasing and restful to the eye."

The Durbar itself took place on 12 December. It was a scene of almost mediaeval magnificence. The great canvas city erected outside Delhi covered twenty-five square miles. It consisted of tented camps surrounded by neat green lawns, which had sprung up from the brown wastes as a result of hundreds of men watering them daily by hand. The most imposing camp was the King-Emperor's. It was in the form of a huge semi-circle, the King's suite occupying one arm, the Queen's, lined in pink silk and carpeted with magnificent rugs, the other. It was from here that the royal pair issued on Durbar day – in the absolutely still, hot air of noon – to process to the pavilion where the Indian Princes would make obeisance. To mark the historic magnificence of the occasion the Queen wore her coronation gown and jewels, including the Order of the Garter, the Koh-i-nor diamond and the Durbar emeralds. The pavilion, shimmering in the heat, consisted of a base of three tiers which were ascended by three broad stairways to a central structure on which stood the two thrones. Above the thrones, supported by four slender columns and surmounted by a bulbous gilt dome with a gilded fretwork balustrade, was a canopy of crimson velvet broadly fringed in crimson and gold. In this splendid setting the King-Emperor and his Queen Consort received their loyal subjects undeterred by the crushing heat or the enormous expense: the government of India's camp for

Queen Mary photographed with Middle East dignitaries on her way to India in 1911. As visiting Queen Consort she was allowed privileges not always accorded to women, including the right to be seated in male company.

sixty persons in a country where poverty was of epidemic proportions, had cost 500,000 rupees for one week.

Canada has temperatures as extremely low as India's are high. King George VI and Queen Elizabeth boarded the *Empress of Australia* at Portsmouth for their trip to Canada on 6 May, 1939, and arrived in Quebec twelve days later. They had suffered a two-day delay because icebergs had forced the ship to drop to a speed of only four knots and, for eight hours, to stop altogether. Life, however, was pleasant. Photographs, packed in a barrel with the royal mail on 9 May and thrown overboard for the escort ship, *Repulse*, to take back to Plymouth, showed the Queen being fitted with a lifejacket and the King taking snapshots. A souvenir of the trip highlights the ship's delights: "The main lounge of the *Empress of Australia* is decorated in the Empire style and is eminently suitable for dancing owing to the absence of pillars or other obstructions. A private dining room for the royal party was fashioned out of the liner's smoking room and all the other appurtenances of a luxury vessel, such as gymnasium, swimming pool etc. were prepared for the use of their Majesties and their suite." The 21,800-ton liner, used for long-distance pleasure cruises, had to be considerably adapted for royalty. The King's brass bedstead from the royal yacht *Victoria and Albert* was installed and the Queen was given a modern one with chromium fittings. The return journey was on the *Empress of Britain*, the flagship of the Canadian Pacific Fleet. It required very little alteration to be converted into a 'royal yacht', containing as it did two suites on A deck suitable for their Majesties. Each suite consisted of a spacious bedroom, bathroom, sitting room, verandah and service accommodation and "radio, telephone, and every luxury were installed".

The first royal tour after World War II was to South Africa. The party, which included both the princesses, again travelled by sea. This time, however, there was no conversion of luxury liners. In keeping with the austerity of the post-war period, H.M.S. *Vanguard* was used. The royal family sailed on 1 February, 1947, and arrived in Cape Town on 17 February, having sailed from bitter winter to glorious summer. As this was the Princesses' first time to cross the equator, the traditional ceremonies of 'Crossing the Line' were performed, though modified to spare the Princesses their full rigours.

The tour of South Africa, which lasted for sixty-five days, was the first official visit there of a reigning British monarch and the last anywhere in which all the members of the royal family took part. For the first time, the King's Flight was called into service on a royal tour: twin-engined monoplanes, under the lead of Captain 'Mouse' Fielden, were used for internal flights. The majority of the trip, nevertheless, was taken in the famous White Train specially built in England to the order of South African Railways. It acted as a luxurious mobile hotel for the royal party, who travelled and slept in it. It was the longest and heaviest train ever seen in South Africa. One-third of a mile in length, painted in ivory white and gold, it contained luxuriously appointed private coaches for the King and Queen and a separate coach for the Princesses. In addition to accommodation for their personal staff of private secretaries, ladies-in-waiting, equerries, valets and ladies' maids, which took up ten coaches, a complete coach at the rear, with its own kitchen and dining room, was reserved for the government minister in attendance. It had special facilities so that he could be in constant touch with Whitehall. Along with the minister went a staff of cipher experts; a number of officials from South African government departments; the Commissioner of Police; and several officials of lower rank (catering managers, electricians, personal servants and other persons whom the elaborate programme required to be continually available).

All the way round the Union the White Train was preceded, half an hour ahead, by a pilot train carrying the rank-and-file of the police and railway representatives, newspaper correspondents and photographers, and other individuals such as the King's barber and the supervisor of the flowers in the royal apartments. It had a post office, a telegraph office and even radio communication with the White Train. The railway cortege was completed by a third train, popularly known as 'The Ghost Train', which followed several hours behind and carried spare parts and repairing gear for the railway service.

Princely magnificence was not the sole prerogative of the Indians, as the sharp-eyed James Cameron reported in the *Daily Express*: "Wherever the train is scheduled to pull up, drains are laid, water piped, traffic blocked, grass sown, roads rebuilt, groves of aloes planted, cactus mown, bush cleared and flags flown." If there were no natural screen for the royal train, trees with no roots were hastily stuck in the ground. At every halt the train was met by an army of black cleaners whose scrubbing kept it pristine white. Back-up vehicles, specially manufactured for the South African government by Daimler, consisted of two limousines, two landaulettes and an 'all-weather' tourer. All were dark blue with grey interiors. Fittings included hinged reading lamps and arm rests fitted with smokers' requisites. The landaulettes had transparent roof panels. They were looked after by thirty drivers and two mechanics. When the royal train travelled through the night, the drivers, dressed in overalls because of the dust, would set off on the 200-mile journey between 7 and 8 p.m. The roads were so dusty that even driving a mile apart it was like driving through fog. Arriving after midnight, the drivers would sleep before rising early to clean the cars to an immaculate standard ready for the day. The despatches from the tour which gave such details must have intrigued readers in the United Kingdom, who were suffering from post-war shortages and the most severe winter weather in living memory.

In 1953 the Queen and the Duke of Edinburgh set off on the most ambitious tour of the century. The six-month Commonwealth tour of 1953–54 began with a 10½-hour flight to Newfoundland in a BOAC Strato-cruiser, Canapus. It was fitted with two blue upholstered divans, screened by white silk curtains, and a specially made dressing room. From Newfoundland the royal couple flew to Jamaica and for the rest of the trip their base was the S.S. *Gothic*, a 15,902-ton vessel of the Shaw-Saville Line. In the various countries visited every form of transport was used. In Australia the royal train had an observation platform at the rear and a special whistle code:

three blasts meant that people were ahead and the royal couple would go into action stations to be out and smiling at the crowd; two blasts meant 'all clear' and they could go back and relax. The last leg of the trip, from Malta, was on the royal yacht, *Britannia*, spanking new with its Queen's sitting room, Duke's sitting room and drawing room with panelled walls. The pastel green walls and sage green upholstery of the Queen's room reflected her favourite colours. Next to her ivory telephone, extension 95, were books such as *The Cruise of H.M.S. Drake* and records of 'The Flight of the Bumble Bee' and 'Selections from Band Wagon'.

For foreign tours of any length the royal yacht often goes ahead to act as a floating hotel. It is especially useful for state entertaining. It is an impressive ship: 412 feet long, with a blue hull, white superstructure and buff funnel and masts. It carries the royal coat of arms at the bow and the royal cipher at the stern. Illuminated, it looks as glamorous as any ocean-going liner of the halcyon days of sea voyages: one can imagine clipped Coward voices exchanging deck-rail epigrams. When the Queen is in residence, the Royal Standard is flown. Once on board guests are in a little England. A Royal Marine band plays selections of light music as aperitifs are served in the drawing room. The dining room chairs are Hepplewhite, the cutlery silver, the china Minton and Spode, and the glasses Brierley crystal. The yacht is virtually self-sufficient. Food and wine are loaded in England and even the flowers frequently come from the Windsor gardens. All in all, it is as near to being a floating country house as anything could be.

When the Queen visits foreign countries she travels with British Airways. Planning begins well in advance, often six months ahead, and airline and Palace officials work closely together to ensure a smooth journey. British Airways produce for each trip a confidential 'blue book' (now not normally blue) which contains, in addition to complicated technical flight data, details of the aircraft type, seating plans, lists of passengers and personnel, a detailed operating schedule, loading plans, security arrangements, and sketch maps, diagrams and plans of all airports to be used. The catering manager produces his own 'blue book', equally thick, which contains details of every aspect of food and drink and their service for the trip, the persons responsible for loading and preparing the food, the security and hygiene of all supplies, the arrangements for local purchase of produce and detailed lists of cutlery, crockery, glass and dry goods.

The Queen does not have her own aircraft. She uses a schedule aeroplane which is temporarily removed from service and modified to meet the royal requirements. Nowadays British Airways usually allocate her a wide-bodied Tri-star, which has the ideal amount of cabin space and enormous holds. All seats are removed from the forward cabin, which is transformed into a royal suite consisting of a lounge, dining and sleeping areas for the Queen, and wardrobe and dressing-room space. A wardrobe, dining table and four chairs, lounge seating and two divans furnish the royal cabin. When the Queen first boarded a remodelled Tri-star, on her trip to Delhi in 1983, she told the crew that it was "lovely – just like a little house". She tested the divans by bouncing up and down on them and took some practice twirls

Regardless of the heat and discomfort of India Queen Mary wore the sort of heavy clothes she considered suitable for a Queen Empress when she visited the subcontinent for the Durbar in 1911.

in the swivel chair. Ten days later Mrs Thatcher followed her for the Commonwealth Prime Minister's Conference. Her Tri-star was modified also. The front cabin was stripped of all but the window seats as she wished to hold an in-flight cocktail party. When told of the Queen's comment she agreed, but added that by her standards it was like a rather *large* house.

The Queen's entourage takes up the normal seating at the rear of the plane, where passengers are placed in strict accordance with their status. On the Queen's trip to Italy in October, 1980, when staff were also required for the royal yacht, the passenger list was long. The members of the household included Lord Carrington, as the minister in attendance, and the British Ambassador to Rome, both with their wives, the Mistress of the Robes, Lady-in-Waiting, Private Secretary, Master of the Household, Comptroller of the Lord Chamberlain's office, Press Secretary, Medical Officer and Equerry-in-Waiting. The Duke of Edinburgh's household staff brought the total to fifteen. Officials, clerks and police officers added another fourteen passengers, a group of twenty-five more included the Queen's assistant dresser, her hairdresser, the royal chef, the head chauffeur, the Queen's page, yeomen of the plate pantry and glass and china pantry, the page of the Presence, sergeant footman and three ordinary footmen. The trip is estimated to have cost more than £35,000. In addition supplies for the royal yacht, sent by commercial flights at the rate of £1.22 per kilo, cost the Palace £2,176.

The cabin crew consists of senior personnel who are hand-picked according to their experience and known performance. The Cabin Service Officer and Stewardess A are responsible for all service in the forward cabin, occupied by the royal party. The stewardess also looks after the dressing room and forward toilets. The starboard front toilet is reserved for the Queen's exclusive use and is equipped with her choice of fragrances and her favourite Chanel soap. All staff are given strict instructions concerning dress and demeanour. They are to be at their most formal for the reception and disembarkation of the royal party. They must stand to attention and not greet or speak to any member of the royal family unless spoken to. The Cabin Service Officer waits by the entrance foyer, salutes her Majesty and 'persons of rank' and directs them to their seats. Stewardess A curtseys when the Queen enters, but does not salute at any time. All staff are expected to know the rank and title of every passenger. An aspect of protocol which is taken just as seriously is the flying of the Royal Standard, the Queen's personal standard, or the flag of the country being visited. The blue book gives precise instructions on how to fit the flag to the mast, how to erect it through the hatch and how to fasten the dummy hatch cover in inclement weather. Details as to when the flag is flown are specific: "The Royal Standard will be flown when Her Majesty the Queen is in the vicinity of the aircraft ... the Standard should continue to be flown until shortly before approaching the runway for take-off ... the Standard should be flown as soon as practicable after leaving the landing runway until after Her Majesty has left the vicinity of the aircraft by car."

Nowadays, security on all flights is very strict; for a royal flight, precautions are even more stringent. The aircraft, having been removed from service, undergoes a thorough maintenance check, is fitted with new tyres and receives an air test. It is then fitted with the royal furnishings, cleaned to a 'royal standard of cleanliness' and placed under security control in its own hangar. From this moment it is maintained in a 'security-sterile' condition. No one is allowed access to it who cannot produce a valid Royal Flight Security Pass. These passes are numbered and colour-coded and each stop on the route has its own secret colour. For the 1983 trip to India, for example, Heathrow was white, Akrotiri apricot, Hyderabad grey and Delhi green. Fuel samples are taken at all stages and water supply points are sampled and sent to laboratories at Heathrow for examination. Special care is taken to check all water that may be used to make ice cubes for drinks. If the water supply gives the slightest cause for concern, BA supervisors wash all utensils and and equipment with a germicidal detergent. Every item of raw food is checked before being loaded at any stage in the journey.

When the Queen steps out of the special V.I.P. lounge on the south side of Heathrow and moves towards her aeroplane, she is secure in the knowledge that it and everything aboard, including people, have been most rigorously checked and double-checked. Everything has been done to make her trip pleasant and relaxing. The delicate balance between maintaining the highest standards of service and allowing the royal party its privacy is explained to cabin crew. Fuss, pomposity or any kind of familiarity are simply not allowed in the royal cabin.

Catering proposals are submitted to the Palace well in advance and the menu choice is made by the Queen. She has a choice of four 'starters', four main dishes and four puddings. She chooses one from each group and that meal is served to everyone in her entourage. There is no special food served only in the royal cabin. If the Queen has been, or is going to be, formally entertained on the ground, she will require only something very simple in the air. So, while the entourage may be tucking into Beef Wellington, the meat for which was flown on dry ice from Heathrow and the pastry made by a BA supervisor in Hyderabad, she will merely toy with a lobster mayonnaise 'starter'. She is, at any rate, an extremely light eater, and often has only two courses. Wines are chosen from the normal first-class wine list. The Queen eats at her dining table, often with two or three members of her entourage if she is travelling alone, and her food is served on the special royal-flight bone china. The glasses are Edinburgh crystal and the tablecloth is Irish linen. After dinner the royal-flight silver cigar box appears. It is a unique record of all royal flights, with details of each one engraved on its sides. The Queen's drink trolley contains decanters of whisky, port, sherry, and brandy, with their silver labels, and after dinner the royal party frequently dismiss the steward and merely help themselves. They can then relax over the English daily papers, which British Airways make available at all stops within twenty-four hours of publication, and the normal first-class selection of magazines, such as *Cosmopolitan* or *Good House-keeping*, augmented by the royal choice of those like *The Lady* and *Scottish Field*.

The Queen's favourite foods and drinks on board the aeroplane are a carefully guarded secret. No one has forgotten the case of the mineral water leak some years ago on a visit to Vienna. The Queen had asked for Malvern Water to be included in the bar supplies. The order went to Schweppes along with the request for standard items such as tomato juice and tonic water. However, when the goods were delivered to Heathrow, it was discovered that the Malvern Water had not been included. A telephone call explaining whose flight the water was for soon produced the required number of cases. As the Queen's lady-in-waiting left the aeroplane in Vienna, she picked up two bottles to place in the Queen's bedroom. The headline in a Viennese newspaper read, "We are happy you are here, even if you do not trust our water". How the leak occurred no one knows, and although it was hardly a serious matter, it caused embarrassment to the Queen. The lesson has not been forgotten. No information concerning royal preferences is allowed to slip out. So the Queen can relax with British Airways. On the return trip she "lets her hair down and has a knees-up" with her entourage, distributes small gifts and signs the leather-bound visitor's book, which is carried on all royal flights, as a token of her approval of the faultless service she has received in flight.

Quite apart from the transport arrangements, any tour of major importance and length requires infinite planning and organisation if the objects of the visit are to be fully realised. Along with engendering goodwill between Great Britain and the country which is being visited, a royal tour 'shows the flag' in such a way that British standards of efficiency and style are judged by it. Although a royal tour is never undertaken on any sort of commercial basis, it is obviously viewed as a reflection of Great Britain. In an obscure, but real, way a smooth, efficient and gracious royal tour encourages foreign governments to take British industry seriously. An increase in trade very often follows a royal tour. Another good reason why nothing should go wrong is the enormous cost involved. The *Britannia*'s running costs are on average three million pounds a year. The Queen's Flight costs slightly less than five million pounds a year. As far back as 1948, when King George VI was forced to cancel his projected Australian tour, the insurance claims against the cancellation amounted to an estimated £250,000.

Planning meetings take place twice yearly and events are organised at least a year in advance. Major tours may easily be planned two years ahead. Tours are always made at the invitation of the host country, which proposes the bulk of the programme and submits it to the Palace for approval. Protocol must be observed and the visit must not be used for overtly political or commercial ends; otherwise, the Palace rarely makes any major changes. Planning, however, does not stop there. The royal machinery of polished perfection goes into action. *Every* detail of *every* minute and *every* step is worked out. The Queen's state visit to Brazil in 1968 involved twelve drafts of the arrangements and planning began two years before the event, even though the visit was only of eleven days' duration. Her 1973 tour of Canada was minutely planned by the Canadian government with former chief-of-staff, Lieutenant-General Howard Graham. He was assisted by the Master of the Household, a private secretary to 'walk the route' with a stopwatch and a body-

The wardrobe which Queen Elizabeth took to South Africa in 1947 was created in an atmosphere of austerity and shortages but Hartnell still managed to design evening dresses of the right degree of splendour, and to create silk crepe ensembles "for afternoon receptions".

The Queen wore a white hopsack rayon dress (left) frequently in South Africa. Princess Elizabeth celebrated her 21st birthday in this Hartnell dress (centre); the taffeta dance dress was in her favourite colour: lime green.

guard to check security arrangements. Seven separate committees involving seventy-four people were required to organise everything. Canada's under-secretary for external affairs twice flew to London for discussions and royal aides flew to Canada.

In addition to staff a tour requires the press. There is no point in making a success of things if the success is not reported to the world. Journalists must be accredited if they are to gain access to royal occasions. For the Brazilian tour there were 800 accredited press men of whom almost two-thirds were from Latin America. Their major stories were daily translated for the Queen and given to her at breakfast time. All press, British and foreign, work to clearly laid down standards of protocol and security. No reporter or photographer is permitted to address the Queen or Prince Philip (or indeed any member of the royal family) directly. Nor may they take photographs of them eating, drinking, or 'negotiating a hazard'. To help the press, daily briefings are arranged and handouts are distributed. These handouts give details and timings of each day's events. They normally now include a description of the clothes worn by the Queen and the name of the designer or the couture house. For the royal tour of North America in the spring of 1983, each day's outfit was described for the press, along with details of jewellery where appropriate.

THE QUEEN'S CLOTHES (27 February) San Diego/Palm Springs
Pale mauve and white check wool dress and jacket with matching hat of mauve felt.
Ian Thomas

THE QUEEN'S CLOTHES (20th Century Fox dinner)
Evening dress in white chiffon with bodice embroidered in orange Californian poppies.
Hardy Amies

THE QUEEN'S CLOTHES (28 February) Los Angeles
Blue printed woollen coat-dress with detachable cape. White felt bowler with blue straw trimming.
Hartnell

THE QUEEN'S CLOTHES (dinner on 28 February)
Fuchsia printed chiffon evening dress with soft pleats. Embroidered with self-coloured stones. Dress has three-quarter length sleeves.
Hartnell

THE QUEEN'S CLOTHES (1 March) Santa Barbara
Dress of petrol blue, black and tan printed wool, with hat of petrol blue felt with feather trimming.
Ian Thomas

THE QUEEN'S CLOTHES (2 March) arrival in San Francisco
Dark green and red printed dress and jacket
Hartnell

THE QUEEN'S CLOTHES (3 March) San Francisco
Coat in peacock wool. Matching dress in crêpe de chine with self spots and belt. Matching chiffon hat with rolled brim and veil.
Hardy Amies

THE QUEEN'S CLOTHES (3 March) De Young Museum dinner
Evening dress in champagne taffeta with ecru (light fawn) and gold lace sleeves trimmed with bows. Pearl and diamond necklace and earrings. Pearl and diamond tiara.

Hardy Amies

The same details are given when the Princess of Wales is on a visit, but, as she does not have official dressmakers 'By Appointment', the designers' names are omitted. This seems an ill-advised policy. There is such intense world-wide interest in the Princess and her clothes that publicity for her designers would help trade and exports.

On any royal visit abroad the clothes must be carefully considered well in advance. For the Queen's Commonwealth tour of 1953–54 Hartnell had a weekly audience months before the departure to submit designs and discuss the many types of fabric required for a tour which took in such a wide range of climates. As early as the 1905 Indian trip, clothes had been a preoccupation. Queen Mary's Aunt Augusta wrote from Strelitz: "your dresses amuse me to read about: so many too! and *who* is to pay? the one for the tiger's hunt gave me the shivers". The death of the King of Denmark during the tour meant that Mary had to go into mourning. "It is tiresome too;" she wrote to Augusta, "on account of my clothes as I can only wear white now, and all the coloured clothes upon which I had to pay hundreds have had to be put away." As we have said, white as an official mourning colour for royalty re-surfaced in the 1939 state visit to Paris of George VI and Queen Elizabeth. The effect on the world's fashion capital was stunning. Several years later, in 1948, Princess Elizabeth visited France and, according to Marian Crawford, her "wardrobe of dresses sent a ripple of excitement through the fashion capital". Miss Crawford even claimed that Dior, the doyen of French dress designers, could find no fault. "'She is magnificent,' he told one of the royal party. 'I never knew from pictures that she could be so lovely or wear her clothes with such distinction.'" And when, in 1957, the Queen returned to France, *Picture Post* declared in a headline, 'Queen Conquers France'. Trevor Philpott, possibly a more impartial observer than Miss Crawford, described in an article for the magazine the Queen's major fashion triumphs – two sumptuous and spectacular evening dresses by Hartnell. For a gala evening at the Opera House Hartnell created a full-skirted dress in "ivory satin thickly encrusted with pearls, topaz and gold, with fleur-de-lys, poppies and a tiny gold bee – Napoleon's symbol of industry". The gown fulfilled the function of a gala dress on an overseas visit: it impressed, while subtly flattering the host country. The magnificence prompted Philpott to muse on the nature of royal dressing. "In a century in which clothes have become simpler and simpler – when a large sparkle too often shines from a large jewel of paste – where understatement and restraint often seem to be the only heralds of genuineness, there is a certain superlative in dress that perhaps only a Queen can attain. For her, the question 'I wonder if it is real?' can never be raised even to be denied."

This really is the whole point of royal dressing at all times but especially on tours abroad. The Queen is seen as a symbol, not only of British attitudes and culture, but, in many cases, of Western civilisation and history. Everything that the Queen stands for must be reflected in her clothes. For male members of the party matters are somewhat easier, since uniforms are frequently worn. No nation's uniform is the same as another's and it is so well known that it automatically acts as a national symbol. The Queen does not wear uniform in foreign countries. The nearest she gets to formalised, symbolic dressing is when she wears an ornate long dress, tiara and Garter sash to perform a state ceremony. Most of the time she wears clothes that make her look confident and attractive, but also slightly distant: over-excited foreigners rushing up for a kiss would certainly not do. On the other hand, her appearance must not be too formidable. Majesty that is too formal intimidates spectators and calls forth merely respectful cheers at a respectful distance. Rigid adherence to protocol must be tempered with a degree of friendliness and accessibility.

Certain unwritten rules must also be obeyed. Outfits already seen in Great Britain are not normally worn on formal occasions in foreign countries; a dress worn for an important occasion in one major city of a tour cannot be worn again in another city; clothes worn on an important tour such as the North American one of 1983 cannot be seen on a tour of, say, Australia (although it must be said that clothes do reappear on tours to less Westernised countries). In addition, local customs and attitudes must be respected: in Muslim countries, for instance, protocol demands that, when the host King is present, long dresses which cover neck, ankles and elbows be worn. Again, any visit to the Vatican requires a full-length black dress with long sleeves and a decent head-covering. Many royal tours take place in countries with high levels of temperature and humidity. Hot, clinging materials are therefore impossible, and the designers tend to use natural fabrics like silk, cotton or fine wool. Modern synthetics are used, but cautiously – damp patches on royal backs and underarm sweat marks on Queenly clothes are quite unacceptable.

The final decision on colours, fabrics and styles although taken in accordance with advice concerning the countries to be visited, is a personal one. Queen Mary's yellow flowered chiffon gown and straw hat which she wore when arriving in India in 1911 was one of her favourites and she wore it four times during the trip. Even in those halcyon days of royal privilege, the popular belief that a Queen wore a dress only once was as untrue as it is now. In addition to the coronation gown worn for the Durbar in Delhi, twenty-three 'special' dresses were taken. There were three clear favourites. A white satin broche was worn five times, a cream-and-gold silk broche six times, and a cream-and-gold Indian muslin five times. A list of the remaining dresses, with the number of times worn, shows the range of colours and materials which appealed to Queen Mary.

Pink-and-silver brocade (four)
Yellow flowered chiffon (four)
China blue chiffon (four)

In Venice the Queen Mother looked typically English, wearing a pale blue coat and flattering off-the-face hat.

White chiffon with hollyhocks (three)
Mauve flowered chine silk (three)
Pinky-mauve charmeuse (three)
Pale mauve chiffon (two)
Cream silk moire with rose bouquets (two)
Cream quipure gown (two)
Grey-and-silver brocade (two)
Sapphire-blue and gold (two)
Pale blue satin with blue bows (two)
Pale blue crêpe de chine (two)
Mauve-and-grey chiffon (one)
White pompadour satin (one)
Mauve stamped velvet (one)
Pink satin gown with Indian embroidery (one)
Pale green silk poplin (one)
Chine silk and lace gown (one)
Deep yellow satin (one)

With a wardrobe like that it seems likely that Queen Mary managed not to be overshadowed by the lavish and colourful tented city at Delhi.

Clothes for the South African trip in 1947 were not so lavish. Fabrics were still in short supply and the Board of Trade wartime restrictions continued in force. All clothes required coupons and there were no exceptions to the number to which each person was entitled, not even for Royalty. Hartnell, who was in charge of the Queen's wardrobe and designed the majority of the Princesses' dresses, had therefore the tricky job of producing glamorous clothes in straitened circumstances. Various ruses were resorted to and ingenious solutions found. Some of the Queen's pre-war clothes were cannibalised, especially for trimmings and linings, old stocks of buttons and odd rolls of pre-war fabric were brought out and all outfits were designed to be flexible. Photographs of the tour show that the Princesses in particular wore the same clothes on many different occasions. As the *Daily Mail* reported, their daytime wardrobes contained "sensible inter-changeable outfits requiring only one set of accessories, such as a wool three-piece of skirt, jacket and princess-style coat with exactly matching crêpe dress and crêpe blouse. They each have a stone-coloured linen coat that will tone well with all summer frocks." Both Princesses had wedge-heeled sandals in 'elastic' doeskin combined with whip-snake in contrasting colours designed by Rayne. He provided the Queen with her favourite high-heeled, peep-toed, ankle-strapped sandals with a built-up sole in six different materials from oyster satin to white suede. For Princess Elizabeth Captain Molyneux created a polka-dot, turquoise silk day dress and a Grecian-style white chiffon evening dress with a diagonal gold stripe and a gold kid belt. The Queen's outstanding evening dresses included an oyster satin crinoline with a quilted skirt ornamented with pearls and an off-the-shoulder neckline bordered with antique lace, re-embroidered in pearls and copper. The dress was a tribute to Hartnell's high skills. A richly embroidered skirt to catch the lights and shine glamorously would have required an unobtainable number of sequins and paillettes, but Hartnell achieved a similar effect by quilting, which broke up the surface, and the addition of only a few seed pearls produced a shimmering richness. Again, the substitution of copper embroidery for gold or silver shows his ingenuity. He had learned during the war, recalling his theatrical days, that decorative painting on gowns could also eke out meagre embroidery resources.

In exotic countries the competition from the local architecture and flora can be formidable, as this description of the surroundings in which Queen Elizabeth II opened the 1954 Ceylon Parliament, taken from *The Queen's Tour* by L.A. Nickolls, makes clear.

> Above the Queen, as she sat with the Duke on the throne dais, was a great purple lotus flower worked in glistening silk. In front of that was a white silk lotus. To right and left of the Queen, set against the golden-coloured draperies forming the background for the dais, were two emblems of royalty. These took the form of gold plaques, each set upon a six-foot long staff. One, showing a glittering face, represented the sun. The other, which carried a crescent-shaped face plus a rabbit, represented the moon. The hope expressed in these emblems, my neighbour informed me further, is that royalty may flourish so long as sun and moon shine in the sky. Between the 'sun' and the 'moon' was the national crest of Ceylon.

The temperature was in the nineties and the humidity in the seventies but the Queen wore her coronation gown, even though it weighed thirty pounds. She had decided that for the first Commonwealth tour of her reign, as many of her subjects as possible should be given the opportunity to see it. She had, at any rate, already learned to cope with heat during her visit to South Africa. In Cape Town, which she had visited in 1947 with her family, the royal party had listened to a speech lasting thirty-five minutes in a temperature of 100° in the shade – they were standing in the open. On the same visit she also learned to choose the right clothes, especially shoes. On an excursion to Cecil Rhodes' burial place in the Manotopo Hills, twenty miles from Bulawayo, the terrain was so difficult that her mother could not walk in her high-heeled, peep-toed shoes. Princess Elizabeth learned from her mother's mistake. She had to give up her shoes to the Queen and go barefoot.

The Canadian tour of 1951 taught Princess Elizabeth important lessons about travelling abroad. Good will was promoted by sitting for Karsh of Ottowa, whose photographic portraits were used as official Dominion souvenirs. The Princess wore the mink coats which had been Canadian gifts for her wedding. She frequently displayed her mother's diamond maple-leaf brooch and her wardrobe included a maple-leaf coloured jersey suit with a matching felt hat of "Napoleonic line, with a cockade on the left side". Like the Queen on her 1939 trip, Princess Elizabeth dutifully climbed into the cab of the royal train's locomotive; indeed she went a step further and drove the train on the way to Edmonton. She also learned the problems of exposure: she and the Duke were 'trapped' on a launch in a lock as the water slowly fell to the level of the river. One of the bystanders was a press man who lowered a microphone in front of the Duke's face and tried to interview him. However, she garnered the rewards of a dignified, but light-hearted, approach. When she and the Duke went square dancing, her outfit was a brown-and-white checked shirt and a dirndl skirt "of steel blue with amusing appliqué figures", while the Duke wore jeans, loafers and an evidently hastily purchased checked shirt – it still had the price tag on. The result of this carefully balanced informality was that the students of McGill University in Montreal cheered her with "Yea, Betty, Yea Windsor; Yea yea, Betty Windsor; Rah, rah, rah!" When the royal party visited Washington, the *Star* said that "the Princess ought to be told the simple truth . . . that she has charmed and captivated this city to such an extent that our oldest inhabitants, searching around their memories, are hard put to it to remember the name of any past visitor comparable to her": a nice compliment and a just reward for shaking hands with no less than 1,574 guests at a splendid British Embassy reception there.

Her clothes were carefully judged. Coming from a country still attempting to recover from the convulsion of war, but also from a Europe in thrall to Christian Dior's New Look, the Princess had to steer a careful course between austerity and ostentation. Going to a country which, at that time, was distrustful of oversophistication and upheld egalitarian attitudes meant that super-fashionable clothes would not be acceptable. Princess Elizabeth and Hartnell trod a middle path: day wear was based on a modified New Look, with coats which flared, but were not too flared, and skirts which were not too long (mid-calf length being judged as the right point). Evenings were glittering, sparkling occasions with embroidered dresses, tiaras and jewellery. Dignity and comfort during the day and glamour at night is the royal formula, at home or abroad.

With such trips behind her it was no mere tyro who set off around the world to see and be seen by her Commonwealth in her post-coronation world tour. By air, sea and land the royal party travelled 44,000 miles across the southern hemisphere in heat which ranged from the pleasant to the oppressive. The Queen's wardrobe consisted of 150 dresses, as many as possible in what her dressmakers referred to as 'disciplined' fabrics, that is, ones subject to the minimum amount of creasing. Most were in silk. To look after them the Queen's personal dresser, Miss MacDonald, and her two assistants spent the tour packing and unpacking, checking, sending trunks ahead and endlessly ironing. One of the Queen's designers swears that, in later years, dresses were chosen with Miss MacDonald's help not only for their suitability or attractiveness, but also for the ease with which they could be packed and maintained! Moving dresses, accessories and priceless jewellery around the world without damage or disaster is no easy matter. The Queen's luggage for a major tour is colossal. Her Baggage Master has at his disposal a separate plane which takes all luggage in advance. In addition to the clothes intended to be worn, alternatives are

The problems of looking regal during the day are highlighted in this photograph of the Queen in the Solomon Islands. She could be opening a church fete in the Home Counties were it not for the Prime Minister holding a protective parasol.

packed against unforeseen emergencies, such as the disastrous weather which the Queen encountered in California in 1983.

Peggy Hoath and May Prentice are the personal dressers who travel in the Queen's party now that Miss MacDonald is too old. Their job is to prepare every outfit the Queen will wear. Pressing, dry cleaning, brushing and polishing are their daily life. They lay out all the items which the Queen requires for each change, from underwear to jewellery. They are responsible for making sure that everything is ready when required and put away in its correct box, container or trunk after use. Not surprisingly, they spend much of their 'spare' time away from the ironing board anxiously going over lists and checking the contents of wardrobes.

The art of packing has been largely lost in these days of non-crease, non-iron clothes. The days of preparation and packing which were required to get an Edwardian lady away for a house party or weekend trip are over. For Royalty, however, packing remains a complicated affair. It is absolutely no use packing an item for a long trip if several cases have to be rifled through before it can be found. So lists are essential. Hartnell always presented Miss MacDonald with small black pocket-books containing coloured sketches of all the clothes provided for a visit with details of matching hats, gloves, handbags and shoes. The contents of all cases, trunks and hat boxes are written on duplicate lists, one of which is kept by the dressers and the other stuck to the inside of the container's lid. If anything is mislaid the responsibility is the dressers'. Ironing being a constant chore, they take the actual packing very seriously. To keep creases to a minimum, masses of tissue paper are used for each outfit. The shoulders and collars are padded with it and every fold is interlined with several sheets. Important evening dresses and state gowns travel separately on their hangers, shrouded in cotton wool and dark tissue paper (to prevent tarnishing) and zipped in plastic protective covers before being placed in their individual containers. Dresses and coats travel in large wardrobe trunks, dark blue and labelled 'The Queen'. Accessories are in separate trunks: to prevent them being dented hats are placed on suspended ribbons secured to the sides of the trunks; umbrellas and shoes are packed separately. When the royal family were living on the White Train in South Africa, the cramped space made it doubly important that royal maids should be able to unpack the appropriate garments without ransacking a dozen trunks; each trunk was therefore labelled – 'Hartnell dress No. 1', 'Thaarup hat No. 1', and so on. Thaarup wrote in his biography *Heads and Tales* that the designers could never forget the difficulties of climate – humidity, for instance, caused hat pins to rust overnight if precautions against this were not taken.

In addition to clothes the Queen always carries personal items such as her own pillow, Earl Grey tea, Malvern water and homoeopathic medicines prepared for her by Dr Marjorie Blackie. To counteract the sinus trouble which sometimes strikes her unexpectedly, she takes homoeopathic pills containing arsenic, deadly nightshade and onions. She does not rely wholly on these, however. One of her doctors always travels with her and her personal records, including her blood group, are normally sent on ahead to the country to be visited. She also lets it be known in advance what her likes and dislikes are, especially in food. The Queen eats no curry and no garlic, for obvious reasons.

Travelling within Great Britain is very much easier for everyone. Although an increasing number of trips are taken by aeroplane, the royal train and royal cars still play a vital role. Until well into the fifties they were the major means of transport within the United Kingdom. The royal train in Edwardian times was a very grand and ornate affair. In 1903 the King took delivery of two magnificent new twelve-wheeled saloons from the Wolverton works. Designed by the London North West Railway carriage superintendent, Mr C. Park, they were painted dark carmine lake in the lower half and milky white in the upper. Elaborate gilding, including carved lions' heads on the door handles and hand-painted heraldic coats of arms, prepared one for the opulence inside. The day areas had gold fittings, the bedrooms silver. The Queen's saloon contained a full-sized bedroom with two silver-plated beds, heavily draped with pink silk hangings, for her Majesty and Princess Victoria. The carpets were peacock blue, the soft furnishings, from Waring and Gillow, largely blue with pink trimmings, and the lamp shades pink. Queen Mary found this saloon somewhat overpowering and had the pink hangings swept away, along with the second bed. She also had a partition erected so that her dresser could have a small sleeping compartment next to her. Her favourite saloon was the smoking room created for Edward VII. She and King George normally spent their journey sitting in its green leather chairs, surrounded by black mahogany panelling inlaid with rosewood and satinwood and unburnished gilt fittings.

The East Coast Group royal train, with King's and Queen's saloons 395 and 396, was built between 1908 and 1909 to the same high standards, following the design of Mr Nigel Gresley. In 1925 the bedrooms in the saloons were scrapped when it was decided to use the 1903 train exclusively for overnight journeys. Ceramic baths and basins were fitted in 1941 – with a horizontal red line painted to show the maximum water-level permissible if spilling were to be avoided when the train was in motion. That problem, indeed, was normally taken care of by instructions such as this one from the forties: "hot water for Her Majesty's bath to be available about 6.30 a.m. on the morning of Friday, September 29th and the timing of the train is slowed down to enable the bath to be taken in comfort".

The third set of royal saloons, designed by William Stanier, and delivered in 1941, were originally provided with auxiliary armour-plating and steel-shuttered windows. After the war was over they were removed. When the King and Queen visited badly bombed cities throughout the country, they used the saloons as a hotel, the train being 'stabled' in secret sidings overnight. The two saloons were luxuriously furnished and fitted at considerable cost: 798, for King George VI, cost £3,584 and 799, for Queen Elizabeth, cost £3,297. For about £7,000 (at 1939 prices) their subjects could have bought a terrace of twenty semi-detached, three-bedroomed houses, or six Rolls-Royce cars. The royal bedroom took up one-third of the saloon, which also contained a bathroom and a room for a maid or valet. A side corridor led to the lounge. The Queen's lounge was decorated mainly in pale grey with a distinctive yellow, grey and white carpet, yellow and grey curtains from Marion Dorn of Bond Street and Gordon Russell furniture. Her bedroom was carpeted in mulberry and painted in Worcester Blue eggshell enamel.

The 1941 train was used by the present Queen until 1977, when it was replaced by high-speed modern stock. The fittings for the new train were chosen by the Queen and the Duke of Edinburgh with the advice of Sir Hugh Casson. Mahogany panelling has given way to melamine and P.V.C. and the interiors are business-like rather than luxurious. The Queen's saloon is fitted throughout with slate blue carpet; her lounge has an upholstered settee and easy chair in pale blue and a second chair in jasmine yellow. Desk and wall cabinets are faced in royal silk natural-coloured P.V.C. and their tops are painted cream to match the walls. The same colours and materials are used in the Queen's bedroom, which has a three-feet-wide spring divan bed with storage space for luggage underneath. The royal bathroom separates the Queen from her dresser's bedroom and bathroom. The other coaches of the royal train have been built at various times since the fifties and include a royal dining car for the family and a restaurant car for the royal household.

Queen Victoria was nervous of trains and refused to travel faster than forty miles per hour. She also disliked eating on board and demanded frequent refreshment stops. Her son, Edward, instituted very strict rules governing the way royal trains were run. He introduced the pilot train, which 'cleared' the line by running ten minutes ahead of the royal train. From then until the royal train passed all trains on lines parallel to its route were stopped; level crossings were locked; bridges (which had already been examined) were guarded by platelayers with flags; tunnels were patrolled; and all station masters on the route were expected to be on duty with as many of their staff as possible. There was a secret bell code to signal the pilot engine and the royal train had chief railway officials travelling on board. Security was even higher when foreign royalty were also travelling. Then the entire route was lined by patrols in sight of one another. Although such extreme measures are long gone, British Rail still treats all details of the running of the royal train as high-security classified information. Timetables are never divulged, nor the diagram of the train. The diagram, which shows the composition of the train, is based on the exact number of the royal household who are travelling – on first-class tickets paid for by the Queen – so that the number of carriages required can be calculated. In this way, by working out precise measurements and speeds, British Rail can ensure that the royal door meets precisely the royal carpet laid down on the station platform. Edward VII had to send a horse and carriage train two or three days in advance of himself so that coaches, horses and grooms would all be settled in before he arrived; the Queen merely steps into one of her cars which has been driven ahead of her.

The royal connection with cars began with Edward VII. As early as 1902 *The Autocar* was hailing him as "a fearless autocarist ... although he does not drive himself". He bought Daimlers and this royal tradition lasted unbroken until 1960. The first Rolls-Royce, which is now the standard royal automobile, was not bought until well after World War II. All members of the royal family have taken a great interest in their cars and have always liked them to be very grand. In 1903 the Prince of Wales, later George V, bought a 22-horse power Daimler with scalloped front seats and "immediately behind them, two more seats, each of the fauteuil pattern". King Edward's new car, bought the following year, was described in *The Motor* as having electric lighting, blue leather upholstery and blue pile carpet which gave a very 'toney' appearance; the wheels were "shod with Collier tyres". Queen Mary took an especially deep interest in the style and appearance of her vehicles. As early as 1905, when she was the Princess of Wales, she had Mulliner design her first Daimler to her very precise specifications. Walking in the grounds of York House, the Princess was much taken by the contrasting greens of a fir tree. A sample of the foliage was despatched to the carriage-maker with instructions to copy the shades exactly for the paintwork of the new car. The interior which she required was luxurious and included French-polished figured rosewood fittings, royal blue morocco upholstery, silk blinds, a watch case, speaking tubes and electric lighting. Her 1907 Daimler was also in her special greens and had mother-of-pearl fittings. For her 1913 Daimler special a second speedometer was installed in the rear compartment so that she could keep a check on the driver's speed. The first royal drivers were policemen; in 1905 they were earning £3 per week, 'all found', plus a daily allowance of 3/6 and a travelling allowance of 6/–. "I must say I have the greatest confidence in our driver," Queen Alexandra said; but she still kept a close watch. "I poke him violently in the back at every *corner* to go gently and whenever a dog, child or anything comes our way". How long the chauffeurs lasted before handing in their notice is not recorded. If chauffeurs were not too expensive, the cars most certainly were. In 1920 it was planned to buy a new car for Princess Mary at a cost of "approximately £2,000", but in the end she had to make do with a second-hand Daimler at £700.

All royal Daimlers were custom designs created by the carriage-makers, Mulliner or Hooper, to royal specifications, one of the most important being to allow extra headroom for elaborate uniform helmets or high hats. The windows were low and wide so that the occupants could be properly seen. For the same reason King George V and Queen Mary never sat in the back seats, but always very upright in the centre ones. Designing to order, the coachbuilders were able to take into account personal requirements. In 1950, for example, Queen Elizabeth decided that she required somewhere safe to put her hat which she liked to remove when driving from one engagement to another and Hooper's gave her a hinged peg on the inside of the door panel. In later life Queen Mary suffered from sciatica and had great difficulty in bending her head. Her last Daimler, delivered in 1947 for her eightieth birthday, was made especially high so that she could step in and out with dignity and comfort. The space between the step and the underside of the door cantrail was 62¾ inches and the interior headroom was 57 inches. Personalised design for

Hardy Amies designed this coat for the Queen in 1976 but in feeling it is Paris of twenty years before.

royalty even crossed the Atlantic. The Buick used on the Canadian and American tour of 1939 had a specially built body and the fabric, interior trim and upholstery were chosen on the advice of Queen Elizabeth's couturier, Norman Hartnell.

As with every aspect of royal life, the planning, preparation and choosing of everything to do with travel, not least the selection of clothes, require enormous efforts. But the results surely justify them. As L.A. Nickolls said of the 1953 Commonwealth tour, "the Queen had brought with her such an extensive wardrobe that, over a period of weeks, we seldom saw her twice in the same ensemble ... it was interesting to hear some of the New Zealand women journalists

"Honestly, Norman, I much preferred your collection for my American Tour!"

saying that they found some of the colour shades of the dresses so 'subtle' that they found difficulty in describing them as accurately or as definitely as they could wish". Those were the days when as many as six changes a day would be required, with little or no repetition. When King George VI and Queen Elizabeth were in Canada in 1939, Hartnell even designed a dress for train halts in the middle of the night – a sable-trimmed cross between a silk negligee and an evening dress. Wardrobes are much simpler now, but standards are just as high. Mrs Roosevelt said of Queen Elizabeth that she "never had a crease in her dress or a hair out of place". The same could be said of her daughter, Elizabeth II.

The Princess of Wales has learned to accept that wherever she goes a phalanx of pressmen with cameras will face her, jostling each other, calling her name and hoping to get the picture of one of the most photographed people in the world.

7
PRESS AND PALACE

Queen Anne has been described as dull, spoilt, indolent, discontented and rich. Since her reign the monarchy has slowly and gently slid down the road to a kind of middle-class respectability. One aspect of this change has been the projection of the royal *family* as the all-important public face of monarchy. Caroline of Brandenburg-Ausbach, who became Princess of Wales in 1714, wrote of her son, that "my dear first born is the greatest ass and the greatest liar and the greatest canaille and the greatest beast in the world and I heartily wish he were out of it". Such an outburst is unthinkable today. The royal family is 'the firm', as George VI said, and it must present a united front – the quintessential example of the domestic virtues towards which the rest of society should strive. Yet for all that the monarch remains the captain of the team and the quality of the teamwork reflects the standards of the person who sits on the throne.

Each monarch's success is now a success of personality. Failure, a possibility only when a monarch makes decisions which affect government, is hardly considered any longer. Monarchs seem to create an atmosphere in reaction to the tone set by their predecessors. Victoria's straight-laced attitudes made Edwardian relaxation possible; the general 'naughtiness' of Edward's reign led to George V's 'father-figure' dullness. Edward VIII's brief reign was characterised by his rather loose approach, a want of earnestness which made George VI's stability appear all the more attractive, especially since he was so clearly 'a family man'. When George died, tired and worn-out, the youth and vigour of his daughter, Elizabeth II, were seen as the key to the future. "God save the Queen," Sir Norman Hartnell wrote in his autobiography, "and long may she reign – I feel that the whole world needs her." Many of his readers no doubt agreed with him. Certainly, in a century outstanding for the speed with which royal houses have declined and fallen, persons who believe in hereditary monarchy must look with awe and pleasure at the staying power of the British monarchy. Not even the dramatic controversy of the abdication crisis was able to shake permanently the popularity of the royal family or impair its image as the perfect family unit.

Young royal children have traditionally been kept out of the public eye. But after the abdication of Edward VIII, which ruffled royalty's self-confidence even if it did not greatly diminish public regard for the monarchy, the stability of the family unit was emphasised by ·the stress placed on the new King and Queen *and* their daughters. So the making of the Queen started very early. Despite the attempts of her mother and Queen Mary to protect her from over-exposure, she was hounded by press photographers. They would conceal themselves in hedges and lurk behind trees, waiting for her to pass by with her nurses. Dermot Morah, in his book *Princess Elizabeth, Duchess of Edinburgh*, pointed out that efforts to give the little Princess "the sort of natural, homely and intimate nursery life that every little girl ought to enjoy" were frustrated by "imposing scarlet guardsmen at the gate who will go through the stately exercise known as presenting arms" and "grown-up ladies who will sink to the earth before her in the ceremonious gesture of the curtsey". Wherever Elizabeth and her parents went presents were showered upon her. The King and Queen returned from their Australian tour with no less than three tons of toys. (More than ninety per cent of them went to children's hospitals and charities.) On their trip to Paris in 1939, they were presented by the children of France with two dolls for the princesses. Called Marianne and France, the dolls came complete with their own model Citroën cars in light green and periwinkle blue. In 1934 Princess Elizabeth was given a scaled-down model of a Welsh cottage designed by Morgan Willmott, which had running water and electricity – luxuries which millions of her father's subjects were living without. As she grew up the life of unreality continued. And it was chronicled in the most unrealistic way. In 1958 Brigadier Stanley Clarke wrote in his *Palace Diary*, apparently without a hint of irony or humour, that when the Princess accompanied Prince Philip on his naval posting to Malta she "was in the same position as the wife of any naval officer – she was joining her husband on his station. She sent her own car and forty large cases of clothes and personal effects ahead of her, and also a new polo pony for her husband." From childhood the Queen has never had the opportunity to be anonymous or ordinary. Whether as heir to the throne or as Queen, she has always been 'different'.

The present Princess of Wales was not similarly trained to the role of future Queen. Having lived a comparatively normal life, albeit on a luxurious and privileged level, the sudden glare of the spotlight has been harsh. She has, nevertheless, adapted to constant exposure and endless curiosity with some aplomb. She has quickly learned to cope with the peculiar demands made on the royal family by the people. Queen Alexandra, Queen Mary and the Queen were all born royal princesses; the Princess of Wales and the Queen Mother are alike in that their adult role was undreamed of in their youth. They both came from an aristocratic background and enjoyed a wealthy upbringing, but neither was royal: they had to learn the royal 'ropes' when they were adults. The difficulties involved in adapting to a royal life can be dismissed too easily. There *are* problems, there *are* difficulties and there *are* considerable adjustments to be made.

A royal person must keep his head when all around are losing theirs. We are all familiar with the civic nonsense that a visit from royalty so often brings: coal is whitewashed and 'Gentlemen' signs are removed. When the Queen Mother went to a performance of *The Prime of Miss Jean Brodie*, a ten-second sequence of two girls giggling over a picture of a naked man was cut out lest it offend. Much the same thing had happened in the thirties, when she attended a performance of Diaghilev's *Scheherazade*, in which the harem orgy scene had 'specific postures'. The court asked the company to tone down the scene and, amazingly, it agreed. One has to ask what sort of royalty we have and what sort we want when confronted by these essentially insulting attitudes towards them. Individuals are no less surprising in their reaction to the royal presence. Once when the Queen opened a new block of flats in St. John's Wood, the woman in whose flat she took tea marked the bottom of the Queen's chair with a pencil, "so that I don't get it mixed up with the other one of the pair," and planned to have a plaque fixed to its back. In America, when the Queen was to visit the horse-training centre of Mr and Mrs Paul Mellon, Mrs Mellon put timber cradles with cotton covers around the flowerbeds to protect the plants from the cold so that they would be perfect for the visit. In 1969, the *Western Morning News* reported the strange behaviour of Lt. Commander Stephen Emberton, who "to make sure the princess would be able to negotiate the narrow companion-ways, steep ladders and hatchways in a tight skirt, went through a special rehearsal in drag".

Words sometimes speak louder than actions, and professional writers often say things which are highly revealing of our fundamental attitudes towards the royal family. In writing so clearly hagiographic as Marion Crawford's, one can forgive statements such as "our royal family symbolises for us the perfection all would like to attain" and references to the Queen "the woman, who by the grace of God, guides our destiny". Nor, perhaps, should we be surprised by the heightened language in which Godfrey Winn wrote of the Queen's attendance at a gala performance of a Florence Nightingale film when her father was sick: "I have seen many brave acts performed on the battlefield of life but few braver than her dedicated performance that night". This when memories of World War II were still in people's minds and Europe was full of refugee camps! Even writers of the calibre of Elizabeth Longford get flummoxed in the presence of royalty. Of the Queen Mother she said, in an interview with Jean Rook published in the *Daily Express* on 16 July 1980, that "the moment she speaks to you, you feel as if you're the most important person in the world . . . the Queen Mum's as near perfect as they come".

Experienced journalists do not find their perceptions so dulled by royal subjects. Far from it. They learn to be simultaneously intimate and audacious, although, to quote Sylvester Bolan, their sensationalism normally "does not mean distorting the truth. It means the vivid and dramatic presentation of events so as to give them a forceful impact on the mind of the reader." Nothing is more revealing of public attitudes to royal personalities than the way in which their actions are chronicled, with or without commentary, in the daily newspapers. There are various means by which journalists keep royalty 'on the boil', even when their daily doings are routine and uninspiring. When the Queen is 'opening' the tenth hospital in a year, a hospital, moreover, which has probably been functioning for nine months before the ceremony, the desperate press commentator falls back on a description of her appearance and the features editor sparks it up with a hint of criticism. So the copy is born. Concentrating on fashion is one of a variety of approaches which have become acceptable to editors, readers and even, perhaps, the Palace.

One of the most commonly recurring approaches is to suggest that life in the Palace is not so very different from life in a 'semi' in Blackburn or a bungalow in Rhyl. Worldly journalists pretend to believe in a royal family which lives up to the views expressed by the woman interviewed by Tony Parker and published in *The People of Providence*: "Not a word against the Queen will I listen to, not one. I think she's a wonderful person and she does a wonderful job ... deep down she'll always be an ordinary everyday person with a house to run and a family to bring up ... I'm sure in elections and things she votes Labour like all the rest of us ordinary people do." Such ignorance of the real situation seems quite incomprehensible in these days of the mass diffusion of information, until we look at the quality of the information which is fed to the public by the daily press. It is easy enough to forget the Queen's immense wealth and to imagine her sitting by the fireside with a needle when one reads reports like this one from the *Evening Standard* of 21 June, 1971: "Up and down go hemlines; while we plead with our women to wear what suits them, they usually follow fashion ... the Queen appeared at a Smith's Lawn, Windsor, garden party at the weekend in a raspberry-coloured suit which clearly had two hemlines – the old and the new: the skirt was originally made to reach the knee. But it has been let down about three inches. The Queen has always been sensible enough to alter clothes she likes to keep in step with fashion, instead of buying new ones. 'Sometimes she has things which are three years old,' said a Buck House official. 'There is certainly nothing unusual about the Queen making changes to her existing wardrobe to get extra wear from things'."

The *Daily Mail* took a slightly different line to a similar story in its reports of 20 and 21 June, 1979, suggesting that carefulness with money was really meanness. What the *Standard* presented as praiseworthy, the *Mail* found cause for criticism: "the Queen wore a 'make do and mend' dress for the opening of Royal Ascot – with two feet cut off the hemline of a dress she wore in Saudi Arabia in February". That report was followed the next day by a more critical comment: "Our parsimonious monarch was at it again yesterday – she turned up at Royal Ascot in a printed chiffon dress in grey, pink and lavender, with a matching loose coat and lavender straw hat, created by Hardy Amies for the State Visit to Denmark last month". The *Daily Mirror* of 4 June, 1975, was more sympathetic. Here is the Queen being sensible.

The chill winds of economic reality are blowing through the strangest of places these days – even the Queen's personal wardrobe. In what is obviously an attempt to cut down on the high cost of her clothing – the annual bill is

In Portugal in 1985 the Queen donned a student robe as honoured guest. Smiling, relaxed and happy she clearly felt completely comfortable in her yellow coat by Amies.

huge – she has just had four of her Norman Hartnell outfits (they cost around £400 each) copied by a Hong Kong couturier – Soong Salon De Mode Ltd. She visited the little-known Chinese frock maker during her recent Asian tour. He obligingly gave her four fittings, and the patterns of the four Hartnell copies were given to her so that she could order them by mail from Buck House in any colour or quantity.

Norman Hartnell was, understandably perhaps, taken aback when I informed him yesterday of what the Queen had been up to in Hong Kong. "What did you say?" he asked. "The Queen has had some of my clothes copied?" One could hear the doyen of British designers swallowing hard at the end of the telephone. "Did she really?" There was a painful pause and he added, a trifle more chirpily: "Oh well, I suppose imitation is the best form of flattery. In these inflationary times, when things are so expensive, I think it's probably very sensible of her".

The Queen's wardrobe for the trip to the Far East was extensive – 30 dresses, 40 pairs of shoes, 4 diamond tiaras and 15 hats.

The picture of royalty being 'just like us' and having to mind the pennies is also used to highlight the Princess of Wales, as an item from the *Daily Express* of 22 February, 1981, shows. "There was nothing wrong with the blue two-piece suit Lady Di chose for her official picture except that it was a bit too short. So like the economy-minded and sensible girl that she is, she unpicked the hem and let it down an inch or so. Then the girl destined to be the next Queen, got out her needle and thread and stitched it neatly back again."

If part of the population wishes to identify with the royal family as the apotheosis of domestic virtue there are others eager to envy them their privileged super-star status. For them the press is happy to provide carping or even openly hostile comments on the things which can be criticised with impunity – their clothes and general appearance. *The People* plunged in on 21 May, 1972. "The Queen got a dressing down last week over the clothes she wore on the tour of France. The attack came from *Women's Wear Daily*. Why, the paper asked, did the Queen dress so badly? It added scathingly: 'Why must she be the nice Queen in the nice little Chanel-copy?' Even the Queen's accessories upset the newspaper. Why, it asked, did she need 'that dumb handbag'? Was it 'to suggest that she's just like other women who have to carry money and identity cards'?" This is an example of the veiled criticism which is so popular with newspapers. By quoting another source, preferably foreign, the newspaper protects its own reputation for 'patriotism'; it merely passes on news which, however distressing, must be revealed. The technique was used with great skill by the *Daily Express* on 19 August, 1972:

The knockers have been on the Queen for years. They accuse her of dressing dowdily. They say the clothes she wears are dreary and out of date. What a lot of stuff and nonsense!

Her skirt length has not varied much over the years. It usually dips an inch or so below the kneecap. Her hats have come in for a great deal of criticism. Even the most ardent royalist must grudgingly admit that some of the creations which have rested on the royal head are, to be polite, rather strange. Her shoes, somebody once said, were only suitable for retired school-marms. All clump and no glamour.

The *Sunday Express* of 1 January, 1972, knew how to criticise without offending its royalist readers. "The most distinguished lady in the land has got herself a new mink coat, and been publicly photographed in it. As her slightly less distinguished husband is president in Britain of the World Wildlife Fund, dedicated to the preservation of all wild life except pheasants and such things, I suspect that fur coat must have caused some embarrassment. But when the wife is boss what can a man do?"

Criticism of the Queen's clothes has become more aggressive in the last ten years and, frequently under the guise of "advice", no-nonsense comments like one which appeared in the *Daily Mail* of 16 November, 1983, are now acceptable, though they might have been considered offensive a few years ago: "Princess Diana is said to be having a marginal effect on the Queen's terrible clothes. In time, hopefully, she will persuade her to reject the double-breasted coat, the felt hat, the sensible costume, the bow-tied blouse. So the next time she goes through her mother-in-law's wardrobe I suggest she persuades her to chuck out all those frumpish stoles the Queen is partial to clutching to her diamanté-encrusted evening gowns." Earlier in the year, during the Queen's visit to California, her wardrobe had given rise to an avalanche of criticism and we can take this comment from the *Sunday Express* of 2 March as typical: "There ought to be somebody around to save the Queen from wearing silly things ... half Britain must have cringed with vicarious embarrassment when they saw on T.V. and in the papers the outfit the Queen wore on Sunday at San Diego. Her fussy blue and white suit was bad enough, but the matching sailor cap she wore with it was gruesome. She ended up looking like a matronly cinema usherette, circa 1940." When the Queen went to India at the end of 1983 the *Evening Standard*, on 22 November, was critical of her clothes, but angled the comments so that she appeared to be the victim of insensitive and unimaginative designers: "The remarkable thing about the Queen's clothes during the current Royal tour is that they have remained so consistently unremarkable. Safe and sensible seems to be the instruction given to the 3 designers who are responsible for the Queen's wardrobe in Kenya, Bangladesh and now India."

"It is well known that the Queen – happiest in tweeds and walking shoes – refers to her clothes as 'props'. But that does not mean that her designers – Amies, Thomas and Hartnell – could not have shown more of the flair that has just occasionally been visible. For her arrival in New Delhi the Queen looked cool and charming in a pretty tangerine-and-mauve patterned dress which, for once, flattered her figure. But more often than not one was tempted to think, 'It ain't half hot Ma'am', as she pulled at the waistband of yet another long-sleeved, shirt-waisted dress. For her triumphant arrival in sweltering Nairobi she wore such a style in pale yellow and made of *wool*. On her visit to Treetops, the safari hotel, the material was cooler, but the design still formal and the silk fabric fluttered constantly in the breeze, revealing the white royal petticoat. 'I think someone must have miscalculated the weather,' a spokesman said."

The Palace had heard much the same sort of thing earlier in the year from the same newspaper. The following report appeared on 4 March: "With more than a nod in the direction of the frothy style set by the Princess of Wales, the Queen stepped out in a frou-frou of taffeta and lace ruffles for a San Francisco banquet. Her champagne silk taffeta dress, by Hardy Amies, was cut with a voluminous skirt flounced from a dropped waistline. A flurry of gold lace ruffles decorated the puffed sleeves, and giant candy box bows perched on each shoulder. With the glittering tiara, 100-watt diamond drop earrings, and magnificent necklace of dazzling diamonds, even the design team at Hardy Amies now admit the whole effect might have been over the top last night."

The Princess of Wales has been alternately praised and pilloried for her dress sense with such a bewildering series of volte-faces that she must be thoroughly confused. Even before she became Princess the press made huge mileage out of a black taffeta evening dress which was perfectly unremarkable except for being strapless and mildly low cut. The *Sunday Mirror* became over-excited: "It is a dress," it declared on 15 March, 1981, "that will go down in history." The fashion correspondent of *The Times* landed herself in hot water by writing a straight-from-the-shoulder criticism of the dress in the *International Herald Tribune*. However, she was unbowed, and stoutly defended herself in an interview for the *Daily Express*, published on 7 March, 1981: "I defend the piece totally, I do not rescind a single word of it. The piece is directed at the inappropriateness of a particular dress and its construction. In my view it is very rash for royalty to be fashionable. Total anonymity is what you want for Royal clothes. I'm not averse to the dress, I just don't think that the public should be exposed to Lady Di's bosom."

Criticism of the Princess has sometimes pinpointed her extravagance. "The Princess of Wales will be able to indulge her apparently insatiable appetite for elegant clothes while her husband is out grouse shooting," commented the *New Standard* on 17 August, 1981. Sometimes it is more directly hostile. On 12 December, 1983, the *Sun* fired a broadside at the Princess by quoting comments from the compiler of the worst-dressed women list. "Princess Di got a shock new title from a leading fashion expert last night: 'Dowdy Di'. The 21 year old Princess, who last year was voted among the world's most elegant women, was accused of 'invading Queen Victoria's attic and looking old hat'! The astonishing dressing-down came in top Hollywood designer Richard Blackwell's annual list of the Ten Worst Dressed Women. Poor Diana came top of the flop parade ahead of actresses, comediennes and other celebrities. Blackwell, whose acid comments have been ruffling women for 23 years, lashed out with: 'Diana is looking so unlike the marvellous, progressive girl she once was'. Among the outfits which came in for a

The *superstar meets the superstars of Hollywood – Frank Sinatra, Dionne Warwick and George Burns – during her California tour. Her dress by Amies is decorated with Californian poppies as a heavy-handed and not entirely successful compliment to her host state.*

Blackwell blast was a two-piece, low-hipped suit Di wore to a friend's wedding last year. He said 'in the picture I saw the Princess was leaning against a wall – the wind was blowing at her face and clothes. She looked like a 1910 bathing beauty from a Mack Sennet silent movie'."

On 22 July, 1983, the *Evening Standard*'s readers were informed of France's critical attitude to the Princess: "This week the French weekly *Paris Match* comes out with an article headlined 'Oh Diana, Why Do You Have To Dress Like That?' written by one of France's leading fashion experts, Mlle Kathleen Pancol. She described the colours of Diana's clothes as those that might have been chosen by the manufacturers of boiled sweets. Her skirts are too long and 'her hats are ridiculous'." A few weeks earlier the *Daily Express* had drawn its readers' attention to the fact that the Canadians were not happy with the wardrobe which the Princess had chosen for her North American tour. An article of 30 May said that "Canadian fashion designers have taken a swing at Princess Diana for the 'matronly wardrobe' she's been wearing. Some criticised her clothes as 'too severe' and unyouthful. And even the Princess's hats – surely one of her fashion hallmarks – are put down as being 'too old'." On 10 April of the same year criticism from Australia was reported

151

in *The People*: "Princess Di's designers got a real dressing down from the critics for the slip-up they made over the striped pyjama-type suit she wore in Adelaide last week. For the beige and cream outfit – topped by a frilly, clown-like collar – made Di look awkward. For a princess with a model-girl figure and wasp waist the straight up-and-down cot suit disguised all her assets except her face."

By reporting foreign criticism of the Princess, newspapers are able to keep their own hands clean and so avoid loss of sales. Foreign sources, however, help to fill space. There is so little real information available to journalists, and so little that can be written about royal clothes as news, that many a column has been filled with speculation and what could be called rumination on a vacuum. The Queen's handbag has proved a remarkably fruitful area for conjecture over the years. "What is in the Queen's handbag?" wondered the *Sunday Express* on 19 November, 1972. "Royalty does not use ready money – is never in urgent need of a penny. Royalty is never seen to powder its nose in public – or blow it for that matter. Royalty does not require driving licence, cosmetic 'repair kit', dark glasses, face tissues, pens etc. so what's in that royal handbag? Has anybody ever seen the Queen open it?" The answer was supplied by the *Daily Express* on 1 June, 1973. "Like any other woman," the Queen had a psychological need for her handbag. "The Queen seems to feel a great attachment for her handbag. She is never photographed without it, not even when she's strolling across the comparative privacy of her own front lawn. Royal handbags are invariably leather, highly polished, neat and buttoned up. The bags must contain very little, if anything at all. So why do they carry them? There are a few reasons, one very obvious. A bag is something to clutch when nervous, something to busy the hands with during long, awkward moments. It also gives a feeling of security and contentment and it's as private to any woman as a love affair." The same newspaper returned to the how, what and why of royal handbags four years later, in an article of 25 May, 1977, which discussed the Queen's accessories: "Gloves, which are regarded as essential by the Queen, are not only a sign of formality, though rather old-fashioned, but a practical defence for a woman who has in the course of duty to shake so many hands. Although the Queen has perfected a rather limp royal handshake which protects her fingers, she is further guarded by gloves. Fine suede (which has to be cleaned) is more elegant, but the Queen prefers gloves in suede fabric, easily washed, easily removed, easily dyed. As omnipresent and unchanging as her gloves are her handbags. Always copious, always in good quality heavy calf for daytime and silver tissue for evening, often black and occasionally white, never without a loop to hang over her wrists, and never far from her side, they have ignored fashion change and been a frequent subject of criticism."

With the Princess of Wales speculation seems to centre on how she manages to keep warm. On 28 March, 1982, the *Sunday Mirror*'s sharp-eyed reporter discovered the secret: "A sudden gust of wind reveals Princess Di's fashion secret. Instead of tights she preferred to wear knee-length pop sox when she visited a community centre on Tyneside last week." On 10 December, 1983, the *Daily Mail* made another discovery: "The secret of the Princess of Wales' ability to keep out the cold as she goes walkabout is an undercover job. She's into thermal underwear. 'I am a walking advertisement for Damart,' she said. Thermal underwear was invented by her great-great-great-great-great uncle, the second Earl Spencer."

When all else fails, a hard-pressed journalist can always fall back on gossip, as the *Daily Express* did on 9 December, 1981, in an article which detailed the 'downfall' of two royal designers. "Why are the royal wedding dressmakers, David and Elizabeth Emanuel, so needled because their relationship with the Princess of Wales has ripped apart at the seams? What did they expect, after all the colourful stuff they've been turning out, by the yard, to newspapers and TV? The Emanuels should have been sharp enough to realise that someone at Buck House would eventually cut them off for opening up like scissors and making flashy little stabs at becoming TV personalities. And they might have remembered that Norman Hartnell, who had the royal business sewn up for more than 40 years, always kept his lips firmly tacked. You couldn't unravel him on the subject of the Queen, or Queen Mum, with a safety pin." The silly season never closes as far as royalty are concerned, as the following two extracts show. They are separated by ten years, but the trivial attitudes which they exemplify are identical. The *Evening Standard* of 29 June, 1971, found it worthwhile to report on the following: "The staff of a York drycleaners got an unexpected customer yesterday. They were asked to press the Queen's coat which had become damp and creased during her tour of the city. All seven of the staff dropped their work and concentrated on the coat, which was returned in 20 minutes, immaculately hand-finished and without charge. 'A great honour' said Mr Fred Street, manager of the shop." On 21 March, 1981, the *Daily Express* felt that the world should know that "the jeans factory in Labour M.P. George Foulkes' south Ayrshire constituency has been saved – because his suggestion that Lady Diana Spencer wore jeans to her wedding boosted sales". *Plus ça change, plus c'est la même chose.* It is almost as if the press is eager to establish the truth of words spoken by Tom Paine in his address to the people of France, delivered on 25 October, 1792: "In whatever manner we consider it we find in the notion of Hereditary Royalty only foolishness and infamy. What is this office which infants and idiots are capable of filling? Some talent is required to be a common workman; to be a king no more is needed than to have a human figure, to be a living automaton."

8
PRINCESS DIANA

"The Queen is not allowed to wear a crown: nothing less than a halo will suffice. But the halo is neon-lighted." So Kingsley Martin wrote in 1962. Today he would need to be much more emphatic. Since the Jubilee of 1977 the halo has burned with a supernatural light and it now gleams, with the steadiness of a laser beam, above the head of the Princess of Wales.

When Diana Spencer walked out of St Paul's Cathedral on 29 July, 1981, she had changed her life forever. The upper-class English girl had ceased to exist; in her place stood the future Queen Consort of England. Already, the fluffy duckling who had attracted the Prince of Wales was being transformed into a svelte swan. It is hard to imagine a more dramatic physical change than that which the Princess of Wales has undergone. She has lost weight, altered her whole appearance and in record time developed into a highly sophisticated and fashionable figure. The pretty girl has been groomed into elegance and beauty. Taking advantage of her height, five feet and ten inches, she has slimmed down to a model girl's proportions, so that she now has the perfect fashion figure. Her appearance and attitudes to dress raise interesting questions concerning the royals and the people's approach towards them. Are royal ladies to be viewed as sex-symbols like film and pop stars or are they brightly coloured nuns to be viewed with respect and from a distance? The latter was surely the case before 'Shy Di' joined the firm, but since her marriage to the Prince of Wales she has been deliberately exploited by the press as 'Sexy Di' and she and her advisers seem to be willing to live up to the image. As a result, nine-to-five-Nigels dream of the Princess of Wales as their ideal Samantha.

The Princess of Wales can be seen as a perfect success or as a victim in the royal popularity stakes. Certainly she has allowed herself to be exploited as a glamorous clothes-horse; as many women of her age have pointed out, she has done very little to assist the feminist movement. Yet it is difficult to imagine what she could do for such a movement. Marriage to a Prince, especially the heir to the throne, entails a certain kind of behaviour. Vast amounts of money must be spent on clothes, wardrobes must bulge with outfits worn fewer than a dozen times and the press must write ecstatically about her looks. This is all part of the 'bread and circuses'

The Princess of Wales photographed by Lord Snowdon before her trip to Italy in April 1985.

155

role of the young royals. Were she to take a more serious role in society as, increasingly, Princess Anne does, it would be difficult for the press to keep the 'Di' euphoria high – to the detriment of their sales and, possibly, the popularity of the Palace.

Nearly every appearance the Princess makes is hailed by the press as creating a significant fashion statement. Criticism of her appearance is minor and is soon drowned in the general buzz of acclaim. It is an acclaim which is usually deserved. The Princess of Wales often dresses very nicely. The need for a degree of formality often means that she dresses in a much older way than her contemporaries, just as the Queen did in her youth. But the Queen, who grew up secure in the knowledge of her future, did not consider personal adornment to be important. The Princess of Wales clearly enjoys clothes and understands fashion. Not having been closeted in castle and palace, she has always been free to shop around (something the Queen has never done). She has learned street wisdom (the Queen hardly ever went out into the streets at all and was twenty before she took her first bus ride and paid her fare as an ordinary passenger) and she has mixed with a wide range of people, which gives her a unique position in the royal family (the Queen has never met a person in any other capacity than Princess or monarch and has never been treated as an ordinary girl). The Princess knows what real people wear because she has 'street credibility' – although admittedly the streets tend to be within a two-mile radius of Sloane Square. Unlike the Queen, who was constrained by rationing, the Princess has no limits on her buying. Her husband is very rich and, unlike most men, who can never be totally sure of their financial future, he knows that he will inherit an immense fortune. With an income of around £8,000 per week he can afford his wife's clothes' bill. He set off their life together on the grand scale: he is reputed to have paid Garrard's, the royal jewellers, £28,000 for her diamond and sapphire engagement ring.

Like the Queen, who needed 'Bobo' MacDonald to advise her, the Princess of Wales has relied on her 'Bobo's', selected staff of British *Vogue*, who help to guide the Princess's taste. By and large, they and the Princess have chosen soundly. The major problem they face is the unwritten law that members of the royal family should patronise British designers. The most interesting British designers tend to produce irreverent, exciting clothes for the very young or make very strong and uncompromising fashion statements. The Princess cannot wear very young, iconoclastic clothes; neither can she be too much a 'fashion freak' without running the risk of alienating her public. She is circumscribed by orthodox views of how the future Queen Consort should be dressed. It is not possible for her to be a fashion leader, nor indeed a fashionable figure in the way that a girl of her age and wealth would perhaps wish to be. Since she became the Princess of Wales fashion has undergone enormous changes, of which she, as a reader of fashion magazines, is clearly aware. Post-punk looks from the London art school and club scene have been taken to Paris, where Jean Paul Gaultier and Thierry Mugler have tamed and modified them before their return to London to appear in a gentler form on the backs of the well-heeled young. This period has also seen Japanese-inspired layered and torn garments. Alaïa's body-hugging looks and eclectic London street fashion. Such exciting developments have had to be ignored by the Princess of Wales, no matter how much she may be attracted to them simply because they are too fashionable. The Princess must never look anything but demure; she must never look threatening; above all, she must always look like a lady. Modern fashion for the young is about none of these things.

No fashion-conscious woman would have a wardrobe of clothes entirely from one country. Princess Diana is no exception. She is reputed to buy clothes by the Paris designers, such as Kenzo, and the Milanese, such as Versace. But unfortunately, she may not wear them on official engagements. She has been known to drive herself down Bond Street in her blue Cortina and pop into Benetton, accompanied only by a detective. She shops at Harvey Nichols and is sufficiently interested in fashion to have visited the trade stands at Olympia during fashion week, accompanied by Anna Harvey, of British *Vogue*. If she were allowed total freedom of choice there can be no doubt that the Princess of Wales would be a much more fashionable dresser than she is. What is interesting is that her particular brand of well-groomed, high-gloss chic is producing a look which is in some ways more American than British. Some of her more successful outfits would fit in perfectly on Fifth Avenue, whereas in England, even on Bond Street, they might appear too polished and fashionable. The formal, over-all look, which is the basis of smartness for wealthy American women, is not now part of the British fashion scene. Princess Diana's super-enamelled looks are closer to those seen in *W*, the American fortnightly publication for the rich and fashionable or *Town and Country* than to those in *Tatler*, the house magazine of her class, or *Country Life*.

It would, even so, be wrong to say that the Princess is a fashion anachronism. That her clothes find an answering chord in the minds of many women is undeniable. Although under twenty five, the Princess has an appearance which appeals much more to an older age-group. Fashion-conscious girls of the Princess's generation are not interested in the tasteful 'together' look which she presents. They are involved in the exciting world of instant fashion looks and fads. These looks are always vibrant, although to the older generation they are sometimes startling. If they are rich enough to buy designer labels, they are attracted to people like Body Map, and Katherine Hamnett. If they don't have that sort of money, they home in on the shops which have a strong fashion personality at affordable prices, such as Jeff Banks' 'Warehouse' or Miss Selfridge. Their fashion eye is educated by reading magazines like *Honey*, *Company* or *Over 21*. They want their looks and clothes to make a statement about their independence. They do not wish to be pretty, lady-like or charming; they want to be sexy, self-reliant and exciting. They laugh at Barry Manilow and Neil Diamond, but love The Thompson Twins and Frankie Goes to Hollywood. The appearance of the Princess of Wales has little relevance for them. It is women between twenty-five and thirty-five who try to emulate her looks. If they have a reasonable amount of money they will buy at Jaeger, Alexon or the designers

The demure royal look that launched a million imitations; it incorporated three of the Princess's recurring fashion statements: large collars, chokers and very plain shoes.

which the Princess herself uses, such as Arabella Pollen. If their budget is limited they will go to chains such as Next. Whether they have a small or large amount to spend, they probably use local boutiques for many purchases. They keep in touch through reading *Vogue* (probably at the hairdresser), *Woman's Journal* and *Good Housekeeping*. It is on this group, which made the *The Sloane Ranger Handbook* a bestseller, that the Princess of Wales has most impact.

The most instant and powerful fashion fad created by the Princess, apart from her very glamorous and attractive hairstyle by Kevin Shanley, was her hats. Suddenly, large numbers of women who had thought hats suitable only for very formal occasions realised that there were practical alternatives to large picture hats which could be worn for everyday occasions. The Princess's early hats by John Boyd, with their small curved brims and feather trim, looked so striking on her that from 1981 to 1983 the style was copied at every possible price level. The impact of the Princess's hats has weakened now that she wears a much wider, less identifiable, range of styles. There is no longer a 'Princess Di' hat; instead there are many different hats in many moods, chosen from talents as far apart as Freddie Fox and Stephen Jones, in addition to John Boyd. This broadening of the fashion message and subsequent weakening of its impact has happened in all aspects of the Princess's appearance. The frilly necklines that made (and, it must be said, sometimes marred) so many of her outfits became a fad and then slowly died. The same can be said for the pearl choker which fashion journalists soon spotted as a favourite. Jewellers copied it and sold the copies in considerable numbers, but, like everything to do with fashion, its life was limited and is now over. Flat shoes and clutch bags, the other 'Princess Di' fashion statements will, of course, continue; they are part of a way of living (comfort and ease) rather than a way of projecting a fashionable image.

What the new trends will be is not easy to spot. The Princess is not yet a real fashion *leader* because she does not work closely with one designer to create an exclusive and original look. As she grows older it is to be hoped that a latterday, but ultra-modern, Hartnell will appear to create for her a look and image distinctive enough to be her own consistent fashion statement. Whatever the future holds, we may be certain that she will continue to wear her styles and her accessories with such panache that other women will wish to copy them. This is her great strength: she puts together a distinctive look in a way which is the epitome of style. The future of the Princess of Wales in the affection of the people seems assured. The image that she has projected is exactly what is required by her public and, as Kingsley Martin has said, "when the personal and public character of the monarch conforms to the appropriate pattern, there is a natural tendency, which propaganda can easily exploit, to see in him the ideal personification of these qualities which are most admired in contemporary society".

A Princess is expected to be at a distance from life. If she dresses like other girls she destroys the fantasy. Long evening dresses are found in the wardrobes of very few girls under twenty-five and tiaras are even scarcer. Also hats and gloves do not

The Princess of Wales tried the fashionable 'oversize' style for her visit to Venice but looked less than happy in it. The general 'top-heavy' feeling was emphasized by the overproportioned hat.

take up much room. Yet for a Princess these are essential 'props'. At this stage, the Princess of Wales is still playing a fairy-tale role and her dressing must, in a sense, be unreal. Her appearance has all the artificial perfection of a florist's carnation: beautiful but characterless. It was through her appearance that the Princess caught the imagination of the people. Might it now lose her their support? The appearance of the Princess of Wales is perhaps becoming too extravagantly stylish to chime with the times. Outfits like that worn for the christening of Prince Harry give her the distant quality of a femme fatale in forties' movies. The danger is that too much fashion magazine perfection could make her seem as irrelevant as a soap opera character to many of her husband's future subjects of her own age, poor and unemployed as they are. However, it is clear that she understands style and fashion and, as she matures with motherhood, it is probably safe to say that her fashion 'day' will come. Palace officials who hear her criticised for wearing clothes that are too old or outré for her must sigh: it is the same criticism that was directed at the Queen when she was young. The dilemma can only be solved with the passing of years.

Some of Diana's clothes' choices, from designers almost as young and inexperienced as she is, have been worrying. But in her hats, at least, she has been lucky, for John Boyd, *the* milliner to the Princess of Wales, is a craftsman of great skill, knowledge and understanding. He was born and brought up in Edinburgh, where he began his working life, in the late thirties, in the chemical laboratory of a factory. A friend who bought her hats from Thaarup urged him to go to London to become a milliner. The war stopped any hope of that, although he did meet Thaarup, who was in Glasgow doing a promotion, and explained to him that he wanted to create hats. Thaarup, who was once told by a judge in the bankruptcy court that "You loved your fellow men too much", was characteristically helpful. He gave Boyd his fare to London, booked him into the Y.M.C.A. and gave him materials to work with. Thus his career began.

Boyd went to war in the navy and remembers with gratitude returning on leave and going to see Thaarup. "He always left the key under the fire bucket outside the back door and frequently there was a theatre ticket as well." After the war, Boyd worked for eighteen months as Thaarup's assistant, learning as much as he could from him. He was taught how to dye – one of his jobs was to dye veils to the *exact* shade in the upstairs room and then shake them out of the window to dry! In 1946 Boyd opened his own boutique with his sister. They began in the basement of the designer, Clive Duncan, who encouraged his customers to patronise them. Boyd recalls that their first customer was Lady Grenville, the Queen Mother's sister. As business prospered they moved to the Carlton Tower area and then the Brompton Arcade.

Boyd's royal trade began with Princess Anne when she was only seventeen and he has continued to supply her millinery since that time. In those days she came to his shop, but now he frequently takes his hats to her. Another royal customer, Princess Michael of Kent, walks into the shop without any warning or ceremony.

A very glamorous evening dress chosen by the Princess of Wales. It requires a good figure and a considerable degree of poise to be worn successfully.

The Princess of Wales originally came to him through her mother, Mrs Shand Kydd, who had been a client for some years. The Princess telephones about twenty minutes in advance and when she arrives goes upstairs to the workroom to try on the hats with Boyd and the work girls, with whom she is very relaxed. If she likes something which is not quite right, he remodels it and makes it work for her. Boyd also makes hats for Mrs Thatcher. He normally goes to Downing Street at eight in the morning, when he finds the Prime Minister already at work on her papers. She frequently consults him on other accessories – "Now John, do these shoes go with the dress?" – thereby exposing an uncharacteristic lack of certainty. John Boyd's success is based on almost forty years' experience as a practical milliner: when he comes downstairs from his workroom he has a pin cushion hanging round his neck and it is immediately obvious that he works on the hats himself. His future seems assured, but he remembers the bad years about seven years ago when no one needed model millinery. He recalls how embarrassing it was meeting ex-customers in Harrods, who would say how much they wanted to buy hats again but could not because no one did. The fact that this situation has changed is due in no small measure to John Boyd himself.

The Princess of Wales has no 'official' milliners, dressmakers or designers. She shops where she wishes and uses those designers who appeal to her. The first designers to shoot into prominence as a result of her patronage were the Emanuels, who designed her wedding dress, the black strapless evening gown with which the press had such fun pretending to be shocked, and many other 'early' outfits. David and Elizabeth Emanuel met while studying fashion at Harrow School of Art, married and graduated together. They decided to continue their studies and applied for the one-year M.A. course at the Royal College of Art. They were both accepted: the first married couple to be so. Their backgrounds are diverse. David is Welsh and was born at Bridgend, Glamorgan, into a family of eleven children. Elizabeth's father, a stockbroker, is an American who came to England during the war and remained here. Their approach to fashion is not diverse. On the contrary, it is so close that they wished to present a joint collection at the end of the Royal College year in 1977, but this was not permitted. They are united by determination and ambition. Their fortunes inevitably slumped after all the brouhaha of the wedding. The press turned sour, the Palace felt that the Emanuels had used their royal connection rather brashly and the Princess of Wales patronised them less than they had hoped.

The firm of Belville-Sassoon was another of the Princess of Wales' early choices – her going-away outfit came from them – and they continue to provide clothes for her. Their efforts are not always happy. They designed the much-criticised 'dressing gown' dress worn by the Princess at the London Fashion Week reception in March 1985. Belinda Belville began her business more than twenty years ago when she opened a shop in Knightsbridge. In this she followed a family tradition: her grandmother had run a dress shop in London during the twenties. She spotted David Sassoon's work in a Royal College of Art final-year show, liked it and asked him to be her designer. They produce ready-to-wear and couture lines and have specialized in wedding dresses. Belville-Sassoon creations also appear in Vogue Patterns. Another well-established designer who has been patronised by the Princess is Gina Fratini. Her background is complicated: she was born in Japan of an Irish father and English mother, was evacuated to Canada at the beginning of World War II, joined her parents in Burma after the war and lived in India before returning to England to study at the Royal College of Art. For a while the Katherine Dunham dance company in California employed her to design costumes and scenery. With them she toured America, France and Italy. She married an Italian artist. Her first collection was in 1966 and for it she did everything, designing,

The Princess of Wales is most noted for her hats. These two examples from her Italian trip in Spring 1985 show why they are remembered as her 'fashion statement'.

Occasionally the Princess's appearance is
only saved by her radiance and beauty
when her designers create clothes which
seem to be working against her.

making and modelling the clothes herself. Her royal connection began in 1971, when Princess Anne chose to wear her dresses for her official twenty-first birthday photographs.

An increasing favourite of the Princess of Wales is Bruce Oldfield, who studied at Ravensbourne College of Art and St Martin's School of Art, from which he graduated in 1973. He was successful almost immediately and became a 'name' in New York and Paris as well as London. He sold sketches to Yves Saint Laurent, his clothes were stocked by prestigious American stores like Saks, Bergdorf and Bloomingdales and he also designed costumes for films, notably for those starring Charlotte Rampling and Joan Collins. In 1978 he moved to Beauchamp Place and began to concentrate on building up his private clientèle, which is now considerable. In 1984 he began to produce a ready-to-wear range. One of the better known younger designers chosen by the Princess of Wales is Jasper Conran, whose father is Sir Terence Conran of Habitat fame and whose mother, Shirley Conran, is a best-selling novelist. He studied fashion at Parson's School of Art and Design in New York and worked for Wallis before setting up on his own in 1978. Arabella Pollen, another favourite, was born in Oxford and brought up in New York, where her father was president of the art auctioneers, Sotheby Parke Bernet. She was educated in England. After a period in advertising and working in film, she began to concentrate on designing and formed her own company in 1982.

The Princess of Wales' connection with the Chinese designer, Monica Chong, began when she bought a pair of velvet trousers by Chong on one of her early morning shopping trips to Harrods. Monica Chong was born in Hong Kong and studied fashion at Chelsea School of Art, after which she received a sound practical grounding in the rag trade before designing her own range in 1978. Since then she has continued to design collections for her own label. The Princess of Wales is especially fond of the clothes of The Chelsea Design Company, which was founded by Catherine Walker in 1977. Catherine grew up in France, where her family was involved in the woollen industry. She studied at Lille University and then came to London to teach French and run the lecture department of the French Embassy. She married an English solicitor, but was widowed six years later. It was at this point that she turned to dress design: borrowing a pile of cutting textbooks she sat down at her sewing machine and learned from scratch. From this modest beginning she has developed sufficiently to produce a ready-to-wear and couture line that now attracts a regular clientèle. The Japanese designer, Hachiro Nakatsu, whose firm is called Hachi, has been in England for 'about fourteen years'. He was born in Tokyo in 1947 and studied for two years at Kokugakuin University. This was followed by a three-year course in fashion training. Before starting his own company in 1977, he worked in London for various people, including the men's tailor, Tommy Nutter. He came into prominence when the Princess of Wales chose a one-shouldered, slinky evening dress from him.

Of the several other designers whose clothes have been chosen by the Princess, three stand out as people to whom she has consistently returned for various outfits.

The firm of David Neil was founded in 1978. The designers are David Bates, who studied fashion at St Martin's School of Art, and Julia Fortesque, who was educated at the Royal College of Art. After graduating Bates spent some time in Paris before working with Roger Brines, a Frenchman in London who designs for Princess Margaret. On leaving the Royal College, Fortesque trained at Belville-Sassoon and worked with Mattli. Both spent time with Collection 'O' in Knightsbridge before becoming part of David Neil. Donald Campbell is another designer who has been consistently patronised by the Princess. A Canadian, he was born in Cobourg, Ontario, and studied fashion at the Ryerson Institute of Technology, Toronto. After a period working in Toronto's wholesale dress industry, which took him up to the late fifties, he moved to London and got a job with the couturier, John Cavanagh. He worked as Cavanagh's assistant for two-and-a-half years and then left to take up a job in the wholesale end of the market. In 1965 he returned to John Cavanagh as designer for the new ready-to-wear shop. After eight years in this role he left in 1973 and opened his own establishment in Chelsea. In 1978 a second shop was opened in Knightsbridge. The Dutchman, Jan Vanvelden, has also found a degree of favour with the Princess of Wales. Born in Amsterdam, where he studied fashion at the Charles Montaigne Ecole de Couture, Vanvelden has lived in London since the sixties. He studied at the London College of Fashion and worked in retail at Simpsons of Piccadilly and Austin Reed. This was followed by a period designing for the ready-to-wear firm, Salvador, where Vanvelden soon became design director. In 1981 he formed his own company.

It can be seen from this sample of designers that the Princess of Wales has catholic tastes. Although buying British, she chooses designers who came from many parts of the world. Whereas the royal dressmakers appointed by the Queen and the Queen Mother are unlikely to change in the foreseeable future, the situation with the Princess is still very fluid. It is rapidly becoming a distinguishing mark in London design circles not to have had one of one's dresses worn by the Princess. As she continues to move away from frills and bows to a more sophisticated, tailored look, some of the dressmakers presently in favour are bound to be left behind.

Will the Princess eventually appoint a couture house as her official dressmaker? Or will she remain loyal to one of her current ready-to-wear designers and give the royal accolade to a non-exclusive establishment, just as Princess Anne has continued to patronise Maureen Baker? By the time she becomes Queen Consort the 'deformalising' of life, even royal life, may have accelerated to such an extent that ball gowns and grand evening dresses will be a thing of the past and a Queen will buy her clothes from whichever shop pleases her. The concept of a royal warrant-holding designer is in some ways already an anachronism. The informality which the Princess is likely increasingly to bring to bear on her public life may well make the exclusive royal dressmaker as obsolete as that other long defunct warrant holder listed in the *Royal Kalendar* for 1789: Spatterdash Makers: Aeron Easton, Snr & Jnr.

*One of the Princess's most successful
evening outfits in Italy was this one worn
in Florence.*

I love royalty, they're so clean.

Diana Vreeland

APPENDIX A

The royal warrant, granted to tradesmen to the royal household, goes back to the twelfth century. The first 'charter' was granted to the Weavers' Company in 1155 by Henry II, awarded as a sign of royal approval of the high standard of the stuffs provided for the King. To protect the royal family, the Lord Chamberlain produces a book of stringent rules concerning what can and cannot be allowed to a warrant holder, with particular emphasis on the use made of the royal coat of arms. This is a secret volume whose contents must not be divulged to the public. Only warrant holders are allowed to read it.

The warrant holders produced their own book, *Who's Who in Royal Warrant Holders*, in 1924. It was tastefully printed and bound by Samuel Straker & Sons, 'By Appointment' printers, publishers and stationers to His Majesty King George V, with a gravity and precision entirely appropriate to a company whose telegraphic code was 'Wavernon, London'. In the book royal warrant holders wrote about themselves in glowing terms. J. C. Vickery (jewellery, silverwear and leather goods), for example, boldly asserted that 'the very highest-class articles alone are dealt in, and these of able and artistic workmanship', adding authoritatively, 'Vickery's novelties for gifts are well known', before concluding with an impressive list of royal clients, "Their Majesties the King and Queen, H.M. Queen Alexandra, H.R.H. The Prince of Wales, His late Majesty King Edward VII, Her late Majesty Queen Victoria, H.M. King of Spain, Their Majesties the King and Queen of Denmark, H.M. the Queen of Norway, and H.M. the Queen of Sweden". Swaine (photography and portrait painting) pointed out that their 'clientele is practically scattered all over the world, and largely represented in the Colonies, the firm having photographed many Royalties both at home and abroad, and nearly every celebrity of society',

which included the Spanish, Portugese, Norwegian and Swedish royal houses.

G. Adam & Co., court florists, felt no mock modesty about their standards, claiming quite boldly that they were 'experts in every description of florists' work, and are conspicuous for their taste and artistic ability quite as much as for their knowledge of the technique of a business which is not quite so simple as it looks to the uninitiated. Thus, they are specialists in the making of wedding, presentation and ball bouquets, in table decoration, in floral decoration for balls, church decorations for weddings, and everything of that description on any scale. They have quite a reputation for what may be styled the ingenious trifles of the business, such as sprays for ladies and buttonholes for gentlemen.' Other accessory manufacturers included the Indian firm of Girdhar and Hari Das, who manufactured hand-woven gold and silver brocades, fancy saris and 'jewellery of every description'. Their entry mentioned their lucrative line in special scarves, 'The Queen Mary Scarf' and 'The Princess Marie Scarf', which were 'much appreciated for their superior workmanship and designs' by visitors to the city of Benares.

Several court dressmakers, outfitters, tailors and milliners were listed, pre-eminent among whom was Redfern, who gave his Paris, Nice and Monte Carlo addresses as well as his London one. The entry pointed out that the firm was noted for its tailor-made costumes, riding habits and yachting outfits. Its history 'dates back to the early days of the Duchess of Kent and H.M. Queen Victoria, whose distinguished patronage it received, and onwards to all the younger Royal Princesses of the present day.' Another court dressmaker, Phillips of Sloane Street, Belgravia, produced a very full and confident entry explaining that they specialised 'in ladies' coats and skirts in all the fashionable and seasonable styles, and materials of the finest qualities, and nothing is turned out of the establishment but what is of the highest-class description. The dresses and furs in particular are noted for their excellence, and cannot anywhere be surpassed in style or character. The ladies' tailoring department is one of the most complete in England, and its fine productions even recall those of Paris or elsewhere. The distinguished patronage bestowed upon the business extends from Royalty to the leading aristocracy of the West End, and the Continent. It may be mentioned in this connection that all the dress equipment for Her Majesty Queen Mary's visit to India and Australia respectively were specially and exclusively provided by the firm. The extensive business premises have recently been rebuilt, re-decorated and equipped in the best and most complete style, and have lately been honoured by a personal visit from her Gracious Majesty the Queen. It should be further noted that everything turned out by the firm is made in the establishment itself. Mr Phillips has been granted Royal Warrants by Appointment to Their most Gracious Majesties Queen Mary and Queen Alexandra.' Threshers, the court dressmakers and ladies' outfitters, more modestly explained that they originally specialised in 'providing outfits for ladies going abroad and for this purpose various members of the Royal family extended their patronage', but thereafter acquiring the dressmaking establishment and connection of Madame Bernard, they were granted the royal warrant in 1914. Jays, the costumiers and furriers, was perfectly confident in its entry. "Jays is perhaps the most exclusive House in the West End for distinctive styles, and throughout the land the judgement and taste of this well-known establishment is accepted as a criterion of fashion. For over half a century it has appealed to that conspicuous minority of ladies who desire a quiet distinction in their *toilette*, and its clientele are to be found in every part of the civilised world. It is not the policy of this House to show illustrations of their exclusive models; therefore, ladies who can make it convenient are respectfully invited to pay a visit to the salons at Oxford Circus, which afford a wealth of choice that gives expression to the most advanced ideas, and accurately reflects the styles that will be in vogue during the season. The reputation this establishment enjoys for originality of design, scrupulous good taste in the matter of trimming, and careful attention to cut and style, is more than maintained by the season's stock, which comprises the most up-to-date model costumes, tea-gowns, blouses, millinery, tailor-made coats and skirts, lingerie, hosiery, etc., etc., indeed the best of everything in feminine attire in the latest style and highest quality. Every garment that bears the *cachet* of this famous House is made from material that can be thoroughly recommended, and in shape and fit leaves nothing to be desired. A Royal Warrant Appointment is held to H.M. Queen Alexandra, granted in 1901".

Aquascutum were praiseworthily matter-of-fact about their goods: 'The specialities of "Aquascutum" are: A pure, new wool, soft and comforting to the touch; efficiently proofed to withstand the heaviest downpour; made in exquisite colourings and designs. "Eiderscutum": luxuriously light and wonderfully warm; an ideal coat for walking and all forms of travel: weighs but little more than a raincoat. "Field" Coatings: present an impenetrable front to wind and rain; identical to the war-famous Aquascutum "Trench" coatings. Further, an unequalled selection of sporting, motoring, and travelling coats is always in stock ready for immediate wear. It is creditable to the firm to learn that over 95 per cent of their staff served with the colour in the late War.' A similarly no-nonsense approach was adopted by Burberrys: 'Burberrys are a firm of experts in weatherproof cloth and garments, which opened a London branch in Haymarket thirty years ago; they were pioneers in the Weatherproof Trade and did much by the quality of their manufactures and zealous propaganda, to substitute overcoats, made of self-ventilating materials, for macintoshes proofed with rubber, which for nearly a hundred years were regarded as the only possible safeguards against getting wet. For purposes of sport, exploration and aviation, the firm's manufactures are throughout the world in great and growing request, so that the demand for them is now universal.'

Liberty & Co., Designers and Makers of Artistic Wares and Fabrics, explained their policies succinctly: 'Dress and furnishing fabrics are made of special designs and colourings, so as to secure a continuance of exclusive excellence. Dressmaking has been added because the professional dressmakers were wedded to the use of stiff and ungainly materials, and were loathe to substitute for them the soft and graceful Liberty fabrics. Silk printing works at Melton Abbey have been established because better results could thus be obtained.' Swan & Edgar, who styled themselves Costumiers, Silk Merchants, Furriers, Fancy Goods, Ladies and Gents Outfitting and General Drapers, felt that a historic approach was appropriate: 'John Pearce, an original partner, was one of the first men in London to learn the news of Wellington's victory at Waterloo by stopping and interrogating the King's messenger who, galloping along Pall Mall, was on his way to the Prime Minister's residence in Grosvenor Square, with the despatches, telling the defeat of Napoleon at Waterloo. The same day he caused a board to be fixed over the *facia* of his firm's building, bearing the words, 'Waterloo House', and the premises retained that name from June, 1815, to July, 1886, when the business and title were transferred to Regent Street and Piccadilly by amalgamation with the old firm of Swan & Edgar, which title is still continued by the Company, and the names "Swan & Edgar" and "Waterloo House" are synonymous throughout the world.

Paris model gowns, party frocks, tea gowns, blouses, cloaks and millinery were claimed as the specialities of Marshall & Snelgrove (Debenhams) Ltd., who produced an entry full of superlatives: 'The house of Marshall & Snelgrove was founded in 1837, and has a world-wide reputation. Situated in the heart of the West End, its position is quite unrivalled, and the firm owes its success to the fact that they have always endeavoured to give superlative value, which may be interpreted as the best of everything at moderate prices. As a fashion house, the firm are noted for their own exclusive creations which are designed by experts, and made by highly skilled workers on the premises, and customers will also find in the ribbon, umbrella and sunshade salons the most unique and exclusive productions. The firm have always been famous for their silks, and hold what is probably the finest stock in Europe of beautiful and exclusive brocades, velvets, and other silk fabrics. Their household linens are always reliable, the prices being the lowest possible compatible with quality. Their stock of modern laces is particularly comprehensive; they have also a unique collection of antique laces, which cannot fail to appeal to all connoisseurs and collectors. The making of really beautiful artificial flowers on the premises has received special attention; these are truly artistic, and compare most favourably with the best Paris creations. The fur department has been recently enlarged.' Against such self-confidence Debenham & Freebody's entry appears quite understated: 'The house of Debenham & Freebody has long been noted for the creation of the most beautiful gowns, garden party frocks, visiting costumes, etc., modelled by exclusive designers and made in the firm's own workrooms. In the Millinery Salon, upon the first floor, customers will find a large and varied selection of the newest Paris models, and upon the ground floor a popular priced department for untrimmed hats, flowers, feathers, and ornaments of every description, in addition to the large stock of laces, many of which will appeal to the connoisseur and collector. In connection with the large fur section, there has been introduced a system of freezing storage for preserving and prolonging the life of furs, which has proved of great benefit and convenience to customers. No visitor, we are

assured, can depart without having felt the advantages of the personnel of the staff, which has been brought together with the greatest care and attention, and which, it is sincerely felt, maintain the high standard and courtesy so much appreciated by the clientele of the firm. It may here be pointed out that customers, after visiting the various departments, can, if they wish, have lunch or tea in the quiet and elegant Restaurant; ladies can read the papers and magazines, can telephone, write their letters and meet their friends in the large Club Room, connected with which is a suite of luxuriously appointed dressing and retiring rooms.'

Royal Warrant holders today no doubt feel the same security as their counterparts did sixty years ago, but they are probably more circumspect about expressing the fact. They certainly know that they are extremely fortunate in having the right to display the royal coat of arms as a proof of their excellence. The royal warrant is granted to firms or individuals providing goods or services for those members of the royal family empowered to grant it. Only the Queen, the Queen Mother, the Duke of Edinburgh and the Prince of Wales appoint royal suppliers. Firms must have provided goods or services for three consecutive years before being eligible to apply for a royal appointment. If their application is accepted they are granted the warrant for a ten year period. During this time it can be removed without any explanation. It is reviewed after ten years.

A list of all royal warrant holders is published annually in December or January as a supplement to the London Gazette. If we look at warrant holders who have supplied goods and services concerned with dress and appearance throughout the century a remarkably consistent picture emerges. Once the decision to use certain designers, milliners and shoemakers has been taken, the royal ladies remain faithful. In the following lists it can be seen that each Queen has her own favourite suppliers who serve her throughout her reign.

QUEEN ALEXANDRA   *1901*

List of Tradesmen who hold Warrants of Appointment from the Lord Chamberlain to Queen Alexandra, with Authority to use the Royal Arms. These warrants do not carry the right to fly the Royal Standard:–

Aitchinson, James	Jeweller	Edinburgh
Atkinson, J. and E.	Perfumers	London
Atloff and Norman	Bootmakers	London
Berthe and Yeo	Dressmakers	London
Blackborne, Arthur	Laceman	London

Brigg and Son	Umbrella Makers	London
Brown, W.C.	Hatter	London
Court, Bruno	Perfumer	Grasse, France
Burger, Isabelle	Manicure	London
Busvine and Co.	Tailors	London
Collingwood and Co.	Jewellers	London
Drion, Madame	Corset Maker	London
Duboc, Madame	Dressmaker	London
Duncan and Co.	Bootmakers	Edinburgh
Dubelleroy, J.	Fanmaker	London
Ede and Son	Robemakers	London
Edmonds and Orr	Outfitters	London
Errington, Annie	Milliner	London
Frederic, Madame	Dressmaker	London
Fryer, Jos.	Hosier	London
Gent and Son	Ladies' Tailors	Birmingham
Givry, V., and Co. Limited	Dressmakers	London
Harborough, John, and Co.	Glovers	London
Heath, Henry	Hatter	London
Helbronner, Mrs.	Embroiderer	London
Holt, Renfrew, and Co.	Furriers	Quebec
Hook, Knowles, and Co.	Shoemakers	London
Isidore, Charles	Hairdresser	London
Lincoln, Bennett, and Co.	Hatters	London
Morgan, John and Son	Tailors	Cowes, Isle of Wight
Pears, A. and F.	Soap Manufacturers	London
Phipps and Barker	Bootmakers	London
Redfern and Co.	Ladies' Tailors	London
Rimmel, Eugene	Perfumer	London

Buckingham Palace,
November 1, 1901

COLVILLE OF CULROSS
Lord Chamberlain to
Queen Alexandra.

QUEEN ALEXANDRA 1903

Aitchison, James	Jeweller	Edinburgh
Atkinson, J. and F.	Perfumers	London
Atloff and Norman	Bootmakers	London
Bagwandas, Copierata	Shawl Merchant	Benares, India
Heath, Henry	Hatter	London
Helbronner, Mrs.	Embroiderer	London
Holt, Renfrew and Co.	Furriers	Quebec
Hook, Knowles, and Co.	Shoemakers	London
Isidore, Charles	Hairdresser	London
La Maison Laferriere	Couturier	Paris
Lambert, Madame	Corset Maker	London
Lincoln, Bennet and Co.	Hatters	London
Morgan, John, and Son	Tailors	Cowes
Pears, A. and F.	Soap Manufacturers	London
Phipps and Barker	Bootmakers	London
Penhaligon and Jeavons	Perfumers	London
Phillips, A.	Ladies' Tailor	London
Poland, G. and Son	Furriers	London
Rimmel, Eugene	Perfumer	London
Seymour and Molyneux	Embroiderers	Windsor
Smith, J.	Ladies' Tailor	London
Sparks, Hall and Co.,	Bootmakers	London
Tayler, D.F. and Co.	Pinmakers	Birmingham
Tessier, Henry	Jeweller	London
Thomas, J.B. and Co.	Jeweller	London
Tiffany and Co.	Jewellers	London
Tirard, A.V.	Hairdresser	London

Buckingham Palace,
January 1, 1903.

COLVILLE OF CULROSS
Lord Chamberlain to Queen Alexandra.

QUEEN MARY 1914

Aitchison, James	Goldsmith	Edinburgh
Atkinson, J and E.	Suppliers of Perfumery	London
Betts, Mrs. A.J.	Milliner	London
Braun, Kate	Lace Dealer	London
Chand, Manick	Shawl Merchant	Delhi, India
Collingwood and Co.	Jewellers	London
Debenham and Freebody	Costumiers and Linen Drapers	London
de Faye, F.G.	Perfumer	Jersey
Durrant, Madame	Dressmaker	London
Duvelleroy, J.	Fan Maker	London
Ede, Son and Ravenscroft	Robe Makers	London

Edmonds-Orr and Co.	Ladies' Outfitters	London
Edward, Mrs.	Ladies' Outfitters	London
Frederic, Madame	Milliner	London
Garrard and Co. Limited	Jewellers and Goldsmiths	London
Graham and Son	Ladies' Outfitters	London
Hook, Knowles and Co. Ltd.	Bootmakers	London
Maison Nouvelle	Milliners	London
Nicol, David	Hairdresser and Perfumer	London
Nicoll, H.J. and Co. Limited	Tailors	London
Pears, A. and F. Limited	Soap Manufacturers	London
Phillips, Albert	Ladies' Tailor	London
Reville & Rossiter, Limited	Court Dress Makers	London
Wilkinson and Son	Robemakers	London
Yapp	Bootmaker	London

Buckingham Palace, January 1, 1914

SHAFTESBURY, Lord Chamberlain to the Queen.

QUEEN ALEXANDRA   1914

Aitchison, James	Jeweller	Edinburgh
Atkinson Limited, J. and E.	Perfumers	London
Aylwin, Madame	Milliner	Paris
Berthe and Yeo	Dressmakers	London
Betts, Mrs. A.J.	Milliner	London
Burger, Isabelle	Manicure	London
Busvine and Co. Limited	Ladies' Tailor	London, Rugby, Paris and Berlin
Cartier and Son, A.	Jewellers	London and Paris
Collingwood and Co.	Jewellers	London
Court, Bruno	Perfume	Grasse, Alpes Maritimes, France
Creamer and Co.	Furriers	Liverpool

de Faye, F.G.	Manufacturer of Perfumery	Jersey
Debenham and Freebody	Silk Merchants, Furriers and Embroiderers	London
Doeuillet Limited	Dressmakers and Costumiers	London and Paris
Drion-Regnier, Madame	Corsetiere	Paris
Duboc, Madame	Dressmaker	London
Duncan and Co.	Bootmakers	Edinburgh
Durrant	Ladies' Tailor, Dressmaker and Furrier	Edinburgh
Duvelleroy, J.	Fan Maker	London
Ede, Son and Ravenscroft	Robe Makers	London
Edmonds, Orr and Co. Limited	Outfitters	London
Edwards, Madame	Milliner	London
Frederic	Dressmaker	London
Gent and Son	Ladies' Tailors	Birmingham
Graham and Son	Lingerie and Outfitters	London
Heath Limited, Henry	Hatters	London
Holt, Renfrew and Co.	Furriers	Quebec
Hook, Knowles and Co Limited	Shoemakers	London
Isidore, C.	Hairdresser	London
Laferriere, Maison	Couturiere	Paris
Lambert, Madame D.	Corset Maker	London
Morgan and Son, John	Tailors	Cowes
Penhaligon, Walter	Perfumer	London
Redfern Limited	Ladies' Tailors	London
Rimmel Limited, Eugene	Perfumers	London
Roche, Miss	Dressmaker and Milliner	London
Seymour and Molyneux	Embroiderers	Windsor
Streur, M.H.F.	Fournisseur	London
Sturrock and Sons	Hairdressers	Edinburgh
Tayler, D.F. and Co. Limited	Pin Makers	Birmingham
Tiffany and Co.	Jewellers	London
Vernon	Ladies' Tailor	London

Marlborough House, S.W. January 1, 1914

HOWE, Lord Chamberlain to Her Majesty Queen Alexandra.

QUEEN MARY — 1925

Name	Trade	Location
Aitchison, James	Goldsmith	Edinburgh
Angrave Limited	Milliners	London
Atkinson, J. and E. Limited	Suppliers of Perfumery	London
Betts, Mrs. A.J.	Milliner	London
Braun, Kate	Lace Dealer	London
Brigg and Sons	Umbrella Manufacturers	London
Chand, Manick	Shawl Merchant	Delhi, India
Collingwood (Jewellers) Ltd.	Jewellers	London
Debenham and Freebody	Costumiers and Linen Drapers	London
de Faye, F.G.	Perfumer	Jersey
Durrant, Madame	Dressmaker	London
Duvelleroy, J. Limited	Fan Makers	London
Ede and Ravenscroft	Robe Makers	London
Edward, Mrs.	Ladies' Outfitter	London
Forrest and Sons Limited	Costumiers and Silk Merchants	Dublin
Garrard and Co. Limited	Jewellers and Goldsmiths	London
Girdhar Das, Raghunath Das	Jewellers and Embroiderers	Benares City, U.P. India
Hook, Knowles and Co. Limited	Bootmakers	London
Liberty and Co. Limited	Silk Merchants	London
Nicol, David	Hairdresser and Perfumer	London
Pears, A. and F., Limited	Soap Manufacturers	London
Phillips, Arthur	Ladies' Tailor	London
Reville, Limited	Court Dress Makers	London
Revillon Frères (London) Ltd.	Furriers	London
Sturrock and Sons	Hairdressers and Perfumers	Edinburgh
Tayler, D.F. and Co. Limited	Pin Manufacturers	Birmingham
Wilkinson and Son	Robemakers	London
Yapp, Peter	Bootmaker	London

Buckingham Palace, January 1st, 1925

ANGLESEY
Lord Chamberlain to the Queen.

QUEEN ALEXANDRA — 1925

Name	Trade	Location
Aitchison, James	Jeweller	Edinburgh
Atkinson Limited, J. and E.	Perfumers	London
Bhagwan, Dass Gopinath	Brocade and Shawl Merchant	Benares, India
Burger, Isabelle	Manicure	London
Busvine Limited	Ladies' Tailor	London, Rugby and Paris
Cartier	Jeweller	London and Paris
Collingwood (Jewellers) Ltd	Jewellers	London
Creamer and Co. W.	Furriers	Liverpool
Debenham and Freebody	Silk Mercers, Furriers and Embroiderers	London
Derry and Toms	Furriers	London
Doeuillet Limited	Dressmakers and Costumiers	London and Paris
Durrant	Ladies' Tailor Dressmaker and Furrier	Edinburgh
Duvelleroy, J. Limited	Fan Makers	London
Ede and Ravenscroft	Robe Makers	London
Edmonds, Orr and Co. Limited	Outfitters	London
Edwards, Madame	Milliner	London
Fowler, Mrs. Ann	Lacemaker	Honiton
Ganeshi, Lall and Son	Jewellers and Shawl Merchants	Agra, India
Gent and Son	Ladies' Tailor	Birmingham
Haywards	Lacemen	London
Heath Limited, Henry	Hatters	London

Holt, Renfrew and Co. Limited	Furriers	Quebec
Hook, Knowles and Co. Limited	Shoemakers	London
Kirby, Beard and Co. Limited	Pin Makers	Birmingham
Kishan, Chand and Sons	Shawl Merchants	Delhi, India
Lambert, Madame D.	Corset Maker	London
Liberty and Co. Limited	Goldsmiths and Silversmiths	London
Manick, Chand	Shawl Merchant	Delhi, India
Morgan and Sons, John	Tailors	Cowes
Penhaligon, Leonard Hugh	Perfumer	London
Phillips, Albert	Ladies' Tailor	London
Rimmel Limited, Eugene	Perfumers	London
Roche	Dressmaker and Milliner	London
Seymour and Molyneux	Embroiderers	Windsor
Smithe and Graves	Furriers	London
Streur, M.H.F.	Fournisseur	London
Sturrock and Sons	Hairdressers	Edinburgh
Tayler and Co. Limited D.F.	Pin Makers	Birmingham
Tiffany and Co.	Jewellers	London
Vernon	Ladies' Tailors	London

Marlborough House,
January 2nd, 1925.

HOWE,
Lord Chamberlain to H.M.
Queen Alexandra.

QUEEN MARY   *1936*

Allan, James & Son, Ltd.	Boot and Shoe Makers	Edinburgh
Benzie, Simpson	Jeweller	Cowes, Isle of Wight
Braun, Kate	Lace Dealer	London
Chand, Manick	Shawl Merchant	Delhi, India
Collingwood (Jewellers) Ltd.	Jewellers	London
Debenham and Freebody	Costumiers and Linen Drapers	London

de Faye, F.G. Ltd.	Perfumers	Jersey, C.I.
Ede and Ravenscroft	Robe Makers	London
Edmonds-Orr and Co. Ltd.	Ladies' Outfitters	London
Foster and Co.	Robe Makers	Oxford
Fowler, Mrs.	Lace Maker	Honiton
Ganeshi, Lall and Son	Jewellers and Embroiderers	Agra, U.P. India
Garrard and Co. Limited	Jewellers and Goldsmiths	London
Girdhar Das, Hari Das, Raghunath Das	Jewellers and Embroiderers	Benares, City, U.P. India
Handley-Seymour, Ltd.	Court Dressmakers	London
Nicol, Maison, Ltd.	Hairdresser and Perfumer	London
Pears, A. and F. Limited	Soap Manufacturers	London
Phillips, Albert	Ladies' Tailor	London
Rayne, H. & M. Ltd.	Shoe Makers	London
Reville Limited	Court Dressmakers	London
Revillon Frères (London) Ltd	Furriers	London
Wilkinson and Son	Robe Makers	London
Yapp, Peter, Ltd.	Boot Makers	London
Yardley & Company Limited	Perfumers	London

Buckingham Palace,
January 1st, 1936

ANGLESEY,
Lord Chamberlain to The
Queen.

QUEEN ELIZABETH   *1945*

Carrington & Company Limited	Jewellers and Silversmiths	London
Collingwood (Jewellers) Ltd.	Jewellers	London
Ede and Ravenscroft	Robe Makers	London
Emile, Limited	Hairdresser	London
Handley-Seymour, Limited	Dressmakers	London
Hartnell, Norman, Limited	Dressmakers	London
Jacobus, Jack, Limited	Shoe Makers	London
Marcyle, Madame	Corsetiere	London

Rita, M.	Hats	London
Swaine, Adeney, Brigg & Sons, Limited	Umbrellas	London
Tayler, D.F. & Company, Ltd.	Pin Makers	Birmingham
Wartski	Jeweller	London
Yapp, Peter, Limited	Shoemakers	London

Buckingham Palace,
1st January, 1945

AIRLIE,
Lord Chamberlain to The Queen.

Smith, W.H. & Hook Knowles Ltd.	Boot Makers	London
Threshers, Ltd.	Tropical Outfitters and Dressmakers	London
Wilkinson & Son, Ltd.	Robe Makers	London
Yardley & Co. Ltd.	Perfumers	London

Marlborough House,
1 January, 1945

ANGLESEY,
Lord Chamberlain to H.M. Queen Mary.

QUEEN MARY 1945

Allan, James & Son, Ltd.	Boot and Shoe Makers	Edinburgh
Atkinson, J. & E. Ltd.	Suppliers of Perfumery	London
Benzie, Herbert Simpson	Jeweller	Cowes, Isle of Wight
Debenham and Freebody	Costumiers and Linen Drapers	London
de Faye, F.G. Ltd.	Perfumers	Jersey, C.I.
Duvelleroy, J. Ltd.	Fan Makers	London
Ede and Ravenscroft	Robe Makers	London
Fowler, Mrs.	Lace Maker	Honiton
Ganeshi, Lal & Son	Jewellers and Embroiderers	Agra, U.P. India
Girdhar Das, Hari Das, Raghunath Das	Jewellers and Embroiderers	Benares City, U.P. India
Handley-Seymour, Ltd.	Court Dressmakers	London
Liberty & Co. Ltd.	Silk Mercers	London
Maison Nicol, Ltd.	Hairdressers and Perfumers	London
Pears, A. & F. Ltd.	Soap Manufacturers	London
Rayne, H. & M. Ltd.	Shoe Makers	London
Reville, Ltd.	Court Dressmakers	London
Revillon, Ltd.	Furriers	London
Swaine, Adeney, Brigg & Sons Ltd.	Glove Makers and Umbrella Manufacturers	London

QUEEN ELIZABETH II 1955

Amies, Hardy Ltd.	Dressmakers	London
Burberry Ltd.	Weather-proofers	London
Calman Links (Trading) Ltd.	Furriers	London
Carrington & Co. Ltd.	Silversmiths	London
Cartier Ltd.	Jewellers and Goldsmiths	London
Collingwood (Jewellers) Ltd.	Jewellers and Silversmiths	London
Day, Kate, Ltd.	Milliners	London
Emile, Ltd.	Hairdressers	London
Ford, Miss, Ltd.	Dressmakers	London
Hartnell, Norman, Ltd.	Dressmakers	London
Lillywhites, Ltd.	Outfitters	London
Rayne, H. & M. Ltd.	Shoemakers	London
Rigby and Peller	Corsetieres	London
Southall, James & Co. Ltd.	Shoemakers	Norwich
Wartski	Jewellers	London
Weatherill, Bernard, Ltd.	Riding Clothes, Outfitters and Livery Tailors	London

Privy Purse Office,
Buckingham Palace,
15th July, 1955

TRYON,
Keeper of the Privy Purse.

QUEEN ELIZABETH, THE QUEEN MOTHER — 1955

Allan, James & Son Ltd.	Shoemakers	Edinburgh
Aquascutum, Ltd.	Makers of Weatherproof Garments	London
Collingwood (Jewellers) Ltd.	Jewellers	London
Ede and Ravenscroft	Robemakers	London
Emile, Ltd.	Hairdressers	London
Hartnell, Norman, Ltd.	Dressmakers	London
Hayford, W. & Sons	Glove Makers	London
Jacobus, Jack Ltd.	Shoemakers	Ballater
Marcyle, Madame	Corsetiere	London
Rayne, H. and M. Ltd.	Shoemakers	London
Rita, M.	Milliner	London
Swaine, Adeney, Brigg & Sons, Ltd.	Umbrella Makers	London
Wartski	Jewellers	London
Yapp, Peter, Ltd.	Shoemakers	London
Lillywhites Ltd.	Outfitters	London
Paris House, Ltd.	Beltmakers	London
Pringle of Scotland, Ltd.	Manufacturers of Knitted Garments	Hawick
Rayne, H. & M. Ltd.	Shoemakers	London
Redmayne, S. & Sons, Ltd.	Tailors	Wigton
Rigby and Peller	Corsetieres	London
Simpsons (Piccadilly) Ltd.	Outfitters	London
Southall, James & Co. Ltd.	Shoemakers	Norwich
Thaarup, Aage, Ltd.	Milliners	London
Wartski, C. & H. Ltd.	Jewellers	London

Buckingham Palace, 1st January, 1955

AIRLIE
Lord Chamberlain to Queen Elizabeth the Queen Mother.

QUEEN ELIZABETH II — 1965

Amies, Hardy, Ltd.	Dressmakers	London
Anderson, William & Sons, Ltd.	Tailors and Kiltmakers	Edinburgh
Billings & Edmonds, Ltd.	Tailors and Outfitters	London
Burberry, Ltd.	Weatherproofers	London
Calman Links (trading) Ltd.	Furriers	London
Custance & Sons (Tailors) Ltd.	Tailors	King's Lynn
Cyclax, Ltd.	Suppliers of Beauty Preparations	London
Driscoll	Tailors	Eastbourne
Emile, Ltd.	Hairdressers	London
Hartnell, Norman, Ltd.	Dressmakers	London
Horrockses Fashions, Ltd.	Dressmakers	London
Johnson, Herbert (Bond Street) Ltd.	Hatters	London

Privy Purse Office, Buckingham Palace, 1st January, 1965

TRYON,
Keeper of the Privy Purse.

QUEEN ELIZABETH II — 1984

Amies, Hardy, Ltd.	Dressmakers	London
Burberrys Ltd.	Weatherproofers	London
Calman Links (Trading) Ltd.	Furriers	London
Cartier Ltd.	Jewellers and Goldsmiths	London
Collingwood of Conduit Street Ltd.	Jewellers	London
Daniel, Neville Ltd.	Hairdressers	London
Driscoll	Tailors	Eastbourne
Fox, Frederick Ltd.	Milliner	London
Grima, Andrew Ltd.	Jewellers	London
Hartnell, Norman, Ltd.	Dressmakers	London
Horrockses Fashion, Ltd	Dressmakers	Milton Keynes
James, Cornelia Ltd.	Glove Manufacturer	Brighton
Johnson, Herbert (Bond Street) Ltd.	Hatters	London
Kinloch Anderson	Tailors and Kiltmakers	Edinburgh
Lillywhites, Ltd.	Outfitters	London
Lock, S. Ltd.	Embroiderers	London
Mirman, Simone	Milliner	London
Rayne, H. & M. Ltd.	Shoemakers	London
Redmayne, S. Ltd.	Tailors	Carlisle
Rigby and Peller	Corsetieres	London
Rony	Belt Maker	London

Thomas, Ian	Dressmaker	London
Wartski Ltd.	Jewellers	London

QUEEN ELIZABETH THE QUEEN MOTHER   *1984*

Allan, James & Sons, Limited	Shoemakers	Edinburgh
Aquascutum, Limited	Makers of Weatherproof Garments	London
Arden, Elizabeth, Ltd.	Manufacturers of Cosmetics	London
Asprey and Co., PLC	Jewellers	London
Bronnley, H., & Co., Ltd.	Toilet Soap Makers	London
Calman Links (Trading) Ltd.	Furriers	London
Chess, Mary Ltd.	Perfumers	London
Collingwood of Conduit Street Limited	Jewellers	London
Ede & Ravenscroft Ltd.	Robemakers	London
Hartnell, Norman, Limited	Dressmakers	London
Maurice & Robert	Hairdressers	London
Mirman, Simone	Milliner	London
Pow, Kathy, Beauty Care	Manicurist	Chalfont St Peter
Pringle, of Scotland Ltd.	Manufacturers of Knitted Garments	Hawick
Rayne, H. and M., Ltd.	Shoemakers	London
Riche of Hay Hill, Ltd.	Manicurists	London
Rudolf	Milliner	London
Robert Shephers	Hairdresser	Aberdeen
Steiner Products	Cosmeticians	London
Swaine, Adeney, Brigg & Sons, Limited	Umbrella Makers	London

APPENDIX B

Professional hostesses keep a record of their menus, table dressings and floral arrangements so that their establishments do not become predictable or repetitious. In much the same spirit royal ladies keep a record of what they wear. The hostess' job is to entertain in a way that pleases guests; much of the job of Queens is to be looked at: to appear to their best advantage. After the couturiers, fitters and cutters have done their job and the jewellers, milliners and shoe-makers have added their part, the actual business of putting together an outfit is the job of the individual. In this, Queens are no different from their subjects. They often rely on their dressers, as royal ladies' maids are always called, to help them make decisions and they expect them to make a note of what is to be worn, with what jewellery, for public appearances. Decisions are made, and notes taken, at conferences between dresser and Queen in the same way that a hostess discusses menus and entertainments with her cook or housekeeper. These conferences, which are normally informal, take place a little in advance of the occasion so that the dresser can ensure that everything is in order before laying out the clothes and accessories to be worn. It must be remembered that Queens have a bewildering choice of outfits. Their wardrobes groan with tight-packed clothes for every occasion and have to be as well organised as any other aspect of the machinery of majesty. Hats, shoes, and bags are normally designed to 'go' with one or, at most, two outfits and they are all docketed before being put away. If a Queen's coat requires a blue hat it is not a question of any blue hat in the millinery cupboard; it is *the* hat for that particular coat and it will be labelled and listed so that no mistakes are made. A dresser is the equivalent of an officer's batman, responsible for her mistress' comfort and required to ensure that everything is to hand when required.

To discover the degree of planning and the extent of the records kept it is instructive to consult the clothes 'bibles' of royalty: the dressers' diaries. These private and confidential diaries, kept by the dressers to note down the public engagements and the clothes worn for them through the royal year, are very rare. Containing essentially ephemeral information, they are normally cleared out a year or so after the events. However, the Royal Archives at Windsor contain six diaries kept by various dressers to Queen Mary between 1911 and 1941. The Queen Mother's early dressers' diaries have not survived but, after personally searching for them, Her Majesty graciously allowed me to consult diaries for 1978, 1979 and 1980. Together, the diaries of these two Queens show the differing patterns of their lives and their preferences in colours and materials in a way that brings their engagements and their personalities vividly to life. There are points of similarity, especially in colour choice. Over the years, Queen Mary's palette can be seen to have been dominated by pink, mauve, china blue, pale blue, sapphire and turquoise. The same colours have been favourites with the Queen Mother for years. As everyone knows, Queen Mary dressed very much in her own fashion, but she followed current modes in colours and freequently wore champagne, cream, white, and grey when they were the fashionable shades of the day. The Queen Mother has rarely been seen in these colours and for several years now has chosen her tones with little regard for current fashion trends. Her choice is taken from the colours of flowers but, as commentators have noted, they are essentially English flowers. Not for her the exotic hues of the hibiscus; the iris, lilac and sweetpea are the basis of her shades.

The most famous items in Queen Mary's wardrobe were her toques' which made her instantly and uniquely recognisable. They were classic substitutes for a crown, large, top-heavy, heavily swathed and trimmed. Everything was done to make their volume and height impressive. Although in later years they were worn constantly by Queen Mary, it is not until 6 July 1920, that they are first mentioned in the dresser's diary: 'new toque with aigrette'. Until then the Queen had worn a variety of hats, though, in the mode of the time, they were always large and trimmed to impress. With the toque she found the basis for her style. She wisely ignored what James Laver called 'the tyranny of the cloche hat', which required short hair tucked underneath and was the natural party to dropped waists, short skirts and no bust. Queen Mary would undoubtedly have wholeheartedly agreed with his little verse:

> The Almighty cannot bear to see
> The female leg above the knee.
> It simply isn't fit to show;
> He made it – so he ought to know.

Certainly she turned her back on what she considered unsuitable developments in fashion. It is sometimes believed that she alone was distanced from the flappers by her adherence to long skirts and discreet *décolletage*, but this is incorrect. Queen Mary dressed like the majority of women of her age. The twenties did not see fifty-year-old women tossing off their corsets and hitching their skirts up to their knees. Flapper fashions were for the young and fashion-conscious – only a portion of society at any period. Even in the thirties she was not dressed so differently from the majority. What made her stand out was the formality and theatricality of her clothes. Except for her hats, her silhouette was much like that of her contemporaries. It was only during the forties and fifties that her appearance came to seem anachronistic. Theatricality is also part of the Queen Mother's fashion statement and is characterised by a particular item which has become as unique to her as toques were to Queen Mary. The panels falling free from the shoulder, which have been a recurring theme for many years, are known to the Queen Mother and her dressers as 'floaters' and appear in the diaries repeatedly. They are a very clever choice for a small woman who wishes to project her femininity. They break up the silhouette and create movement while camouflaging the figure. The effect is soft, lively and fluid.

Reading the three diaries of the Queen Mother's dressers, bound in red and tooled in gold by the British Commonwealth Ex-Services League and bearing the motto 'Lest We Forget', we can learn much about the organisation of royal appearances. The diaries are concise, efficient lists of all the information required to ensure that there is no confusion over what is to be worn for each function. In addition they contain the informa-

tion which a lady's maid needs about her mistress' appointments. Visits from the doctor are noted and, more importantly for the dresser's purposes, the Queen Mother's appointments with her chiropodist, Mr Steiner, hairdresser, Mr Maurice, her milliners, Mr Rudolph and Mme Mirman, and, of course, Hartnell, her dressmaking firm. The Queen Mother's two dressers, Betty and Angela, must note which of them is on duty at any time. Normally, engagements are entered in red and dress details in blue. As a general rule details of jewellery are not entered as fully as they were in Queen Mary's diaries, but a note is always made of regimental badges to be worn. Once a choice of outfit has been made there seems to be very little royal dithering or indecision, although occasionally outfits are changed. For example, the entry for 28 February, 1978, records that 'Her Majesty will lunch with the American Ambassador and Mrs Kingman at Embassy. Green and white floater [crossed out but underlined]. New blue figured taffeta dress, velvet coat and hat [crossed out]'. One assumes that the 'floater' was vetoed – and then reinstated. In both Queens' dressers' diaries it can be seen that many outfits are almost identical copies and are distinguished by 'older' or 'new': for the Trooping the Colour in 1931 Queen Mary's dresser laid out her 'older apricot lace gown' and in May, 1978, the Queen Mother's dresser avoided confusion by noting that Her Majesty would wear her 'new green linen coat'.

The diaries kept for the two Queens reflect the decline in the number of formal occasions held to honour foreign royalty and heads of state. On 15 May, 1912, Queen Mary wore a new mauve tweed coat and skirt with a violet trimmed hat to match to meet the Emperor of Germany. For the arrival of the King and Queen of Denmark on 9 May, 1914, she wore a 'rose red chiffon and soft satin gown with its cloak of ruby velvet, trimmed with sable'. The banquet held for the Crown Prince of Japan in 1921 saw her in an opalescent sequin gown worn at court the year before. The Queen of Spain visited in July, 1926, and Queen Mary favoured grey that month: Reville's fringed grey georgette dress and cloak with a feather-mounted, silver tulle hat, first seen at Olympia, was also worn to visit Hendon and the Reading Show. At the beginning of 1937, while in mourning, Queen Mary received Prince and Princess Chicibu in a long, black beaded dress with pearls; in May, still in mourning, she chose a pale grey, beaded gown by Busvine to meet the Queen of Egypt. In 1938 she attended a state dinner at Buckingham Palace for the King of Romania wearing an encrusted gown: silver paillettes, diamanté and fine crystals embroidered in a design of cascading waterfalls.

The Queen Mother's diaries reflect the changes in monarchy

since the days of Queen Mary. In three years no European crowned head visited London. Of the visiting royal houses entertained by Queen Mary most have lost their thrones. In November, 1978, however, the President of Portugal was given a state banquet to which the Queen Mother wore her 'best gold and white evening dress' with the Order of the Garter, the Family Order and a diamond tiara. In February, 1979, the King and Queen of Tonga popped in for tea at Clarence House and in June Princess Chicibu, who had visited Queen Mary in 1937, called upon Her Majesty. For the state visit of the King and Queen of Nepal in November, 1980, there were two banquets. For the first, at Buckingham Palace, the Queen Mother wore a silver-and-white evening dress; two days later, at a banquet held at Claridges, she appeared in a white dress embroidered in gold, wearing a diamond and ruby tiara and necklace.

For formal evening affairs the Queen Mother almost always wears a diamond tiara and necklace, the Order of the Garter and Family Orders. Queen Mary's jewellery was more elaborate. For one dinner at Windsor in 1911 she wore a diamond comb, a ruby-and-diamond collar, an emerald-and-ruby necklace and a ruby spray brooch. For a court in 1935 there was even more grandeur. To match Busvine's gold lamé gown embroidered in crystal on gold net with its train of Belfast lace over gold lamé the Queen wore a diamond diadem 'with the lesser stars of Africa', a large diamond buckle and the Koh-i-nor diamond. It is clear that Queen Mary considered a regal appearance should be a sparkling one. Even during the day she was often lit by a fantastic light playing off the jewellery she wore in such abundance. For a Jubilee drive through North London in 1935 she wore a gold coat with ermine collar and cuffs and two rows of pearls, a pearl-and-diamond bow, large pearl-and-diamond earrings and Lord Cambridge's long diamond brooch. At state banquets the Queen was smothered in jewellery, the very icon of majesty, even more magnificent than Elizabeth I. The following description from 1937 is typical: 'A white chiffon gown embroidered with diamanté over silver lamé ornaments of pearls and diamonds – Russian diamond tiara – City collar, four rows of diamonds and two of pearls – Richmond brooch, with 5 pearl drops – part of the pearl and diamond stomacher with three drops – pearl and diamond necklace on the shoulder with two pearl and diamond brooches at each end – Order of the Garter – Victorian Order Badge – King George VI's Order – King George V's Order – Indian Order – two pearl and diamond bracelets'.

Even by pre-war standards such elaborate dressing was exceptional. The Queen's normal daytime appearance was much less extravagant and relied on material and colour for its impact. Before World War I she favoured charmeuse, chiffon and silk in soft mauve, pale yellow and, above all, blue. Blue, in fact, can be considered the colour of Queens throughout this century. Its varying shades have been chosen more frequently than any other colour and it has been a clear favourite of Queen Mary, the Queen Mother and Queen Elizabeth II. An indication of Queen Mary's fondness for blue is seen in her choice of dresses for February 1914:

13 February: blue brocade with a train of Honiton Lace
23 February: pale blue brocade
26 February: turquoise blue velvet
28 February: sapphire blue satin brocade.

Her favourite shades were periwinkle and aquamarine, to which she added apricot, cerise, rose pink, beige and grey.

Throughout her life Queen Mary rarely wore a printed or patterned material, but she was very fond of embroidered surfaces, especially of gold-shot Indian fabrics and gold and silver brocades. In royal circles there is still a clear preference for plain materials. They have a dignity and timelessness, whereas patterns and designs change so rapidly that a printed material as recent as 1980 would now look dated. The Queen Mother, who is fond of floral-patterned chiffons, overcomes this problem by choosing softly printed, all-over patterns in similar colours which, from a distance, look unified, with interesting variations. In her dresser's diaries we find repeated reference to this sort of patterning: pink and red chiffon; blue and green floral-figured silk chiffon; yellow figured chiffon; blue and mauve flowered silk. As with Queen Mary, blue predominates: pale, deep, peacock, turquoise and kingfisher are chosen over and over again.

Apart from standard events in the royal year such as visits to Eton, carol services and staff Christmas parties, the diaries record details of many dinners attended and the gowns worn for them. For example, in April 1913 Queen Mary's engagements included private dinners with Lord Grannards (mauve and gold brocade); Lord Roseberry (Indian pink and gold brocade); Lord Farquhars (rose pink and silver); Count Mensdorff (Indian pink and gold brocade) and the French Ambassador (rose pink and silver). The Queen Mother's engagements tend to be less with individuals and much more with societies. Although there are the occasional dinners with the Prime Minister at Number 10 (white-and-gold embroidered evening dress, diamond-and-ruby tiara and necklace) and semi-private luncheons with groups like the directors of Coutts & Co., most of the Queen Mother's engagements are official: dinners at the Royal Horticultural Society or with the officers of the London Scottish regiment are typical entries. A certain amount of time is spent each year sitting for portraits commissioned by regiments and societies, wearing the appropriate badge or brooch.

Queen Mary's dressers' diaries show that she employed several different designers over the years, though the entries for 1911–1919 rarely give the names of dressmakers. Outfits are identified by materials and colours. Individual dressmakers are occasionally identified: 'Balmoral – Gillie's Ball – Frederic's pink soft satin' (8 September, 1911) or 'Naval and Military Tournament: Durrant's new black silk crepe gown'. (14 May, 1914). After 1920 individual designers and suppliers are mentioned with greater frequency. In 1920 two dresses from Harrods are specified; a beige charmeuse and georgette gown and a blue gown and coat. One of the appointed dressmakers most favoured by Queen Mary was Reville, whose name is first noted in 1921, when the Queen wore 'Reville's new pink chiffon gown' to Ascot. For the rest of the decade Reville was worn almost exclusively. The entries for June, 1926, are typical: 11 June: 'Reville's grey georgette gown, grey morocain coat and chinchilla collar'; 14 June: 'Reville's new mauve gown and hat with shaded mauve flowers'; 15 June: 'Reville's new white embroidered chiffon'; 21 June: 'Reville's grey georgette'; 23 June: 'Reville's grey georgette'; 26 June: 'Reville's white gown, white hat and Jacquard cape'. It was probably this trusted dressmaker's influence which led the Queen to place less emphasis on blue in her wardrobe and to broaden her colour choice, although 1926 and 1927 were dominated by mauve and grey as the Queen was in mourning for Queen Alexandra, who died in 1925, and her brother, Prince Dolly, who died in 1927. It was not until June, 1932, that the diaries contained the name of Mrs Handley-Seymour. For the next seven years the initials H.S. were written almost daily by the dressers. The Queen especially liked her coats and often wore them with dresses by the court dressmaker, Busvine, who, like Mrs Handley-Seymour, was one of the Queen's appointed warrant holders. The Queen was still being supplied by Reville and frequently obtained gowns from M. This initial is regularly found in entries of the late thirties, but the dressmaker whose name it stood for is not known. No designer with this initial appears in the lists of royal warrant holders. It is possible that M. stands for Captain Molyneux, but this seems as unlikely as the other speculation Marshall and Snelgrove, who were at that time providing a high-class dressmaking service for society ladies. It most likely stands for Madame Mangas, a private dressmaker who is known to have made some items for the Queen.

The first mention of Hartnell was on 9 November, 1937. The entry reads 'Tuesday Dinner at Marlborough House. Norman Hartnell's mauve paillette'. His way with paillettes, sequins, lace and crystal clearly suited Queen Mary and his name soon came to dominate the dresser's diary. In 1939 Hartnell gowns were worn by the Queen each night from 18 to 23 April. By then Hartnell was also providing all the clothes for Queen Elizabeth. He has created her clothes for the rest of his life and she has continued to patronise his house after his death. Her dresser's diaries for 1978–1980 do not even mention who designed the outfits, it being taken for granted that they are provided by the house of Hartnell. It is interesting to learn how frequently her dressmakers wait on the Queen Mother throughout the year. Their appointments are normally for the morning, between 11 and 12, and, as one would expect, most of them take place in the early spring, when the Queen Mother organises her wardrobe for the rest of the year. What is, perhaps, surprising is how few appointments there are. In 1978 Hartnell saw the Queen Mother only five times, between February and May.

Norman Hartnell died on 8 June, 1979. No doubt the death of the man who had created her clothes for over forty years left the Queen Mother feeling somewhat in a vacuum, especially since her eightieth birthday was to be celebrated in the following year and the demand for new clothes for the various special occasions had to be met. The decision was made to continue with the house of Hartnell, where her needs were so well understood. 1980 was a busy year for Hartnells: they had thirteen appointments with the Queen Mother, beginning in February and ending in December. The normal spring rush continued well into June and there were five appointments in November and December. Of the many new dresses designed during this birthday year the most important was surely the 'smoky mauve chiffon' worn on 15 July for the morning Thanksgiving Service at St. Paul's Cathedral. It was a quintessential 'Queen Mum' dress and it encapsulated the strongly individual look which client and couturier had evolved over the years. The spirit of Norman Hartnell was seen to be still very much alive.

APPENDIX C

ORDERS AND DECORATIONS

The Queen is the sovereign of all the Orders of Chivalry and, as such, is entitled to wear their insignia and decorations. Other recipients of the Orders are personally chosen by her. Although the monarch has always taken an interest in how the Orders are worn, until the beginning of the century this was largely left to the taste of the individual. Not surprisingly, perhaps, most of those who were members of more than one Order liked to wear them all together and they tended to place them where the fancy took them.

However, the sight of men wearing excessive insignia at court levees displeased George V and he issued an edict that no more than four stars of the Orders might be worn at any time. This included Orders given by foreign countries, rather too many of which it was considered had been worn together in the past. The order of precedence in the positioning was also laid down. As it always was, it is according to the date of origin of the Order. In the descriptions below the Orders are placed according to precedence. The Victoria Cross and the George Cross take precedence over all Orders of Chivalry. The badges of the Orders are worn on the left side of the body above the stars of the Orders. Ladies who are members of the Orders wear their insignia in exactly the same manner as men do, with two exceptions. Ladies of the Garter wear their 'garter', not below the knee of the left leg, but on the left arm above the elbow, and whereas gentlemen wear badges around the neck, ladies wear them suspended from a riband, in the form of a bow, in the colour of the Order. This riband is worn across the bodice.

No foreign Orders can be accepted or worn by a British subject without the permission of the monarch. There are two kinds of permission. Unrestricted permission means that the Order can be worn on all occasions when British insignia are worn. The Queen's signed approval is required for this and is published in the London Gazette by the Secretary of State for Foreign Affairs. Restricted permission means that the foreign insignia may be worn only under the following circumstances:

(a) in the presence of the sovereign, reigning prince or head of state of the country concerned
(b) in the presence of any member of the royal family of the country concerned
(c) at the embassy of the country concerned
(d) on all official occasions in the country concerned.

Regardless of their date of origin all foreign insignia are worn after British Orders and decorations. The only exceptions are the circumstances above, when precedence is taken by foreign Orders.

THE ORDERS

The list below is of those Orders worn by the Queen and by Queen Elizabeth, the Queen Mother. The Princess of Wales is not a member of the Orders.

THE MOST NOBLE ORDER OF THE GARTER
"The Order of the Garter exceeds in majesty, honour and fame all Chivalrous Orders", according to the historian, Selden. Certainly it predates all others by several centuries. It was founded in 1348 by Edward III to consist of the monarch and twenty-five knights companion. Non-Christians were not eligible and are still not. The origins of the Order are now lost in history, but the popular version could well be true. The story goes that a lady, possibly the Countess of Salisbury, lost her

garter at a court ball. Embarassed by the laughter of the courtiers she lost her composure and was rescued only by the king's gallant behaviour. Bending to pick it up he chided the sniggering courtiers for being ungallant with the remark, _'honi soit qui mal y pense'_ ('Dishonoured be he who thinks evil of it'). He tied the garter around his left leg saying, 'I shall turn this into the most famous garter ever worn'.

The mantle of the Order is of dark blue velvet, lined with white taffeta. The hat is of black velvet lined with white taffeta. A plume of white ostrich feathers is fastened to the hat by a gold and enamel garter badge. The Garter is a dark blue velvet riband with the motto, _'Honi soit qui mal y pense'_, embroidered on it in gold. The collar, fixed to the shoulders of the mantle by white satin robes, has suspended from it The George: a gold and enamel badge representing St George slaying the dragon. The Lesser George also represents St George slaying the dragon. It is surrounded by an oval band bearing the motto and is worn suspended from a sash of Saxon blue which passes over the left shoulder and under the right arm with the badge resting on the hip. The gold collar consists of twenty-four red Tudor roses within dark blue Garters, which bear the motto in gold, and twenty-four lovers' knots. Roses and knots are placed alternately and are joined by gold links. The star has eight points. It is fashioned in silver and has a white enamelled medallion in its centre. The medallion has a red cross on it and is surrounded by the blue Garter and motto.

THE MOST ANCIENT AND MOST NOBLE ORDER OF THE THISTLE

Although its origins are much older, this Order was not established until James II revived it in 1687. It consisted of the sovereign and twelve knights. In 1821 George IV temporarily increased the number of knights to sixteen and in 1827 this number became permanent. The mantle of the Order is of green velvet lined with white taffeta; the collar and badges are worn over it and secured to the shoulders by white satin bows. The badge appendant is a gold image of St Andrew, in a green habit, holding a white enamelled cross in front of him. The collar is gold and consists of alternate, enamelled thistles and pines. The star is of silver. It is a combination of the St Andrew's cross and a four-pointed star. In the centre is an enamelled medallion surrounded by a band with the motto of Scotland, _'Nemo me impune lacessit'_ ('No one can injure me with impunity'). The riband is green and passes over the wearer's left shoulder and under the right arm so that the investment badge, a gold figure of St Andrew holding the Cross, rests on the right hip.

THE MOST HONOURABLE ORDER OF THE BATH

The knights of the Bath are a very ancient institution, but the Order came into existence only in 1725, when it was created by George I. The Order has a military and a civil division. Only Knights Grand Cross wear the mantle. It is of crimson satin, lined with white taffeta. The badge is a white enamelled Maltese cross tipped with gold balls. At the centre is an enamelled medallion with a rose, thistle and shamrock with three crowns, surrounding by a red-enamelled band with the motto, _'Tria Juncta in Uno'_ ('Three joined in one'). The eight-pointed star is of silver. It has a superimposed gold Maltese cross. The central medallion contains three crowns, has a red surround bearing the motto and is enclosed in a laurel wreath which issues from a blue scroll with the motto of the Prince of Wales _'Ich Dien'_ ('I serve'). The collar, of white enamelled knots, contains crowns alternating with enamelled groups of roses, thistles and shamrocks. The crimson riband is worn over the right shoulder and under the left arm, so that the badge rests on the left hip.

THE MOST DISTINGUISHED ORDER OF SAINT MICHAEL AND SAINT GEORGE

The history of this Order is linked with the Mediterranean. It was founded by George III in 1818 to reward the people of Malta and the Ionian islands for services to Great Britain and the peoples of Great Britain for services to the Mediterranean. There are three classes within the Order. The mantle is of Saxon blue satin and is lined with scarlet silk. The badge of the Order is a gold star with seven points. It is enamelled with a white medallion of St Michael surrounded by a blue band with the motto, _'Auspicium Melioris Aevi'_ ('Token of a better age'). The badge is surmounted by a gold crown. The star has seven silver arms alternating with gold rays. The central medallion of St Michael is on a red enamelled cross. The collar of gold has eight white enamelled Maltese crosses alternating with eight gold lions. The riband is dark blue with a red stripe down the middle.

THE ORDER OF MERIT

Edward VII founded this Order in 1902 as a personal reward for military excellence and outstanding achievement in literature, art and science. The number of members is restricted to twenty-four. The badge is a gold and red enamelled cross with dark blue enamelled edges. It is surmounted by a gold crown. The riband is blue and red.

THE ORDER OF THE COMPANIONS OF HONOUR

Awarded for work of national importance, this Order was

founded by George V in 1917. It is restricted to sixty-five members. The oval badge is a gold medallion of an oak tree, a shield of the royal arms and an armoured knight on a horse. It is surrounded by a blue border with the motto, 'In action faithful and in honour clear'. The riband is crimson bordered with gold.

THE ROYAL VICTORIAN ORDER

This Order is conferred as a reward for personal services to the sovereign. It was founded in 1896 by Queen Victoria and has five classes. The badge is an eight-pointed Maltese Cross, enamelled white with a crimson enamel oval at the centre bearing the royal cipher of Victoria and surrounded by a blue enamelled band containing the word 'Victoria' in gold. The Imperial crown surmounts it. The star of the Order is a silver Maltese cross with silver rays between the arms. At the centre is a silver badge. The collar is gold and contains the words Victoria … Britt … Reg … Def … Fid … Ind … Imp … separated by gold pieces enamelled in blue with a gold rose. The riband is blue with red and white stripes on the border.

THE MOST EXCELLENT ORDER OF THE BRITISH EMPIRE

Founded in 1917 by King George V, this Order was a reward to British and Allied subjects who had rendered services at home and in the Dominions and Colonies. In 1918 it was divided into military and civil Orders. The badge consists of a pearl enamelled cross, surmounted by the Imperial crown. At its centre is a medallion with effigies of King George V and Queen Mary, encircled with the motto 'For God and the Empire'. The star is an eight-pointed one with the effigies at its centre. The silver-gilt collar has twelve chain links of an Imperial crown between two sea lions with tridents alternating with six medallions of the Royal Coat of Arms and six medallions of George V's cypher. The order has a riband of pink with grey border stripes.

THE DISTINGUISHED SERVICE ORDER

Conferred on officers mentioned in dispatches and instituted by Queen Victoria in 1886, the Order has only one class and its badge is worn on a chest riband of red with blue border stripes. The badge is a gold cross, enamelled white, with a green laurel wreath and a gold Imperial crown on a red background.

Each Order has its own chapel where its chivalry services take place and where its banners and coats of arms are hung. The Garter chapel is St George's Chapel, Windsor, and the Garter service takes place every year on 23 April, St George's Day. The banners and coats of arms of the Knights of the Thistle are hung in St Giles' Cathedral, Edinburgh, and the day of the Order is 30 November, St Andrew's Day. The chapel of the Order of the Bath is the Henry VII chapel in Westminster Abbey, where the chivalry service takes place every four years with the monarch attending every eight years. The Order of St Michael and St George holds an annual service in the chapel of the Order in St Paul's Cathedral, but the monarch attends only once in every eight years. The monarch always attends the Royal Victorian Order service, held every four years at St George's, Windsor, as it is the Crown's personal Order. The British Empire Order has its chapel in the crypt of St Paul's Cathedral.

THE ROYAL FAMILY ORDERS

In addition to the Orders of Chivalry, there are personal Orders for female members of the royal family which are known as the Family Orders. These are awarded at the monarch's discretion and are given personally. The tradition of these Family Orders goes back to George IV, who first presented them in 1820. Since then, they have been awarded by every monarch except Edward VIII. The Family Orders are miniature portraits of the sovereign suspended from bows. They are worn on the left shoulder of evening dresses at formal occasions where Orders and decorations are being worn.

The Queen wears the Family Order of her father George VI and her grandfather, George V.

The Queen Mother wears the Family Order of George VI and that of the Queen.

The Princess of Wales wears the Queen's Family Order, which she received in 1982.

In addition the Queen has awarded her Family Order to Princess Anne, Princess Margaret, Princess Alice, the Duchess of Gloucester, the Duchess of Kent and Princess Alexandra. Princess Margaret also wears the Order of George VI.

The Queen's badges are made by Garrards and the miniature they contain is painted on ivory by Hay-Wrightson. It shows her in evening dress wearing the riband and star of the Order of the Garter, pearl drop earrings and a diamond necklace which was part of a wedding present from the Nizam of Hyderabad.

The miniature is surrounded by brilliants and baguette diamonds set in platinum. The riband is two inches wide and is of chartreuse-yellow watered silk tied in a bow. King George VI's Family Order shows him in the uniform of Admiral of the Fleet and wearing the star and riband of the Garter and the Royal Victorian Chain. The portrait is surrounded by an oval band of large diamonds and the riband is of rose pink. The family Order of George VI shows the monarch in the same uniform with the star and riband of the Garter and the badge of the Royal Victorian Order. The diamond-surrounded badge is on a riband of light sky blue.

In adition to Orders of Chivalry and Family Orders, the Queen and the Queen Mother wear the badges of the regiments and corps of which they are Colonel-in-Chief.

BIBLIOGRAPHY

Princess Alice of Athlone   *For My Grandchildren* Evans Bros., 1966

Allen, C.J.   *Royal Trains* Allan, 1953

Amies, Hardy   *Just So Far* Collins, 1954

Amies, Hardy   *Still Here* Weidenfeld & Nicolson, 1984

Arts Council   *The Thirties* 1979

Bagehot, Walter   *The English Constitution* Fontana, 1963

Barwick, Sandra   *A Century of Style* Allen & Unwin, 1984

Battiscombe, Georgina   *Queen Alexandra* Constable, 1969

Beale, Erica   *Memories of Three Reigns* Nash and Grayson, 1928

Beale, Erica   *Royal Cavalcade* Stanley Paul, 1939

Beale, Erica   *Sovereign Progression* Hodge, 1937

Beaton, Cecil   *The Glass of Fashion* Weidenfeld & Nicolson, 1954

Beckles, Gordon   *Coronation Souvenir Book* Daily Express, 1939

Bevan, Ian   *Royal Performance* Hutchinson, 1954

Blunt, W.S.   *My Diaries, Being a Personal Narrative of Events 1888–1914* Secker & Warburg, 1919

Bocca, Geoffrey   *The Uneasy Heads* Weidenfeld & Nicolson, 1983

Brown, Michele   *Ritual of Royalty* Sidgwick & Jackson, 1983

Cadell, Patrick   *Royal Visits to Scotland* H.M.S.O., 1977

Campbell, Judith   *Queen Elizabeth II* Peerage Books, 1979

Cathcart, Helen   *The Queen Mother* W.H. Allen, 1965

Channon, Sir Henry   *Diaries* Weidenfeld & Nicolson, 1953

Churchill, Randolph   *They Serve the Queen* Hutchinson, 1953

Clark, Stanley   *Palace Diary* Harrap, 1958

Crawford, Marion   *The Queen Mother* Newnes, 1951

Cunningham & Lucas   *Costume for Births, Marriages and Deaths* A. & C. Black, 1972

Davis, Reginald   *Elizabeth Our Queen* Collins, 1976

De La Bere, Ivan   *The Queen's Orders of Chivalry* Spring Books, 1964

Devon, Stanley   *The Royal Canadian Tour* Pitkin, 1952

Dodd, Christopher   *Henley Royal Regatta* Stanley Paul, 1981

Drummond, Maldwin   *Salt Water Palaces* Debrett, 1979

Duff, David   *Alexandra – Princess and Queen* Collins, 1980

Duncan, Andrew   *The Reality of Monarchy* Heinemann, 1970

Edgar, Donald   *Happy and Glorious* Barker, 1977

Edwards, Anne   *The Queen's Clothes* Rainbird, 1977

Fawcett, Frank Burlington   *Court Ceremonial and the Book of the Court of George VI* Gale & Polden, 1937

Fawcett, Frank Burlington   *Their Majesties' Courts Holden at Buckingham Palace and at the Palace of Holyrood House* Belgravia Publications, 1937

Ferrier, Neil   *The Queen Elizabeth Coronation Souvenir* Robinson, 1953

Feversham   *Great Yachts* Blond, 1970

Fisher, Graham & Heather   *The Queen's Life* Robert Hale, 1976

Forbes, Angela   *Memories and Base Details* Hutchinson, 1921

Fortescue, J.W.   *Narrative of the Visit to India of Their Majesties King George V and Queen Mary* Macmillan, 1912

Glynne, Prudence   *In Fashion* Allen & Unwin, 1978

Hall, Stuart and Whannel, Paddy   *The Popular Arts* Hutchinson, 1964

Hallows, Ian Sinclair   *The Rolls Royce Motor Car* Anthony Bird, 1975

Hartnell, Norman   *Silver and Gold* Evans, 1955

Helliker, A. *Debrett's Season* Debrett, 1980
Hieronymussen, Paul *Orders, Medals and Decorations of Britain and Europe* Blandford, 1967
Hudson, K. and Pettifer, J. *Diamonds in the Sky* Bodley Head, 1979

Jenkins, Alan *The Twenties* Heinemann, 1974
Jenkins, Alan *The Thirties* Heinemann, 1976
Jenkins, Alan *The Forties* Heinemann, 1977
Jenkinson and Townsend *Palaces on Wheels* H.M.S.O., 1981
Junor, Penny *Diana, Princess of Wales* Sidgwick & Jackson, 1982

Keay, Douglas *Royal Pursuit* Severn House, 1983

Lacey, Robert *Majesty* Hutchinson, 1977
Lansdell, Avril *Wedding Fashions 1860–1980* Shire Publications
Latour, Anny *Kings of Fashion* Weidenfeld & Nicolson, 1958
Laver, James *Between the Wars* Vista, 1961
Laver, James *Edwardian Promenade* Hulton, 1958
Laver, James *Women's Dress in the Jazz Age* Hamish Hamilton, 1964
Liversidge, Douglas *The Queen Mother* Arthur Barker, 1977
Longford, Elizabeth *The Queen Mother* Weidenfeld & Nicolson, 1981
Longford, Elizabeth *Elizabeth R* Weidenfeld & Nicolson, 1983
Lyle, R. *Royal Newmarket* Putnam, 1945

McGowan, A.P. *Royal Yachts in the Maritime Museum* H.M.S.O., 1977
McLintock, J. *Royal Motoring* G. T. Foulis, 1962
Madol, H.J. *The Private Life of Queen Alexandra as Viewed by Her Friends* Hutchinson, 1940
Mansfield, Alan *Ceremonial Costume* A. & C. Black, 1980
Martin, Kingsley *The Crown and the Establishment* Hutchinson, 1962
Milton, Roger *The English Ceremonial Book* David & Charles, 1972
Montague-Smith, Patrick *The Country Life Book of the Royal Silver Jubilee* Coutry Life, 1976
Morrah, Dermot *Princess Elizabeth, Duchess of Edinburgh* Odhams, 1950
Morrow, Ann *The Queen* Granada 1983

Mosley, Leonard and Haswell, Robert *The Royals* Frewin, 1966

Naish, G.P.B. *Royal Yachts* H.M.S.O., 1964
Nares, G. *Royal Homes* Country Life, 1953
Nicholson, Sir Harold *Diaries and Letters* Collins, 1966
Nickols, L.A. *The Crowning of Elizabeth II* Macdonald, 1953
Nickols, L.A. *Royal Cavalcade* Macdonald, 1949

Ormond, Richard *The Face of Monarchy* Phaidon, 1977

Parker, Tony *The People of Providence* Hutchinson, 1983
Picknett, Lyn *Royal Romance* Marshall Cavendish, 1980
Pope-Hennessy, James *Queen Mary* Allen & Unwin, 1959
Pringle, Margaret *Dance Little Lady* Orbis, 1977
Pullar, Philippa *Gilded Butterflies* Hamish Hamilton, 1978

Raglan, Ethel *Memories of Three Reigns* Nash & Grayson, 1928

Sampson, Anthony *Anatomy of Britain* Hodder and Stoughton, 1962
Smith, Brian *Royal Daimlers* Transport Bookman Publications, 1976
Spencer Shew, Betty *Royal Wedding* Macdonald, 1947
Stamper, C.W. *What I Know: Reminiscences of Five Years' Personal Attendance upon His Late Majesty King Edward The Seventh* Mills & Boon, 1913
Stevenson, Pauline *Edwardian Fashion* Allan, 1980
Strong, Roy *The English Icon* Routledge & Kegan Paul, 1969
Strong, Roy *Splendour at Court* Weidenfeld & Nicolson, 1973

Talbot, Godfrey *The Country Life Book of the Royal Family* Country Life, 1980
Talbot, Godfrey *The Country Life Book of the Queen Mother* Country Life, 1978
Taylor, Lou *Mourning Dress* Allen & Unwin, 1983
Thaarup, Aage *Heads And Tales* Cassell, 1956
Tingay, Lance *Royalty And Lawn Tennis* Wimbledon Lawn Tennis Museum, 1977
Tschumi & Powe *Royal Chef: Recollections of a Life in Royal Households from Queen Victoria to Queen Mary* William Kimber, 1954
Thomas, Wynford Vaughan *Royal Tour* Hutchinson, 1954
Thompson, Paul *The Edwardians* Weidenfeld & Nicolson, 1975

Wakefield, Geoffrey *Thirty Years a Queen* Robert Hale, 1968

Warwick, Christopher *Two Centuries of Royal Weddings* Arthur Barker, 1980

Whiting, Audrey *Family Royal* W.H. Allen, 1982

Whittington, B *A Short History of the Royal Warrant* Straker & Co. for the Royal Warrant Holders' Association, 1961

Woodward, Kathleen *Queen Mary* Hutchinson, 1927

Wolff, Louis *Elizabeth and Philip* Sampson Low, 1947

Wolff, Louis *Queen Of Tomorrow* Sampson Low, 1946

Wolff, Louis *Silver Wedding* Sampson Low, 1948

Young, Sheila *The Queen's Jewellery* Ebury, 1968

Ziegler, Philip *Crown and People* Collins, 1978

INDEX

PICTURE CREDITS

Cecil Beaton (courtesy of Sotheby's London) p. 21
The Bridgeman Art Library p. 62
BBC Hulton Picture Library pp. 2, 13, 41, 43, 73, 74, 85, 101, 119
Fredderick Fox p. 33
Tim Graham pp. 114, 135, 147, 151, 159
Peter Hope-Lumley Limited p. 32
House of Hartnell pp. 38, 39
Anwar Hussein pp. 10, 90, 131, 142, 162, 163, 166
Illustrated London News Picture Library pp. 48, 50, 78
Kensley Picture Service p. 28
London Express News Service pp. 92, 112, 140
Simone Mirman p. 33
Paul Popper Limited p. 69
P. A. Reuter p. 25
The Royal Collection, Lord Chamberlain's Office p. 67
Athol Shmith p. 32
Snowdon p. 154
Syndication International Limited p. 60
Denis Thorpe (The Guardian) p.92